Religion and Social Cohesion

RELIGION AND SOCIAL COHESION

Western, Chinese and Intercultural Perspectives

Edited by

ANDRÉ VAN DER BRAAK, DEDONG WEI &
CAIFANG ZHU

VU UNIVERSITY PRESS, AMSTERDAM

VU University Press
De Boelelaan 1105
1081 HV Amsterdam
The Netherlands

www.vuuniversitypress.com
info@vu-uitgeverij.nl

© 2015 texts by the authors

Design jacket: Haags Blauw, The Hague (Netherlands)
Type setting: Titus Schulz, Arnhem

ISBN 978 90 8659 703 1
NUR 706

CONTENTS

III MEETING BETWEEN CULTURES

List of Contributors

ANDRÉ VAN DER BRAAK is Professor of Buddhist Philosophy in Dialogue with other World Views, Faculty of Theology, VU University Amsterdam

GOVERT BUIJS is Professor of Political Philosophy and Religion, Faculty of Philosophy, VU University Amsterdam

CINDY DE CLERCK is a Ph.D. Candidate at Catholic University Louvain, Louvain and VU University Amsterdam

ANNETTE COMBRINK is Professor Emerita of English Literature and Translation Studies, and at present Director of International Advancement, North-West University, Potchefstroom Campus, South Africa

YASER ELLETHY is Assistant Professor of Islamic Studies, Centre for Islamic Theology, Faculty of Theology, VU University Amsterdam

KATHLEEN FERRIER is a specialist in international relations with focus on human rights and migration. She is a former member of the Dutch Parliament and the former chairwoman of SKIN (Platform of migrant churches in the Netherlands)

MANUELA KALSKY is Edward Schillebeeckx Professor of Theology and Society, Faculty of Theology, VU University, Amsterdam, and Director of the Dominican Study Centre for Theology and Society, Amsterdam

AB KLINK was the Minister of Health in The Netherlands, and is at present Professor of Healthcare, Labor Market and Political Control, Faculty of Social Sciences, VU University Amsterdam

DANIELLE KONING obtained her Ph.D. at the Faculty of Theology, VU University Amsterdam

YONGSI LIU is Assistant Professor, Department of Philosophical and Religious Studies, Minzu University of China, Beijing

TYMEN VAN DER PLOEG is Professor Emeritus of Private Law, Law Faculty, VU University Amsterdam

YUJIE WANG is Professor of Islamic Studies, School of Philosophy, Renmin University of China, Beijing

DEDONG WEI is Deputy Dean of the School of Philosophy, Renmin University of China, Beijing

BIN YOU is Professor of Christian Studies, and Director of the Institute of Comparative Scripture and Interreligious Dialogue, Minzu University of China, Beijing

XUNMOU ZHANG is Director of the Research Center, State Administration of Religious Affairs (SARA), Beijing

ZHIGANG ZHANG is Professor of Philosophy and Religious Studies at the Department of Philosophy, Institute of Foreign Philosophy, and Director of the Academy of Religious Studies, Peking University, Beijing

CAIFANG ZHU is Researcher at the International Center for Buddhist Studies, Renmin University of China, Beijing

8

Introduction

André van der Braak

On October 9-12, 2012, the second Sino-Ned Religion Conference was organized in Beijing by the VU University Amsterdam (Faculty of Theology), the Renmin University of China, Beijing (School of Philosophy and Religion), and the State Administration of Religious Affairs (SARA) in China. The conference, a continuation of the first Sino-Ned conference held in the Netherlands in 2009, was called: *Religion and Social Cohesion: Culture, Identity and Practice* and was attended by scholars from Renmin University of China and other Chinese universities, senior administrators from the Chinese State Administration of Religious Affairs (SARA), scholars from VU University in Amsterdam, from South Africa, Hong Kong and Belgium, as well as a number of Dutch politicians. During this lively conference, the participants discussed the role of religion in Western and Chinese society; they exchanged information on current religious developments and looked at how these developments could be addressed through multi-disciplinary and intercultural research. In the various lectures and discussions which were shared during the conference, a basis for mutual trust and cooperation was created, which led to a free and open exchange of views. Most of the papers presented at the conference have now been bundled together in this collection of essays. For it to have as broad an impact as possible, the Sino-Ned dialogue on religion and social cohesion at the conference was conducted not only by academics, but also by government officials and (former) politicians. The contributions in this volume, therefore, represent a wide range of opinion from a variety of multidisciplinary approaches. Yet, in all their diversity, perhaps even because of it, an accurate account of the widely diverging aspects that are involved in the question of religion and social cohesion has been produced.

1 Religion and Social Cohesion

Both in the West and in China, it is increasingly recognized that religion is not merely an individual matter, but a social force that has an important impact on society. And whereas the focus often lies on the potential negative social impact of religion (the threats of fundamentalism, violence and terrorism), religion has also often been an important factor in the arising of social capital and social cohesion, as the social history of Europe reveals.

This volume of essays focuses on the relationship between religion and social cohesion, as thematized in three ways:

1 How does religion manifest itself in culture today, what role does it play in the development of a civil society, and should the state be active in this process? In China, the government increasingly appears to recognize the importance of religion for promoting social and cultural harmony. How does this compare to the role that religion plays in Europe?

2 What are the boundaries of 'religion' and 'religious identity'? In a time when notions of identity are rapidly shifting, religious identity is often characterized by hybridity and multiplicity, both in the West and in China. The formation of a 'new we', not only in the Netherlands or in Europe, but also in China and on a global scale, is of crucial importance for dealing with cultural and religious diversity.

3 How do the general trends of (1) and (2) translate to the specific social practices that result from, or inform, religion? Both in China and the Netherlands, the state actively supports religious education at universities, and values the charity efforts of religiously inspired NGOs. This seems like a very fruitful area for mutual exploration and comparison.

A Western-Chinese dialogue on the topic of religion and social cohesion must recognize that social cohesion has been framed differently in China than in the West. Western societies have had one dominant religious tradition, consonant with theological paradigms of religious exclusivism. Therefore, social cohesion has been framed in terms of the relationship of the dominant religion to the rest of society, and the problem of how to relate to minority religious communities. In China, the religious, the social and the political were not clearly separated until the twentieth century.

2 Religion and Social Cohesion in the West

In the West, the sociology of religion is currently experiencing a paradigm clash between contested discourses. Traditionally, a secular discourse within the social sciences tended to view religion as an illusion that was irrational, ignorant and foolish, and therefore incompatible with modern secular society.[1] The natural result of such a secular discourse has been the secularization thesis, which has proven to be outdated by most scholars of religion.[2]

These days, within the social sciences, the 'religious markets' approach is becoming quite popular in American sociology of religion.[3] This paradigm frames religious activities as taking place in a market place, consisting of competing vendors each offering a religious product. Such a liberal discourse that frames the religious question in terms of markets, views religious affiliation as an individual choice, comparable to other life style choices that are to be made. From within such a discourse, there is relatively little attention to the impact that religion can have on social cohesion.

From an anthropological perspective, religion is closely associated with culture, thickly described by Clifford Geertz as 'a historically transmitted pattern of meanings embodied in symbols, a system of inherited conceptions expressed in symbolic forms by means of which men communicate, perpetuate, and develop their knowledge about and attitudes toward life.'[4] Therefore, some scholars have preferred an ecological discourse on religion. They maintain a holistic view of all the forms of religiosity in a given society, which attempts to describe the religious landscape in that society without the narrow definitions that have constrained the theological and secular discourses on religion in the past, in order to make room for the dynamic processes of interactive change, adaptation, and innovation, that characterize religion as a social phenomenon, and cause its components and boundaries to be constantly contested. Goossaert and Palmer, therefore, prefer the ecological discourse to the market discourse, because it views the 'religious landscape as part of an evolving ecology of elements in constant interaction with one another, and in which a major change in one element, or the addition of a new element, may lead to a cascade of changes in the rest of the system.'[5]

3   Religion and Social Cohesion in China

Some may be surprised to read about religion and social cohesion in China. It is generally believed that while China might have a rich religious history, it is today a thoroughly secular country. The Western study of 'religion in China' has been dominated thus far by sinologists, who have usually claimed that there is no religion in modern day China, and have focused instead on historical research into Confucianism, Daoism and Buddhism. Recent empirical data seem to confirm this picture. In a major questionnaire survey carried out among Han Chinese in 2005, 8.7 percent identified themselves as religious, 52.3 percent as non-religious, and 26.1 percent as anti-religious (firm atheist). However, when asked about religious beliefs and practices, 27.4 percent reported to have paid homage to or worshiped Buddhas or Bodhisattvas, 21.6 percent had prayed to the God of fortune, 12.5 percent to other spirits, while 28.6 percent said that they felt comforted or empowered through these religious activities.[6]

This apparent discrepancy between religious identity and religious practice is related to the hermeneutical complexities surrounding the notion of 'religion' in China. In the classical Chinese language there was no equivalent term for the Western notion of 'religion'. In the nineteenth century, the term *zongjiao* was coined, consisting of the words *zong* (ancestral tradition) and *jiao* (teaching). However, this term has always had a pejorative connotation for most Chinese, suggesting superstitions, dogmas and institutions. The dictionary meaning of *zongjiao* is 'a social ideology and an imaginary reflection of the objective world which urges people to believe in God, ghosts, spirits and retribution for sin, and places hope on the so-called kingdom of Heaven or next life.'[7] Many educated Chinese people have, therefore, tended to distance themselves from *zongjiao*, using terms such as *xue* (learning) or *jia* (family) to refer to their way of life (for example Confucianism or Daoism).

But, regardless of such secular interpretations of religious practices, religion-as-lived is increasingly recognized as being very present in China today. In their recent work *The Religious Question in Modern China*, Vincent Goossaert and David Palmer comment on the rapidly changing perceptions of religion in modern China:

> Until little more than a decade ago, popular and scholarly discourse on China relegated religious practices to the domain of the quaint customs of a rapidly fading past and the lofty platitudes of ancient sages. Whether the subject was yearly offerings to the Kitchen God or the abstruse learning of Confucius, these traditions, if they could even be called religion, were never considered to have much bearing on the real life of Chinese society today. But since the end of the twentieth century, a clear shift in perception has been taking place. The Chinese world has not been immune from the global resurgence of religion and from the growing impact of religion on social and political life.[8]

Indeed, religion is back as a social reality in contemporary China (perhaps it never really left), just as religion remains a social reality in the West, in spite of the dire predictions of secularization theorists such as Peter Berger about its impending demise. There is currently a great deal of interest among Chinese intellectuals, government officials and scholars in what has been called 'the religious question' (*zongjiaowenti*). Also, among Western scholars, the interest in religion in China today is steadily increasing. The study of religion in contemporary China (rather than just the history of Chinese religious traditions) has opened up as an important new field of study.

The American Chinese-born sociologist of religion Fenggang Yang has extended the religious markets paradigm for the situation in China.[9] Because of the limited supply of religious options in China due to government restrictions, he claims, the market collapses into a threefold market: the red, black and grey. The 'red market' of religion in China, in which 'the red stain [of communist ideology] is reflected in the rhetoric of clergy, theological discourse, and practices of the sanctioned religious groups'[10], consists of all legal (officially permitted) religious organizations, believers, and religious activities (the five religious traditions of Buddhism, Daoism, Islam, Catholicism and Protestantism). The 'black market' consists of the illegal (officially banned) religious organizations, believers, and religious activities (such as house churches). The 'grey market' consists of all religious and spiritual organizations, practitioners, and activities which have ambiguous legal status, and refers to a wide range of religious practices that are subsumed under nonreligious labels such as health or Chinese culture, in order to secure the legitimacy and legality of the practices.[11]

But is the market metaphor really appropriate? As Goossaert and Palmer note, 'Since the market provides the greatest realm of freedom in socialist China, couching religion in the language of supply and demand is one strategy for legitimating it. And, to be sure, commercialization and commodification are obvious characteristics of much religious activity in China today […]'.[12] However, applying economic concepts to the discourse of religion also has its downsides. Although markets for religious services and commodities do exist in China, the many configurations of social relations in China's religious landscape today may be too complex and manifold to be reduced to the market metaphor.

4   Toward a Sino-Ned Dialogue on Religion and Social Cohesion

There is an important reason why the more holistic ecological discourse on religion might be more fruitful for a Sino-Ned dialogue on religion than the liberal market discourse: it leaves more room for important differences between the Chinese and the Western religious ecosystems. These differences might be most fruitfully elucidated from within a theological discourse. From a theological point of view, the notions of religion and *zongjiao* uphold fundamentally different concepts of the sacred and the secular, and the relationship of the human to the divine.[13] Western notions of ontological transcendence tend to be out of place in the Chinese world view. Whereas in Western theology, the positions of exclusivism (claiming an exclusive access to religious truth for one's own tradition) and inclusivism (claiming a superior access to religious truth for one's own tradition) have been widely spread, often drowning out attempts by intercultural theologians to come to a theology of religions based on pluralism, it could be argued that pluralism has been the norm rather than the exception in Chinese religious history. Religious adherence in China has mostly been characterized by a mixing and matching of various religious traditions. Within Western theology, this has often pejoratively been framed as syncretism. But a new paradigm within intercultural theology speaks more neutrally of 'multiple religious belonging'.

These days, such multiple religious belonging is also rapidly becoming a reality in religion-as-lived in Western societies, opening up possibilities to new forms of social cohesion that are not informed by fixed and exclusive religious identities, a 'new we'.[14] In this sense, the West might be becoming more like China.[15] This is ironic in light of twentieth-century Chinese attempts at becoming more like the West by establishing exclusive religious identities such as the five religions paradigm (Buddhism, Daoism, Islam, Catholicism, Protestantism) and establishing Western church style institutions. But religion-as-lived keeps resurfacing in a bewildering variety of forms outside such categories.

This difference between formal religious identities and informal 'religion-as-lived' in China has famously been conceptualized by sociologist of religion C.K. Yang as institutionalized and diffused religion.[16] These days, the notion of 'popular religion' is frequently used to describe such religion-as-lived that falls outside formally recognized religious identities. Research into the different senses of religious identity in China and the West can be an important part of any Sino-Ned religious dialogue.[17]

5   The Essays in this Volume

In the first part of this volume, the emphasis is on religion and social cohesion in Europe and South Africa. It contains five essays on the relationship between religion and culture, and the contribution that religion can make to social cohesion and the development of a civil society.

Political philosopher Govert Buijs writes about the way to bring about a civil society. Apart from financial capital, one needs social capital, the ability to cooperate and experience mutual trust. Religion can be either a frustrator or a promotor of social capital. As a case study he analyzes some of the developments in medieval Christianity which led to the creation of the current Western civil societies, as well as the five threats to the development of social capital: possessivism (unrestrained pursuit of wealth), perfectionism (utopianism), power pressure from adverse state-structures, privatism (individualism and group-ism) and pride (being immune to criticism).

Legal scholar Tymen van der Ploeg gives an overview of government policy towards religion in the Netherlands and some other Western European countries. The legal personality of religious communities in the Netherlands is sketched in the context of various regulatory systems in other European countries, such as state church, recognition, and the registration of religious communities. In the Netherlands, the government and religious communities meet each other on subjects like pastoral care in (closed) institutions, religious education in public schools, tax facilities, subsidies for social work etc. and subsidies for monuments. In the conclusion, the legal approach to religious communities by law and government is evaluated.

Former Dutch Minister of Health Care Ab Klink reflects on the historical relationship between religion, civil society and the state in the Netherlands. Should religion be pushed back to the private sphere? Or is it an important pillar in society? Can religion be a source of culture and civil society?

Religion scholar Daniëlle Koning investigates the evangelism of immigrant churches. Can the practice of evangelism be seen as a contribution to civil society? In her Ph.D. research, she investigated fifteen immigrant churches in the Netherlands. Do their missionary practices have a civil potential? Koning analyzes evangelism as a form of social action and as a bridge to other communities.

South African scholar Annette Combrink reflects on religion and culture in the new 'rainbow nation' of South Africa, which is characterized by a great diversity in culture and religion. Although the transition to democracy brought a sense of hope to South Africa, corruption still flourishes. What is needed, in her eyes, is an approach of social and cultural openness.

The second part of this volume consists of essays that approach the topic of religion and social cohesion in China. Since the end of the Cultural Revolution, the Chinese government has placed religion under the supervision of the State Administration of Religious Affairs (SARA). Under its direction, each religion is administered by its own national association: associations for Buddhists, Daoists, Protestants, Catholics and Muslims. Under the law, religious followers must register with one of these five recognized faiths in order to take part in religious activities. Places of worship, priests and heads of churches or temples have to be agreed upon, or approved by, the authorities at the appropriate level. In the first essay, dr. Xunmou Zhang, Director of the Center of Studies of Religion at SARA, gives a brief overview of the official Chinese government policy towards religion. He addresses the three main tasks of SARA: adhering to the policy of freedom of religious belief, promoting religious harmony, and supporting religion to play a positive and active role.

The remainder of the articles in this section show that this apparently clear-cut government policy of the five recognized faiths leads to complexities when applied to the often unclear and chaotic lived reality of the Chinese religious landscape. Zhigang Zhang writes about the process of Sinicization by which Christianity melded into Chinese culture and the Chinese nation. Religious ecological imbalance (see the earlier description of the ecological paradigm) may be a reason for the rapid growth of Chinese Protestantism. There is the feeling that Christianity was used as a tool to Christianize China, a tool for imperialist aggression in the modern history of China to infiltrate the country by Western hostile forces. Nowadays, new developments of interreligious dialogue are a hot topic among Chinese Christians.

Religion scholar Yujie Wang addresses the challenges that Islam in contemporary China currently faces. For Chinese Muslims, it is difficult to establish a relationship between their ethnic identity (which is related to their being a Muslim) and their Chinese national identity. In addition, there is the problem of ethnic boundaries for Chinese citizens who want to convert to Islam. They are often not seen as Muslims because they do not have an Arabic identity.

Buddhist scholar Caifang Zhu describes the social-religious phenomenon of the Little Courtyard in Shanxi Province, Northern China; a phenomenon which has caused controversy due to its ritualized and overtly devotional practice which has converted many families and extended families. Zhu proposes that the practice be viewed as a health and healing-oriented Buddhism.

The model of the five recognized faiths does not leave room for other forms of religiosity, which are often lumped together under the label of 'popular religion'. Popular religion in modern China is difficult to circumscribe as its character is diffused and there is a lack of fixed doctrinal and institutional cores. Religion scholar Yongsi Liu distinguishes three types of popular religion in modern and contemporary China: sectarian groups, liturgical tradition groups, and communal religious groups.

Cindy De Clerck looks at religion and social cohesion in China through the phenomenon of autism. How do Chinese parents describe autism as a medical category, as a socio-cultural category, as a way of perceiving the world and as connected to religious values and norms? De Clerck performed fieldwork with non-governmental organizations. Most are catholic, and are sponsored by American and German organizations. The way Chinese parents think about autism is connected to their world view.

In part three of this volume, various intercultural and dialogical perspectives are explored. Islamic theologian Yaser Ellethy writes about religious-cultural identity and multiculturalism with regard to Islam and pluralism. He investigates the notion of 'Muslimness', and its relationship to 'otherness'. The places where Muslim identities are negotiated, celebrated or resisted matter as they influence how these identities are experienced by Muslims and non-Muslims alike. Muslim intercultural diversity creates the need for, and the challenge of, cultural integration.

Philosopher André van der Braak investigates the differences between the way that Chan Buddhism is practiced in China and in the Netherlands. He uses the Dutch Maha Karuna Chan Buddhist community as a case study in order to reflect on multiple religious belonging, a new religious paradigm in the West, but well known in China.

The notion of multiple religious belonging is elaborated further by theologian Manuela Kalsky, in her description of 'Project We', a Dutch interreligious multimedia project that aims to contribute to social cohesion. She addresses various questions related to diversity and pluralization: what is needed for a 'new we' that binds people together and makes differences fruitful? What is needed to be able to be flexible and connect all those who aim at a good life for all? In search for a mutual connection in facing the differences and making them fruitful, how can believers and non-believers engage in dialogue without having to become the same?

Philosopher Bin You writes about the comparative study of scripture as a

Chinese experiment in interreligious dialogue. Texts from different religions are read together by people from different religious backgrounds. Such a comparative reading has three phases: exegesis, personal interpretation, and reflection on one's personal tradition.

This volume of essays concludes by a personal contribution by former member of Dutch Parliament Kathleen Ferrier, in which she reflects on her own background in Suriname, and her experience as a coordinator of migrant churches in the Netherlands. She passionately pleads to see religion not as a threat, but as the strong driver for social cohesion and welfare that it is, and points out the benefits that are involved for both the state and religious organizations in looking for better ways for further and closer co-operation.

The present collection of essays mainly serves as a first exploration of religion and social cohesion in the West and China, in an attempt to identify topics that are suitable for further study. The explorative essays in this volume hopefully serve as a solid foundation for a continued Sino-Ned dialogue between VU University Amsterdam, Renmin University and SARA.

1   Sociologists Stark and Finke give an extensive description of the history of the social scientific study of religion as a child of the 'Enlightenment': R. Stark and R. Finke, *Acts of Faith: Explaining the Human Side of Religion* (Berkeley: University of California Press, 2000).

2   See the article by Manuela Kalsky in this volume.

3   For a description of this new paradigm, see R. Stark and W. Bainbridge, *The Future of Religion: Secularization, Revival and Cult Formation* (Berkeley: University of California Press, 1986) and *A Theory of Religion* (New Brunswick, NJ: Rutgers University Press, 1996), and Stark and Finke, *Acts of Faith*.

4   C. Geertz, *The Interpretation of Cultures* (London: Hutchinson, 1975), 89.

5   V. Goossaert and D. Palmer, eds., *The Religious Question in Modern China* (Chicago: University of Chicago Press, 2010), 6.

6   X. Yao and P. Badham, eds., *Religious Experience in Contemporary China* (Cardiff: University of Wales Press, 2007), 30-31.

7   *The Contemporary Chinese Dictionary*, 2002: 2554.

8   Goossaert and Palmer, *Religious Question*, 1.

9   F. Yang, *Religion in China: Survival and Revival under Communist Rule* (Oxford: Oxford University Press, 2011).

10 F. Yang, The Red, Black, and Gray Markets of Religion in China, *The Sociological Quarterly* 47 (2006), 93-122, citation on 97.

11 Yang, *Religion in China*, 85.

12 Goossaert and Palmer, *Religious Question*, 12.

13 See A. van der Braak, 'The Secular and the Sacred as Contested Spaces? A Cross-Cultural Hermeneutical Investigation into Western and Chinese perspectives', in: *Contested Spaces, Common Ground* (Amsterdam/New York: Rodopi, forthcoming), 401-414.

14 See the contribution by Manuela Kalsky in this volume.

15 See the contribution by André van der Braak in this volume.

16 C.K. Yang, *Religion in Chinese Society* (Berkeley: University of California Press, 1961).

17 This important topic is also addressed in a collection of essays edited by theologian Perry Schmidt-Leukel and philosopher Joachim Gentz, *Religious Diversity in Chinese Thought* (London: Palgrave Macmillian, 2013).

PART I

EUROPE
AND
SOUTH AFRICA

Remembering the Future:
Christianity, Social Capital and
the Development of the West

Govert Buijs

1 Introduction

For a whole array of social sciences, one of the most intriguing questions is still: what are—to borrow from the title of Adam Smith's 1776 ground breaking work—'the nature and causes of the wealth of nations'?[1] A much more recent inquiry by David Landes poses the same question in slightly different words: 'The wealth and poverty of nations: why some are so rich and some so poor'.[2] Many factors and actors have been proposed as candidates for the role of the explaining the independent variable: natural circumstances (the availability of water or other natural resources, geographical location, climate) that lead to, for example, the concomitant potential for agricultural surplus creation; political causes (well-functioning states, military power, ability to build an infrastructure); or cultural factors (ethics, religion).

Apart from the work of Adam Smith, another early landmark contribution to the debate has been provided by Karl Marx, who identified economic power relations as crucial for the development of modern capitalism. This made it possible that 'the bourgeoisie, during its rule of scarcely one hundred years, has created more massive and more colossal productive forces than all preceding generations together'.[3], Another contributor is Max Weber, who focused on the role of the moral insights and practices of the various world religions in either discouraging or encouraging economic development, i.e. capitalism. In the post WW-II period, a kind of consensus emerged, mainly expressed by W. W. Rostow, that amounted to the idea that something like a 'law of development' can be identified, according to which societies 'develop' from agricultural surplus creation, via heavy industry, to a consumer society, the supposedly happy end phase of world history.[4]

This consensus did not hold. In recent years, at least one new hypothesis has arisen that puts another element in the explanatory spotlight: social capital. The development of a country is primarily based on the ability and willingness of people to work together, to cooperate, to form networks of trust, and to live by shared norms and values to sustain them. Although not the first one to coin or use the term, the first one to employ 'social capital' as a rather encompassing explanation for societal development was sociologist Robert Putnam in his long-term comparative study of Northern and Southern Italy.[5] Two years later, it was given center stage as an explanatory variable in the broad comparative study of economic development by Francis Fukuyama, entitled *Trust*.[6] Ever since, the concept of 'social capital' has enjoyed an impressive career in various branches of the social sciences.[7]

Curiously enough, this hypothesis is a marked departure from other currently dominant interpretations of development, which place all the emphasis on the allegedly blissful operation of capitalist free markets, which are supposedly driven by the individual self-interest of all the actors involved (interpretations that have become immensely popular in recent decades with the rise of what can broadly be called 'neo-liberalism').

In this essay, it is not possible to even scratch the surface of this immense debate. Without giving further reasons in favor of it, for the sake of argument I will assume that the social capital approach to development is a promising research paradigm. What I intend to highlight, within this paradigm, is the role of religion in fostering social capital. However, I will argue that religion can not only provide the social capital that is an essential ingredient of development, it can also provide substantial ideas about what 'development' actually is—and therefore, it may turn out to be critical as well with regard to certain instantiations of development that it deems wanting. In other words: religion may produce its own ideas and ideals about what a good society is—and this may cause tensions with actual social developments. For example, adherents of certain religions may criticize the nihilistic materialism that can be the outcome of development, or they may criticize the injustice that may be the result of certain modernization processes. Is 'development' simply equal to the maximization of the Gross Domestic Product, or does it have something to do with establishing a just and humane society, in which all citizens enjoy certain basic rights and what Amartya Sen and Martha Nussbaum have called 'capabilities'? Paradoxically, it is exactly because religion produces these substantial ideas about a good society and about development, that the critical side of religion may be as important for a healthy society as its positive side is.

Because the central thesis of this essay, as I have just laid it out, is rather complex, I first illustrate it by briefly discussing Max Weber's famous essay on *The Protestant Ethic and the Spirit of Capitalism*. Hidden in this work is a prefiguration of the thesis that I would like to defend in the remainder of this essay. Afterwards, I will argue my own thesis by giving a particular interpretation of the role of Christianity in the development of the West, with special reference to the start of the rise of the West of what later has been called the 'medieval' period.

The reader will have noticed that, in this field of research, a variety of different, and seemingly interchangeable, terms come up time and again: progress, development, capitalism, wealth creation, modernization, and so on. All carry their own load of associations and reference. I choose in this paper to use the term 'development', exactly because the term is so contested, and therefore does not have one clear meaning: the term 'development' opens up a wide spectrum of different views. I can easily add one more tree to the forest.

2 Weber, Bell and the Cultural Contradictions of Capitalism

In his 1905 essay on Protestantism and capitalism, Max Weber argued that it was Protestantism that inculcated in the populace of North-Western Europe the virtues that almost accidentally created the cultural preconditions for the capitalist take-off.[8] Protestantism broadened the notion of 'vocation' to include everyday existence as well. It no longer only referred to the 'religious' life in a monastery or as a priest but also, and equally, to the work of the carpenter or the farmer. The holy life was preferably to be lived within this world ('inner-worldly asceticism'), not beyond it ('other-worldly asceticism'). The exhortation to live a holy life discouraged the spending of money on luxury as well. Thrift, therefore, was a characteristic quality of the Protestant saints. From these elements, an ethic emerged that strongly advised working hard, and simultaneously discouraged virtually all the ways of spending one's money. The result: earning without spending automatically creates a surplus. This surplus, again, should be used wisely and responsibly, which means that it should be rationally invested—the start of capitalism.

Weber argued, long after religious inspiration had evaporated, that the essential ingredients of the Protestant ethic lived on, culminating in the rise of rational utilitarianism, in which the twins—utility and efficiency—became the sole yardstick for one's decisions. Moreover, while the Protestants chose to live that way, later generations were simply forced to do so. The entire social order was now shaped according to this template. No escape was possible from this 'iron cage'. In later analyses, he writes about the loss of freedom that is the consequence of the rationalization of the modern world.

The implication of this analysis is that capitalism, after it severed its connection to the religion that engendered it, developed into an uncontrolled and uncontrollable mechanism, which could even become a threat to mankind. Weber had to stop his analysis here at this very point, because his ideas about 'value free science' prevented him from further developing any ideas about a good society, and fully elaborating his implicit pessimism about the modern 'disenchanted' world. But he was nevertheless on the brink of analyzing something that Daniel Bell later came to call 'the cultural contradictions of capitalism': an unrestricted development of the capitalist market system may turn out to undermine the cultural preconditions that enable it to function. Bell developed Weber's analysis further, and paid special attention to the rise of 'post-bourgeois' values, especially among artists, which were more and more widely dispersed throughout society. While society is structurally organized around values such as efficiency and rationality, many people disavow them and opt for the 'free creative spirit at war with the bourgeoisie'. Bell claims that since the 1920s,

> in effect the Protestant Ethic as a social reality and a life-style for the middle class was replaced by a materialistic hedonism, and the Puritan Temper by a psychological eudaemonism. But bourgeois society, justified and propelled as it had been in its earliest energies by these older ethics, could not easily admit to the change. It promoted a hedonistic way of life furiously—one has only to look at the transformation of advertising in the 1920s—but could not justify it. It lacked a new religion or a value system to replace the old, and the result was a disjunction.[9]

Bell attributes this rise of hedonism to the development of capitalism itself.

Weber and Bell have been presented here to illustrate a rather complex thesis that will be elaborated below. In short: development may develop into something that undermines (healthy) development. The very culture that made it possible can be destroyed by it later on. Therefore, for development to be culturally sustainable, it may be necessary, in some way, to have recourse to the original moral impulses that engendered it.

3 An Interpretation of Western Development (1): How it Started

What did engender Western development? In this paper, I start from the assumption, already very much present in Marx, but now shared by quite a few other researchers, that Western development did not start in what is commonly called 'early modernity' (the sixteenth and seventeenth century) but that we have to search for its origins in the time that the feudal structures were attacked and superseded by the rise of what Marx pejoratively called 'the bourgeoisie,' and what I prefer to call 'burgher culture'.[10] The economic take off of the West took place in medieval towns. Here the recipe for economic success was forged, although almost accidentally. However, in contradistinction to Marx's interpretation, I would like to argue that it was Christianity which provided the spark that ignited this development.[11] The emphasis on Christianity, rather than on Protestantism, also puts me at some distance from Weber's thesis which was briefly discussed above.[12]

Attributing a key role to Christianity may seem awkward, for the seemingly definitive rejoinder is ready to be formulated: Christianity has been the dominant religion in at least two civilizational areas. Apart from the realm of Western Christendom, there is also that of Eastern Orthodoxy (not to mention Christianity's influence in Asia Minor and the Middle East prior to the rise of Islam). And this latter realm is usually not singled out as a particular frontrunner of modernity. So how is it possible for one religion to have these two almost contrary effects? Upon closer inspection, however, this preliminary rejoinder to my central thesis does not hold water. For the key difference between Eastern and Western Christianity is the continuity of empire. Empires, as we know from various contexts, can have a strong impact, either stimulating or frustrating, on the degree to which a development potential can be actualized. Just remember, for example, how after one imperial decision made by the new emperor Hong Xi in 1424, the entire exploration fleet of tens of mammoth ships led by admiral Zheng He suddenly had to remain in the harbor, to just rot away.

In the realm of Eastern Christianity, the empire, with its virtual identification (symphonia) of spiritual and political powers, did not leave any room for a more or less independent materialization of Christianity. In the West, by contrast, after the breakdown of the Western Roman empire there was a power vacuum, in which all kind of different actors positioned themselves, but always with a very limited scope: local feudal lords, monasteries, bishops, at times, for a couple of decades, an emperor, or in some regions a king or an emerging royal house (the latter mostly in a very delicate balancing act with the local and regional nobility, so absolute kingship was unknown in medieval times). Thanks to this rather anarchic situation, in which all kinds of different movements and social initiatives popped up (and went under as well), free spaces emerged in which various groups of people were able, almost by way of experiment, to organize themselves on the basis of Christian principles and insights.

These social experiments were preceded by, and an outgrowth of, attempts to tame and Christianize the 'Germanic soul'. Various historians inform us about the culture of violence that characterized Western Europe, first in what can be called the tribal phase (roughly the fifth to the eighth century C.E.) to be continued in the feudal phase (roughly the ninth to the eleventh century C.E.). The Carolingians each year summoned all their friends, bishops, and so on, and every spring started a big festival of destruction, slaughter, rape and looting. Even at that time, the effective control of the king over the warlords was minimal. Later on, the warlords became local despots, and Europe became an anarchistic archipelago of local kingdoms, in which the poor and the farmers were exploited at will by the lords.[13] The representative icon of a successful man in this period therefore was the warrior, later more specifically the knight:

> For him the real or fictitious war was central; it was war that gave color to life. [...] This culture, deeply marked by what inspired men of war, was based almost entirely upon the pleasures of plunder, rape and aggression.[14]

In this context, the Christian missionaries arrived with a message about a Lord who allowed himself to be crucified, about a God who had created all men equal and was the protector of especially the poor and the weak. In order to receive any hearing at all, the message had to be somewhat adapted to fit its audience (in the *Heliant*, a kind of Germanic Gospel, Jesus has been given some of the traits of a victorious feudal lord), but it was still different enough to confront the Northern Europeans with a clear moral and existential choice: to either persist with the chivalric ideals, or adhere to the new ideals. Many lords chose to adopt the new faith, sometimes under physical threat, but often out of a complex mixture of pragmatic, political, social and existential-religious reasons. They often summoned their household, vassals and serfs to follow suit.

Once the first outward, collective stage of conversion had passed, the missionary activity had to enter into a new stage, influencing individual outward behavior. The Belgian historian Martine de Reu has studied the Christian sermons that were delivered during the successive stages of missionary activity. The sermons in this second stage may not be all that surprising to modern 'civilized' (?) ears, but one has to consider the possibility that they were hard for Germanic ears to hear. De Reu produces a list of do's and don'ts that constitute the central thread running through the sermons. Apart from ritual practices and beliefs, there are the following moral oppositions:[15] murder vs. love of peace; theft vs. hospitality; usury vs. love of neighbor; hatred vs. forgiveness; lying vs. honesty; sexual laxity vs. chastity; vanity vs. humility; gluttony or drunkenness vs. sobriety; attending cruel spectacles vs. meditation on religious subjects. What a blow this must have been in several (not all) respects, to the Germanic soul! Here we can already find much of what would later be called 'bourgeois virtues'.[16] The end of the feudal age is already looming here, right in these early, ninth and tenth century sermons.

Increasingly, the burning question must have been how to embody this new ethic in concrete social contexts. The first opportunity that presented itself was the monasteries. Around the year 1000, the so-called Reformation of Cluny generated more than thousand new monasteries throughout Western Europe within a couple of decades. They were exempted from local ties, and placed themselves directly under the auspice of the Holy See (notwithstanding how far removed this See actually was).

But the radical life choice that was implied by the monastic life was, perhaps for many, a bridge too far. A search began for a more mundane, worldly type of holiness, for (to apply Weber's phrase to a much earlier period) an 'inner-worldly asceticism'. This opportunity was provided by the towns. Here, the model of monastic organization—leaving one's own family or clan and joining a new community in which everybody is equal, which has a clear, written constitution (*regula*), to which one commits oneself by oath or promise, and to which one contributes one's labor according to one's talents, while in a free, talent-based election one chooses one's own leader, the abbot or abbess— seemed too attractive to leave it just for the monasteries to implement.[17] The town movement started in Northern Italy around 1050, and spread to Northwestern Europe about a century later. The movement picked up breathtaking speed, especially in the thirteenth century; in Germany, for example, more than two hundred new towns were founded every decade, until the Holy German Empire counted over four thousand towns within its boundaries.[18] The close connection between the monastery and the city is attested to centuries later by Erasmus who wrote in a letter: *Quid aliud est civitas quam magnum monasterium?* ('What is a town if not a big monastery?')[19]

27

In short, the medieval town movement was based on a worldly application of the monastic organizational model, as a means of escaping feudal structures, and creating a social space in which liberty, equality and solidarity were constitutionally guaranteed by a mutual pact (often called *pactum* or *foedus*, hence our word 'federal') and thus based on the freedom *and* responsibility of the participants.

Like all human communities, the medieval towns were not perfect paradises. But what I am concerned with here is identifying the basic idea, the internal logic of the medieval city, notwithstanding the fact that it often didn't live up to it. Cities were consciously and freely constituted communes that gave their members a unique opportunity to realize, in concrete terms, the ontological status that the Christian message accorded them theologically (loved by God, created in his image, created equal), but that the feudal world denied them politically.[20] The town-founding movement was a truly revolutionary movement that frequently came into conflict with the feudal lords and the feudal structures of governance. The claim to freedom— formulated and embodied in communal terms: we are not yet dealing with modern individualism—was based on Christian teachings. Later on, the basic social and political tenets of this Christian message even reached the lowest classes. 'We are human beings, created in the image of Christ, but we are treated like savage beasts!' With this rallying cry, English farmers, according to the chronicler Jean Froissart (1337-1405), rebelled in 1381 against heavy polls and serfdom.[21]

The towns were indeed the cradle of a revolutionary, very delicate experiment: burgher culture. What this revolution was all about, what was at stake, has been grossly misinterpreted, especially since the nineteenth century.

Although the towns certainly merit a key role in any history of capitalism (a central nineteenth century interest), to say that the emergence of capitalism is somehow the essence of the medieval city is not accurate. The cities were not founded to create capitalism. What, then, were they about?

4 An Interpretation of Western Development (2): the Originating Values

Recent research shows, that a more correct view of medieval cities is to see them as an attempt to combine, in a viable political and social order, a number of different moral impulses and intuitions articulated in the West, especially under the influence of Christianity. I will call this a particular 'value coalition'. It is this value coalition that makes up the social capital which could well be the explanatory secret of the economic and social take-off of the cities. What were the key ingredients of this value coalition?

The Value of Peace. First of all, the town associations incorporated key elements of the first great international social movement in Europe, the Peace of God movement (*pax Dei or treuga Dei*), an intriguing example of what we would now call a civil society initiative.[22] This movement, which was initiated and promoted predominantly by the Church or members of religious orders, tried to generate social pressure in order to bridle the almost Hobbesian war of all against all, that the feudal warlords continually waged among themselves. This was done by establishing more and more fight-free days (Friday, Saturday, Sunday) and by pressuring arms-carrying people (such as knights) to vow not to attack innocent or unarmed people like women, children or the poor. Parts of these oaths were incorporated into town constitutions and citizens had to promise that they would resolve their conflicts peacefully. In this way, following the lead of the Church, the attempt was made to create islands of civil peace.[23]

The Values of Liberty, Equality and Brotherhood. The town association provided a social space, in which people could recognize each other as free and equal, and in which participants committed themselves to mutual assistance (*mutuum adiutorium*).[24] Here we find the true birthplace of the civil ideals that we habitually associate with the French Revolution, but which were already very much alive some centuries before: liberty, equality and brotherhood.

This fed into another element which has often been obliterated by modern, sometimes quite ideological historiography: the rudimentary democracy of the monasteries—the free talent-based election of abbots and abbesses—was developed in the cities into quite a full-fledged democracy, with city councils and voting rights for all citizens (often even including women!).

In such a moral and spiritual climate, the institution of slavery simply did not make sense anymore and, during the Middle Ages, it was abandoned throughout Europe, with an appeal to the original freedom with which God had endowed every human being. In Bologna in 1256, for example, 5,600 slaves were freed simultaneously on the terms of the recently passed *Legge del Paradiso* (Paradise Law). On this occasion, an old letter of pope Gregory I was invoked as one of the key grounds of appeal, in which (around 590!) he spoke with truly Rousseauian grandeur of the *pristina libertas*, the original, paradisiacal freedom of every human being.[25] Not until what has come to be known as 'modernity' was slavery reintroduced by Europeans, tempted as they were by the prospects of global dominance and economic prosperity in the colonies far away from their home countries, notwithstanding explicit and repeated protests in various papal encyclicals (but who listens to a pope when huge profits are at stake?).[26]

The Value of Labor. No slaves—this meant that everybody had to put their hands to the plough (if I am allowed this non-urban metaphor here). What was truly remarkable was the extent to which manual labor and professional practices gained a constitutive role in medieval town communities. This is another parallel with Western European monastic communities (the Benedictine *ora et labora*) and is markedly different from the Classical *polis* as analyzed by Aristotle. For medieval citizens, the fulfillment of their humanity was not the time spent in the civic assembly (*ekklesia*), let alone the time spent in reflecting on the nature of the universe (*bios theoretikos, vita contemplativa,* the contemplative life), but their daily lives of work and trade (*vita activa*).[27]

The Value of Community. In medieval towns, living together was taken very seriously. The cities abounded with all kinds of associations. The most eye-catching ones were the guilds (called *collegia* or *universitates*), which even played a central political role, as the governance of the city was basically organized through them.[28] Medieval towns also spawned not only churches, monasteries and guilds, but also Christian lay orders and other groups that were running, for example, local hospitals, poorhouses and orphanages.[29] Here, practices, lasting attitudes and customs were engraved—the social capital that perhaps explains why to this day volunteer work is still highly regarded in Northwestern Europe (an attitude that the settlers took with them to the U.S.).

The Value of Mutual Care. I have already mentioned the hospitals, poorhouses and orphanages. Historian Paul Veyne identifies this mutual care as the most visible and truly unique characteristic of Western cities.[30] In general, perhaps the most central value of the medieval town communities was, in line with the teaching on the Christian virtues, *caritas*, which Paul had identified as 'the highest road', and which had come to be identified as the highest of the three theological virtues (next to hope and faith). The city as a whole saw the care for the poor and needy as a central task (no matter how difficult and contested this may often have been in practice). In this respect, the guilds also were key players: they established and ran educational institutions, and took care of the orphans and widows of deceased guild members.

The Value of the Fair Market. This moral framework included the market: a mutual, talent-driven exchange of goods and services. Calvin, the Protestant Reformer, and a man rooted in the medieval town culture, was later to describe the market in exactly these terms: an expression of the solidarity and readiness of people to support each other. Everybody offered to others the fruits of their own talents and capabilities.[31] In this context, it was to be expected that prices would have to be just (*justum pretium*). Exorbitant, usurious profits were out of the question and even punishable. Until the late eighteenth century, *pleonexia*, our contemporary 'virtue' of always desiring to have more just for the fun of it, was considered a vice. Perhaps for this reason, it is advisable not to speak of capitalism (in the pejorative sense that it is often used today) until the eighteenth century, as there may have been many earlier practices prefiguring capitalism.[32]

5 The Central Aspirations of Western Development (Partly Illustrated by Adam Smith)

Looking back at 'how it all began', one can easily see the contours of an historic world transformation of the ideals concerning living together as humans, the ideals of a good society. Since medieval times, these ideals have increasingly become the driving force, the *dynamis*, of Western history. And through this history, they have even become projected on the global canvas. We can summarize this transformation in three central tenets.

(a) The transition from *homo hierarchicus* to *homo aequalis*. Almost all political and social theories (and practices) of earlier times, and in many other cultures, presupposed a kind of natural order, according to which some people have a higher position than others (Greeks and barbarians; men and women; free citizens and slaves, and so on). Perhaps the most important achievement of the medieval town was the attempt at a non-hierarchical coordination of human action, which was to become the objective of all Western political orders (although failing time and again!).

This transition had, among many other things, one economic effect: as soon as a society starts to make more extensive use of all the talents that each of its members possesses, it will be exponentially more successful than a society that doesn't do that. As Marx and Engels said about the bourgeois society: 'It has been the first to show what man's activity can bring about. It has accomplished wonders far surpassing Egyptian pyramids, Roman aqueducts, and Gothic cathedrals.'

(b) The transition from all-encompassing, 'totalistic' communities to associations of freedom and free associations. Starting in the (formerly so-called) medieval period, the idea that human communities, be they tribal communities, or political communities, should entirely encompass and exhaustively represent all members, has become obsolete. A political community should be limited in scope, allowing for other types of communities to flourish in their own way, standing their own ground: religious communities, social communities, business communities, educational communities, and so on. The intrinsic value of what we today often call 'civil society' has to be acknowledged as one of the key ingredients of political freedom, and of economic development. An independent civil society (of which religious communities can be an active part) is crucial for identifying, and in many instances remedying as well, what in the social sciences is often called 'state failure' and/or 'market failure'. The discovery of the West in this respect is that a free civil society does not have to hinder social cohesion but is actually capable of furthering it.

(c) The transition from the primacy of heroic virtues (being fit for war) toward the primacy of *agape* or *caritas*: the primacy of 'care and flourish values'. A society's success is not to be measured by its dominance over other societies on the battlefield, but by the extent to which it is a society that values all its citizens equally, giving them equal opportunities, promoting and facilitating their flourishing, and restoring their inherent worth and capabilities (when these are violated).

The awareness of these transformations in Western consciousness has had momentous implications for the long trail of revolutions that have occurred in the West (from the medieval revolutions of the farmers and the poor, via the Dutch Revolution up until the Glorious Revolution, the American Revolution and the French Revolution).

First of all, the revolutions were often triggered and stimulated by a covert awareness that an old order had already lost its legitimacy, for by its very existence it had violated some key characteristics of what had become the new order, the order of the transition.

Secondly, these revolutions had a substantial idea, although sometimes still very inchoately present, of the new society that should be established after the revolution (something which is often lacking in revolutions). The series of revolutions that has occurred in the West were not nihilistic destructive revolutions, but 'revolutions with a cause'.

Thirdly, each phase in which some of these ideals were partially realized, sowed the seeds for a next phase in which more of these ideals would be realized. For example, just remember how Martin Luther King could base his entire campaign for racial justice on the already existing Bill of Rights. This is illustrative of many (earlier) Western revolutions. Think about the rallying cry of the English farmers in 1381 (see above).

The extent to which these ideals later became 'bread and butter' without even feeling the need to explicate their specific Christian background, can be illustrated by briefly referring again to the work of Adam Smith. In his massive *An Inquiry into the Nature and Causes of the Wealth of Nations* (already mentioned earlier) one can find a strong sentiment against the nobility, and in favor of working people.

Labor is for him the central key to prosperity, not inherited wealth, or the availability of precious metals. What distinguishes labor from other forms of capital is that everybody can do it; it is not a resource that is only available for the happy few. Choosing labor as the central key to prosperity ensures the full and equal participation of everybody, 'all the ranks of the people'—and that is what a healthy economy is all about for Smith. The market is the platform on which the results of labor activities are exchanged. As Smith argues in the second chapter of Book I (the first part of the work), this propensity to exchange goods is typically human (greyhounds don't do it). 'In a civilized society, man stands in constant need of the co-operation and assistance of great multitudes', Smith continues here. So it is fair to describe a developed society, in his view, as a grand scheme of mutual cooperation. Every participant is therefore obliged to focus on the interests of the other participants: 'Give me that which I want, and you shall have this what you want' (not surprisingly, given Smith's Calvinist background, one hears the echo of John Calvin's idea of the market!).

Everybody has talents that he or she can employ for the interest of others and, in that way, for his own interest too, Smith goes on to emphasize. We have to address ourselves to the self-love (not love of ourselves, as is almost always said about Smith, but) of the other, whether butcher, brewer or baker. This is the way that, as he mentions in the title of Book I, 'produce is naturally distributed among the different ranks of the people'.

But to make this possible, the public should ensure that everyone can participate in it. In often overlooked passages later in the work (Book V), Smith argues for basic education for all people, including girls, to be provided collectively, in case people cannot afford it themselves. One can safely infer that for Smith, society as a system of mutual cooperation is predicated upon social capital, 'sympathy', as Smith would call it, or 'the ability to place oneself in the position of the other', the central concept of his earlier book, The Theory of Moral Sentiments (1759).

6   The Self-Undermining of the Ideal: Five Shadows

During its entire history, burgher culture was accompanied, haunted, by five dark shadows that could (and still can) pervert it from within—and often indeed have done so. These shadows are sometimes hard to identify, for in some cases they start out as apt responses to aberrations within the culture, and therefore have the appearance of legitimacy, precisely on the basis of the key tenets of burgher culture. Often they dress themselves in a religious cloak. They can be seen as an extension and elaboration of what was earlier identified as 'the cultural contradictions of capitalism'. These five shadows, the cultural contradictions of the burgher culture, can be briefly identified using five Ps: possession, perfection, power, pride and privacy. They undermine the socio-moral infrastructure that supports the burgher-culture—and can therefore give rise to crises and even to revolutions, and at times they may succeed in disturbing, suffocating or even destroying burgher culture.

Possessivism. The first shadow is what Macpherson has called economic possessivism, the egocentric instrumentalization of the burgher culture as a means of acquiring maximal private wealth, the emergence of a culture of greed.[33] Although we have noted that the cities were not founded as economic centers, people did get the opportunity to use their own talents. And whenever this happens, they reap material fruits and may acquire wealth. But this is only one step removed from self-indulgence and self-enrichment if there is no accompanying sense of social responsibility or gratitude toward the community that enabled one to employ these talents. The bonds of solidarity are severed. An upper class emerges that seizes political power, and considers itself the only important group in town. A rich and self-enriching upper class starts to exclude the lower classes from common civil enterprise. Guilds, for example, may develop into exclusive cartels instead of qualitative communities for the development of artisan or commercial talents. The burgher can indeed develop into a *bourgeois*, an exploitive *homo economicus*. But this is a perversion of the burgher ideal. In such an exorbitant, possession-oriented culture, the delicate socio-moral infrastructure comes under severe pressure. The social capital, the basis of the new social order, leaks away. Capitalism undermines the free market society.

Perfection. The second shadow is cast by the utopian alternative, the utopian radicalization of civic ideals: the spell of perfection. As soon as one realizes that a social order is not a natural phenomenon but can be created, why not create a perfect order? Early in the High Middle Ages, we see the rise of all kinds of revolutionary utopian movements, especially in the cities.[34] These early movements show considerable typological parallels with totalitarian experiments like the one in Munster (1534), and the more recent utopian experiments such as communism and national socialism. They set out to destroy burgher society, a 'quite good' society, in the name of a perfect society that subsequently turned out to be unattainable. On balance, the utopian alternative resulted in an orgy of destruction—of people, social structures, the socio-moral infrastructure, mutual trust, and social capital. Here, a comment by Deirdre McCloskey, which probably applies to all the shadows analyzed here, is particularly apposite: 'they made an impossible Best into the enemy of the actual Good'.[35]

Power. The third shadow is that of the heavy bureaucratic power structures that form in and above burgher society, and often originate in a kind of obsession with national power, or an attempt at realizing some parts of a utopian agenda. In burgher society, a government has to protect the space for citizens'

33

free associational initiatives, but there is a constant temptation to intrude on that space and take over the initiative. In the history of burgher society, we constantly come across new classes of bureaucrats, often wise governors, but just as often power-drunk *podestàs*, mostly closely connected with the possessivists, who create an exclusive oligarchy.[36] Time and again, burgher society is haunted by groups of managers and bureaucrats who refuse to internalize the associative-federal thinking stimulated by the Christian tradition, and instead opt for hierarchical exclusiveness with no regard for the networks and associations and their inherent social capital.

Pride. The fourth shadow is that of 'civilizational pride'; pride which presents one's own civilization as the acme, the end-point of human history—and from this idea, curiously, legitimizes confronting other civilizations and peoples with standards that are different from one's own. A very early example is the Crusades, which started at the very moment that the knightly way of life, with its permanent mutual warfare, was virtually outlawed by the Church in Europe. Yet, at the same time this knightly way of life was encouraged if the knights were to go abroad, to the Holy Land.[37] Another example was the reintroduction of slavery—though under ecclesiastical protest—in overseas territories, after its abandonment in medieval times throughout Europe.

The key point of this civilizational pride is that it does not see the foundational value coalition of burgher society as an aspiration, but as an achievement. It no longer functions as a transcendent, critical standard of the social order. It has become an a priori stamp of approval, even a divine approval or the approval of world history. An essential part of civilizational pride is that it silences (potential) dissenting voices.

Privacy. The fifth shadow is that of the boundless individualism that vehemently rejects the self-limitation, the 'asceticism' that is a precondition for living together as citizens. This abstract individualism disturbs the delicate civil balance of rights and duties that sustains the burgher culture.

7   Conclusions: Civil Society as Free Space for Social Capital

In this essay, I have attempted to give an interpretation of Western development. An essential element of this interpretation was the idea of a transformation of the social imaginary, a transformation of the social consciousness, from hierarchy to equality, from totality to differentiation, from heroic values to care values. The title that I have given to this essay is 'Remembering the Future'. This title carries at least three intimations for me.

The first is that this transformation of consciousness always had the index of the future attached to it. The old world (of hierarchical, closed, heroic communities) was experienced as something of a bygone age. Christianity induced in Western consciousness a sense of old and new, of past and future, of a new world to come that was already shedding some light in and on the present. And yet, this new advent was attached to—at the time when its message received acceptance in Europe—almost thousand year old texts. In these old religious texts, Europeans remembered a new future.

The second intimation is that the great transformation I have indicated (from hierarchy to equality, from totality to social plurality and from heroic to care values) in a way always is and will remain a 'future event', a call that constantly challenges us: do we actually embody the potential that is entailed in it? The transformation(s) constantly seem to give birth to new, hitherto still unconsidered implications. Therefore, it is at the same time a critical future. Its ontological status can be described as 'transcendent', and yet we encounter throughout history moments of embodiment—in human actions, social initiatives, institutions, and political structures. In such moments, the Christian ideas about a good society (freedom, equal dignity, mutual support, labor, community, care for the weak) found a certain measure of temporary embodiment in concrete social realities. Fragile perhaps, embattled perhaps, but there nevertheless. So, perhaps it is even better to describe its ontological status as 'between immanence and transcendence', between an 'already' and a 'not yet'.

The third intimation of the title is that for me, as the author of the essay, this anamnestic exercise is also directed toward the future. By going back to the past (remembering), my hope and intention is to find some direction for the future: to wrestle from the permanent shadows a healthy society, for which the burgher culture provided the first contours. There are at least three things that I believe can be learned from the story I have presented here (though they would need a much more elaborate argumentation than I can give here).

The first learning point is that a crucial ingredient of a good society, both in terms of 'being economically successful' and 'providing a context for human flourishing' is social capital: although I did not set out to corroborate, let alone prove, this point, a deal of evidence in its favor has been presented. As a research paradigm, it deserves great attention, if only to provide an alternative for the so-called 'neo-liberal' approaches to development. To present a variation on the often misinterpreted statement of Adam Smith: 'It is not from the self-interest of the butcher, the brewer and the baker, that we expect our dinner, but from their willingness and ability to cooperate with others.'

The second point: although religion can play a negative role in development, and can be socially divisive, it can very often play a constructive role and create social cohesion. As the French aristocrat Alexis de Tocqueville noted when he visited the United States of America in the early nineteenth century, religion directs one's attention away from the little inner circle of the self and its own interests, and makes people aware that they are part of a larger whole, within which they have responsibility.[38] In that sense, De Tocqueville even made the bold claim that, for democratic societies, as America already was at the time, religion can be considered to be 'the first of their political institutions', indispensable for the maintenance of republican institutions.[39] Religion, and I have shown this at length for the case of Christianity's role in the West, can provide social capital, and create a sense of responsibility toward others in society, even unknown others, and even those outside one's own society. However, this social capital requires free social space in order to be redeemed and to be concretely embodied.

This brings me to the third point. This regards the thorny question as to whether, and if so, how, the socio-moral infrastructure of a burgher culture can be sustained. Can it escape the cultural contradictions of capitalism, and perhaps even be made immune to the seductive power of the shadows sketched above? There is, I believe, no recipe or philosopher's stone that can achieve that. Time and again, ideas of humane development, of 'development for human flourishing' have been jeopardized. Ideologies, political oppression, totalitarian regimes, economic exploitation by irresponsible corporations, and so on, have all been able to pervert and frustrate a healthy social order in which all people can flourish. Somehow, both states and markets often tend to lose their humanizing potential. When the salt loses its salting power, how can it become salt again? The remarkable thing about the last centuries is that, time and again, the ideals come up again. An essential minimal precondition for this is a free space for civil society—a non-governmental and non-profit sphere, where people can form ideas—and practically embody them—about what a good life is, about how people can flourish. In the short run, this free civil sphere may seem to be a nuisance at times, but in the long run, a society can only profit from having the courage to endow itself with the gift of criticism, the gift of moral inspiration, the gift of the citizen's moral engagement.

Without having something like what we today would call a 'civil society', the development of the West would never have started. Without it, it would never have continued. Without it, Western societies would never have had the courage of self-criticism and constant moral renewal (even after they allowed horrible cruelties to happen). Therefore, in my view, every society should grant itself this precious gift by allowing a free civil society (which includes freedom of religion), if not for reasons of principle then for reasons of pragmatic functionality: making steps forward in the constant development, the permanent march toward a humane and morally engaged society.

1 A. Smith, *An Inquiry Into the Nature and Causes of the Wealth of Nations* (1776). Note: when referring to classical works that have gone through many editions, both in print and on the web, I shall indicate the chapter from which the quotation is taken, so that readers can easily find the reference in their own edition.

2 D.S. Landes, *The Wealth and Poverty of Nations. Why Some Are So Rich and Some So Poor* (New York: W.W. Norton, 1998).

3 K. Marx and F. Engels, *The Communist Manifesto* (Ch. 1).

4 W. W. Rostow, *The Stages of Economic*

Growth: A Non-Communist Manifesto (Cambridge: Cambridge University Press, 1960).

5 R. Putnam, *Making Democracy Work. Civic Traditions in Modern Italy*. (Princeton: Princeton University Press, 1993). See also the contribution by Ab Klink to this volume.

6 F. Fukuyama, *Trust. The Social Virtues and the Creation of Prosperity* (New York: Free Press, 1995).

7 J. Schneider, 'Organizational Social Capital and Nonprofits,' *Nonprofit and Voluntary Sector Quarterly*, XX/X (2009), 1-20.

8 M. Weber, *The Protestant Ethic and the Spirit of Capitalism* (New York: Charles Scribner's Sons, 1958) (Or. *Die protestantische Ethik und der Geist des Kapitalismus*, 1904/1905, rev. 1920).

9 D. Bell, 'The Cultural Contradictions of Capitalism,' *Journal of Aesthetic Education* 6 1/2 (1972), 11-38. Cf. the later book *The Cultural Contradictions of Capitalism* (New York: Basic Books Publishers, 1976).

10 I prefer to use this term to denote a specific culture, comparable to the way we speak of 'Chinese culture', 'Hellenistic culture' or 'Classical culture'. I choose not to use the pejorative term 'bourgeois culture' or more generic terms such as 'civil culture'. The term 'civil society' (which was used for burgher culture in the eighteenth century), has come to denote primarily the non-governmental and non-profit sector of society. Burgher culture emerged in Europe, starting around 1150 in towns, and then gradually expanding up to the present through various different crises and phases.

11 The argument here is presented at greater length in Govert Buijs, 'Christianity and the Vicissitudes of European Burgher Culture,' *Religion, State & Society* 41/ 2 (2013), 103-132.

12 Cf. R. Stark, *The Victory of Reason. How Christianity Led to Freedom, Capitalism, and Western Success* (New York: Random House, 2006), xi ff.

13 G. Duby, *De kathedralenbouwers. Portret van de middeleeuwse maatschappij 980-1420* [*The Age of Cathedrals. Art and Society 980-1420*] (Amsterdam: Contact/Olympus, 2002), 44.

14 Duby, *Kathedralenbouwers*, 51. The picture of the feudal age as an age of the glorification of war and violence was created for the first time by the nineteenth century French historian Guizot, who also introduced the very term 'feudal age', and has by and large stood the test of time via the work of Marc Bloch until Duby's work. A more recent affirming, and even radicalized, restatement of the picture is presented by T. N. Bisson, 'The 'Feudal Revolution'', *Past and Present* 142 (1994), 6-42. For him, the feudal age was a total meltdown of a pre-existing order of justice and the emergence of 'violence that had the potential to mould a new order of power'; violence after the year 1000 became increasingly 'affective' and anarchic instead of constructive, order-creating. See as well D. Barthélemy and S. D. White, 'Debate: the feudal revolution,' *Past and Present* 152 (1996), 205-223. A further critical discussion of Bisson's radical picture is given by T. Reuter, 'Debating the 'feudal revolution'', in T. Reuter, *Medieval Polities and Modern Mentalities* (Cambridge: Cambridge University Press, 2006), 72-88. For an overview of the debate, see the introductory chapter of H. Teunis, *The Appeal to the Original Status. Social justice in Anjou in the Eleventh Century* (Hilversum: Verloren, 2006), 13-24. The debate has not really challenged the observation that physical violence was considered a normal and legitimate element of everyday politics, even at a local level. But it was not 'total violence' aimed at the destruction of the other, but was aimed at establishing a new balance of power and property, violence as an invitation to renegotiate new settlements.

15 M. de Reu, 'The Missionaries. The First Contact between Paganism and Christianity,' in *The Pagan Middle Ages*, ed. L. Milis (Woodbridge: Boydel and Brewer, 1998), 13-37.

16 D. McCloskey, 'Bourgeois Virtues?' in *Cato Policy Report* (May/June 2006). See also D.

McCloskey, *The Bourgeois Virtues: Ethics for an Age of Commerce* (Chicago: University of Chicago Press, 2006).

17 The parallels between monastery and medieval town are developed extensively by L. Mumford, *The City in History* (London: Penguin/Peregrine, 1987), 269 (original ed. 1961): 'It was in the monastery that the ideal purposes of the city were sorted out, kept alive and eventually renewed. It was here, too, that the practical value of restraint, order, regularity, honesty, inner discipline was established, before these qualities were passed over to the medieval town and post-medieval capitalism, in the forms of inventions and business practices: the clock, the account book, the ordered day.' See also H. Berman, *Law and Revolution. The Formation of the Western Legal Tradition* (Cambridge, MA: Harvard University Press, 1984), 361 ff.

18 B. Hamm, *Bürgertum und Glaube. Konturen der städtischen Reformation* (Göttingen: Vandenhoeck and Ruprecht, 1996), 20 ff. Of course, it should not be forgotten, as Hamm also emphasizes, that around 1500, almost at the end of this movement in the German Empire, there were still around 80% of the people living in the countryside. Most of the cities were small, with about 2000 inhabitants.

19 In *Epistola ad Paulum Volzium*, quoted in Hamm, *Bürgertum*, 81.

20 In addition to the books of Mumford and Berman, already mentioned, my understanding of the medieval towns and their social-moral infrastructure and aspirations has been greatly enhanced by A. Black, *Guild and State. European Political Thought from the Twelfth Century to the Present* (New Brunswick/London: Transaction, 2003) (or. *Guilds and Civil Society* (London: Methuen, 1984); U. Meier, *Mensch und Bürger. Die Stadt im Denken spätmittelalterlicher Theologen, Philosophen und Juristen* (München: R. Oldenbourg Verlag, 1994), 23-61. Cf. U. Meier and K. Schreiner, „Bürger- und Gottesstadt im späten Mittelalter,' in *Sozial- und Kulturgeschichte des Bürgertums*, (Bürgertum.

Beiträge zur europäischen Gesellschaftsgeschichte, Band 18), ed. P;. Lundgreen (Göttingen: Vandenhoeck und Ruprecht, 2000) as well as G. Dilcher, *Bürgerrecht und Stadtverfassung im europäischen Mittelalter* (Keulen: Böhlau Verlag, 1996).

21 J. le Goff, *De cultuur van middeleeuws Europa* (Amsterdam: Wereldbibliotheek 1987), 376 (or. *La Civilisation de l'Occident Médiéval*, Paris 1984); N. Cohn, *The Pursuit of the Millennium. Revolutionary Millenarians and Mystical Anarchists of the Middle Ages* (London: Secker and Warburg, 1957), 199 ff.

22 Berman, *Law and Revolution*, 90 speaks of the Peace of God movement as 'the first peace movement in Europe'. One could even speak more generally of the first pan-Western European social movement.

23 For the procedures of the tribunals of the Peace of God movement, see Duby, *Kathedralenbouwers*, 46; Berman, *Law and Revolution*, 90f; B. Tierney and S. Painter, *Western Europe in the Middle Ages 300-1475* (New York: Alfred A. Knopf, 1978,3rd. ed.), 269.

24 See Meier and Schreiner, *Bürger- und Gottesstadt* 49; Black, *Guild and State*, 3-31, 44-75.

25 For the history of slavery and the continuous papal rejection of this, see R. Stark, *For the Glory of God. How Monotheism Led to Reformations, Science, Witch-hunts and the End of Slavery* (Princeton: Princeton University Press, 2003), 291-366. For the influence of the letter of Gregory I and the expression *pristina libertas*, see U. Meier, *Der falsche und der richtige Name der Freiheit. Zur Neuinterpretation eines Grundwertes der Florentiner Stadtgesellschaft (13.-16. Jahrhundert)*, in K. Schreiner and U. Meier, *Stadtregiment und Bürgerfreiheit*. (Bürgertum, Band 7), (Göttingen: Vandenhoeck & Ruprecht, 1994), 50 f.

26 The following popes explicitly denounced slavery in various encyclicals, also after Columbus had entered the New World: Eugene IV (bull *Sicut dudum*, against the enslavement of the black inhabitants of the Canary Islands, 1435), repeated in comparable bulls by Pius II (1462) and

Sixtus IV (1475). Paul III's bull *Sublimus Dei* of 1537 (*Against Slavery in the New World*) made making and keeping slaves a ground for excommunication. Other bulls against slavery and the slave trade were issued by Popes Gregory XIV (*Cum Sicuti*, 1591), Urban VIII (*Commissum Nobis*, 1639), Benedict XIV (*Immensa Pastorum*, 1741) and Gregory XVI (*In Supremo*, 1839). Moreover, the Inquisition (!) strongly denounced the holding of slaves in 1686. See Stark, *Glory of God*, esp. 329 ff.

27 In this light, it appears that the transition from the contemplative life to the active life is to be dated much earlier than is claimed, for example, by Hannah Arendt, *The Human Condition*. (Chicago: University of Chicago Press 1958), 289 ff.

28 See Black, *Guild and State, passim*).

29 A recent impression of this in the city of Utrecht in the Netherlands can be found in L. Bogaers, *Aards, betrokken en zelfbewust: de verwevenheid van cultuur en religie in katholiek Utrecht, 1300-1600* (*Earthly, Committed and Self-Conscious: the Interwovenness of Culture and Religion in Catholic Utrecht, 1300-1600*) (Utrecht: Levend Verleden, 2008). The translation of the title ('earthly, committed and self-conscious/proud') tells it all: Bogaers offers an important reinterpretation of the medieval mind.

30 See P. Veyne, *Bread and Circuses* (London: Lane/Penguin, 1990) (trans. of *Le pain et le cirque* (Paris, Éditions du Seuil, 1976): 'When we look down from an aeroplane on a city of the baroque period and the ruins of a Roman city, separated by sixteen centuries, we see in the baroque city everywhere the roofs of convents, hospices, charitable establishments. In the Roman ruins, public buildings constructed by *euergetai* seem to cover more ground than dwellings. The observer thinks that he is seeing the operation of one and the same function, redistribution, in the two towns across the centuries, to judge by its manifestations, which are on the same scale in both places. But this is an illusion.'

31 See A. Biéler, *La pensée économique et sociale de Calvin* (Geneva: Georg 1961), 235 (English trans. *Calvin's Economic and Social Thought* (Geneva: WARC/WCC, 2005). Biéler quotes extensively from the *Corpus Calvinum*, in which the same theme is stressed time and again: labor and exchange of the fruits of labor are services that one person renders to another, and in this way they are bound together in a community. See especially Biéler, *Pensée économique*, 335 ff., 410 ff., 449 ff.

32 The point is illustrated by a famous episode in Boston (USA) in 1644. Robert Keayne was accused of a terrible sin. Keayne was a pious, wealthy man of reputation, who had come to America 'for conscience's sake and for the advancement of the Gospel', a truly model Puritan. However, in a certain business transaction he had taken a sixpenny profit per shilling, which was nothing less than usury. The judges were planning to punish him in court for this gross misdemeanour. However, because of his good reputation, they were lenient and merely imposed a fine of 200 pounds. But when the church of Boston started looking into the case as well, Keayne wanted to make a public confession. In tears, he repented of his selfish, wicked and corrupt heart. The next Sunday, the pastor of Keayne's church, Mr Cotton, capitalised on this opportunity with a great sermon denouncing greed and lust for profit. It is utterly wrong to buy as cheaply as possible and try to sell for as high a price as possible. It is equally wrong to try to compensate for an earlier loss (for example through shipwreck) by raising prices later. It is wrong to attune sale prices to buying prices. 'All false, false, false!' cried the Minister. The story is found in J. Winthrop, *Winthrop's Journal: The History of New England from 1630 to 1649* (vol.1) (ed. J.K. Hosmer) (New York: Charles Scribner's Sons, 1908), 315-319. It also appears in Tawney's classic *Religion and the Rise of Capitalism: a Historical Study* (London: Murray, 1926), 129 ff., and in R. Heilbroner, *The Worldly Philosophers* (New York: Simon & Schuster, 1953), 20 ff.

33 C. B. Macpherson, *The Political Theory of Possessive Individualism: Hobbes te Locke* (Oxford: Oxford University Press, 1970).

34 These were first covered extensively by Cohn in, *Pursuit*. For the late medieval and early modern period, see also G. H. Williams, *The Radical Reformation* (Philadelphia: Westminster Press, 1962). E. Voegelin, *The New Science of Politics* (Chicago: Chicago University Press, 1952), 110-21, offers challenging insights but limited historical material; much better documented material is to be found in his posthumously published work, *History of Political Ideas* (Vols. 2, 3 and 4) (Columbia, MO: University of Missouri Press, 1997-1998). Material from these works which deals specifically with medieval revolutionary sects is collected in one volume by P. Opitz: E. Voegelin, *Das Volk Gottes*, ed. P. Opitz (Munich: Wilhelm Fink Verlag, 1994).

35 McCloskey, *Cato Policy Report*.

36 This is the background of Machiavelli's revealing analyses of the political order, taking a perversion for the true nature of burgher culture and even of politics itself.

37 My reference to the Crusades is all too brief and ignores important nuances. A very interesting recent reinterpretation of the Crusades is R. Stark, *God's Battalions: the Case for the Crusades* (New York: Harper Collins, 2009).

38 See also the contribution by Ab Klink to this volume.

39 A. de Tocqueville, *Democracy in America*, vol. 1, Ch. 17 (*or. De la démocratie en Amérique*, 1830).

2

Government, Legal Personality and Internal Structure of Religious Communities in the Netherlands and a number of other European Countries

Tymen J. van der Ploeg

1 Introduction

Freedom of religion implies both the freedom of religion of the individual person, and the collective freedom of a religious community. For the continuity of the tradition of a religion, it is important that the religious community, as such, is recognized as the bearer of the freedom of religion and that the religious community can exercise its rights independent of any legal form.[1] It is, however, practical—and often necessary—for the religious community to be able to act in society as a legal person. To be a legal person means that the organization/community forms a unity with regard to the outside world for which it needs representatives, and a unity inside (through decision making by competent bodies).

The (management board of a) legal person can act as a representative (of the members) of the community.[2] This legal person could be the owner or renter of a place of worship, who can contract a pastor and other professionals for the community, and be the owner of the money that is collected for the service of the community. If there is no legal person, the contracts have to be concluded by individual members of the community. The property, although intended for the service of the entire community, would then be owned by individual members, which is unattractive for both the religious community and its members.

In this paper I will first describe (Section 2) the relationships between the government and the legal personality of religious communities in Europe, in order to place the situation in The Netherlands in context. It appears that, on this subject, there is much differentiation. In Section 3, the Dutch 'model' is sketched. Following on from this, I describe the involvement of the government in the internal structures of religious communities (Section 4). After these rather formal aspects, Section 5 deals with the governmental facilities that are made available to religious communities, and the differences between countries regarding: pastoral care in military service, penitential institutions and hospitals, religious education in public schools, tax facilities and subsidies. In Section 6, I draw some conclusions regarding the Dutch approach to the legal personality and the governmental facilities of religious communities.

2   Government and the Legal Personality of Religious Communities in Europe

In Europe, several rather different types of relationships exist between the government and religious communities regarding legal personality, which has been caused by different historical developments in these countries. In this section, I will not give a description or an explanation of these historical developments in the countries concerned, but I will sketch the different systems that are in use.[3] There is a great variety throughout Europe.[4] The different systems will be discussed in the order of the closeness of the connection between the government and the religious community.

2.1   The State Church

In some countries, like Denmark, Greece and the United Kingdom, a state church exists. This means that the state has given a particular religious community—in Denmark, the Lutheran National Church; in Greece, the Greek-Orthodox Church; in England, the Anglican Church; and in Scotland, the Presbyterian Church—an official governmental status. In the constitution of these countries, this church has a special place, and it is funded by the state. In Denmark, the church is a part of government, but in England, this is not the case. In countries where a state church is not a part of government, the legal personality will be mostly bestowed by the constitution or by a special law.[5] How strong the relationship between the Anglican Church and the government is, appears from the fact that the bishops are appointed by the crown and some of them participate in the House of Lords. But the state church-model is not a uniform one. The competences of the state in relation to the church and vice-versa are regulated very differently in countries with a state church. As these countries also adhere to the freedom of religion, other religious communities than the state church are allowed. These other religious communities, however, generally have to choose a secular form (see Section 2.4). State churches have a long history; as far as I know state churches have not been established in Europe in recent times. In democracies where there is a separation of church/religion and state, the establishment of a state church would not be obvious.

In the next sub-sections, the religious communities are more strictly separated from the state. The focus is on the *legal personality*. It is worthwhile to keep in mind the advices of the OSCE (Organization for Security and Co-operation in Europe), based on the freedom of religion as guaranteed by the European Convention on Human Rights. According to the guidelines of the OSCE/ODIHR (Office for Democratic Institutions and Human Rights), the laws governing access to legal personality should be structured in ways that facilitate the freedom of religion.[6] When the government makes legal personality available to religious communities through recognition or registration, this should not be applied on discretionary grounds but on clear and public grounds.

2.2 *Concordat*

A special form, in which the legal personality of a religious community is recognized, is the *concordat*, which in some predominantly Roman Catholic countries in Europe is concluded between the Vatican and the state.[7] The Roman Catholic Church (the Vatican) concludes a concordat as a public entity that is internationally recognized. With a concordat, the Roman Catholic Church is guaranteed the right to nominate its own officials in that country (church province), but concluding a concordat doesn't necessarily mean that the Roman Catholic Church of the country obtains a legal personality. In Belgium, for instance, this is not the case.

2.3 *Recognition and Registration*

In many countries, religious communities can be *recognized* or *registered as such* by the government. In this way, they obtain legal personality. In my opinion, one cannot say that the governments are cooperating with religions, as they merely allow them to participate in society.[8] This method is, for instance, used in Austria, Germany, Italy and Spain.

In *Austria* and *Germany*, the national public authorities grant legal personality to religious communities on the basis of some objective conditions, like the number of their believers, their regulations, and their creed.[9] In Austria, a religious community can be recognized as a 'religious community' (since 1874) or as a 'confessional community' (since 1998). For the latter category, less strict criteria are laid down in law. This recognition does not imply an approval of the creed of the religious community. There will be a marginal test of the creed. If it summons violence and other crimes, recognition will be refused. The recognition as a 'religious community' in Austria and Germany converts a community into a legal person of public law. Although recognized religious communities such as these have public law status, they cannot exercise public competences. It also does not mean that the government has a say in the internal affairs of the community. In Austria, for instance, they explicitly enjoy autonomy.[10] The 'confessional communities' in Austria receive legal personality by private law.

In *Spain*, religious communities can obtain legal personality under the organic Law of July 5, 1980 (nr. 7) and the Royal Decree 142/1981 on the Register of Religious Entities by registering their accordance to following given rules. After registering, they enjoy special rights which protect their internal freedom and support their external position.[11] Moreover, when they are 'firmly rooted in the area' and have a certain number of members, they may be given the opportunity of concluding an agreement with the government (state) which enables them to enjoy other economic and legal benefits.

In *Italy*, religious communities other than the Roman Catholic Church can apply for 'recognition' by the government according to the law of June 24, 1929 (no. 1159). This leads to the creation of a legal personality of its central office, not of the religious community itself.[12] These recognized religious communities may also, under certain circumstances, conclude a covenant with the government by which they receive public facilities. It seems that the government has unusual discretionary powers here. In 2007, such a covenant was concluded by the Waldensians, the Seventh Day Adventists, the Assembly of God, the Jewish community, the Baptist Church and the Lutheran Church. The application of the Jehovah Witnesses and the Buddhist Union are pending.[13]

The situation in *Belgium* is rather complicated.[14] The federal government recognizes religious denominations as 'worshipping communities' (*erediensten*), these include the Anglican Church, the Islam, the Jewish religion, the Orthodox Church, the Roman Catholic Church, the Protestant Church and the Humanists. With regard to such recognized *erediensten*, local governments are legally obliged to provide local communities with a place for worship, a salary for the local minister (albeit moderate), and, through an ecclesiastical administration (*kerkfabriek*), to take care of the continuity of religious worship. The rules for such ecclesiastical administrations, which have legal personality, are laid down in regional legislation. In the Flemish part of the country, the ecclesiastical administration has a church council that consists of five elected local church members, and a representative from the church officials. The local religious community can ask the municipality to supply additional funds when there is a financial deficit. As one may rightly suspect, this does not always encourage proper financial responsibility.[15] The recognition of national and local religious communities does not provide them with legal personality. To operate as a legal unity in society, they establish associations (and/or) foundations.

The third way in which a religious community can receive legal personality is by obtaining a legal persons form of private law, such as an *association* or *foundation*. This is a possibility in all countries.

In countries with a state church, the other religious communities can obtain legal personality by choosing a 'secular' legal form. In Denmark they have the status of associations. Apart from that, they can be approved as religious entities, with provides them certain public facilities.[16] In the United Kingdom they can be registered as charities for the advancement of religion.[17] When a country knows 'recognized' or 'registered' religious communities, this doesn't prevent other religious communities from using forms of secular private law legal persons. In *Germany, Italy* and *Spain,* religious communities can use the association form. In *Belgium,* all types of religious communities, whether they belong to a recognized denomination (*eredienst*) or not, may choose the association or foundation form.

In *The Netherlands,* religious communities are free to incorporate as an association or foundation. They are not obliged to opt for a 'church society' (*kerkgenootschap*); see Section 3. A special case is *France.*[18] The French Revolutionists viewed religious and private organizations with great suspicion. It was one hundred years after the French Revolution before French law introduced legal personality for associations and for religious communities. In 1901, the Law on Association was issued and in 1905 the Law on Religious Associations. Religious communities can use both types of associations. The religious association (*association cultuelle*) has as its only purpose the practice of worship (*culte*) and is forbidden to perform any other activities. The other association (*association culturelle*) may perform both worship and other activities. The Muslim communities generally use the general association form. For its legal personality the religious association needs a decree from the State Council; the other associations need to deposit documents regarding their purpose, and so on, at the offices of the regional authorities.

3   The Dutch Model

Compared to the other systems that are used in Europe, as described above, the Dutch model is somewhat different: the legal personality of religious communities is not dependent on governmental recognition or registration. This model has developed over the course of time since the freedom of religion was constitutionally recognized in 1848. The (organic) Law on Church Societies (*Wet op kerkgenootschappen*) originates from 1853.[19] This law did not define what a 'church society' is, but mandated the 'church societies' to register themselves with the Ministry of Justice, and provide it with their regulations (church orders). One could say that a religious community is a 'church society' when it acts as a unity in society, is not part of another church society, and is not established as an association or foundation.[20] The Ministry of Justice was only informed; it didn't recognize the religious communities as such or as legal persons like in the systems mentioned in Section 2.3. In the course of time, the interest of the Ministry in this information faded; the possibility of registration remained, but there was no sanction for not registering.

Legal personality was not dependent on registration with the Ministry of Justice, but it was considered to be a matter of civil law. According to civil law (Book 3, title 10, (old) Civil Code) organizations received legal personality when they were recognized or accepted by the government. For more than 50 years after the Law on Church Societies of 1853, it was still disputed whether the church societies were legal persons by themselves, or that they needed to follow the procedure for associations to become legal persons. The courts and legal authors, however, always considered them to be legal persons.[21]

In 1976 a new Book 2 of the Civil Code (on legal persons) came into force, in which for the first time the 'church society' was explicitly given legal personality by the law in Article 2:2 of the Civil Code. This article, however, neither gives a definition of a 'church society', nor does it provide formal requirements regarding its establishment. This causes uncertainty for religious groups that want to determine whether they are a church society (which means, a legal person).

Until 1988, church societies could feel accepted as such by their registration with the Ministry of Justice (in conformity with the Law on Church Societies of 1853).[22] In 1988, however, the Law on Church Societies was repealed, as it was thought to be obsolete, and replaced by the Law on Public Manifestation. The formal mandatory registration was officially abolished.

The established Christian and Jewish churches, which had already been active for a long time as a legal person and had been registered at the Ministry of Justice, were not in trouble by the removal of the registration. New groups (either Christian or from other religions, such as Islam) that hadn't been registered, felt uncertain if they would be accepted as a church society when they could not show any proof of it. Moreover, for non-Christian groups (especially Islamic communities) the use of the legal term 'church society' is problematic, as the term sounds too Christian. I have found one Islamic group and one Buddhist community using the church society as a legal form. Non Christian or non-Jewish religious communities usually use the secular legal forms of association or foundation (compare Section 2.4), which has some disadvantages from a freedom of religion point of view.[23]

Since 2007, church societies (if they are at the highest level of their church) have to be registered in the Trade Register, according to Article 6, Section 3 of the Law on the Trade Register (*Handelsregisterwet* 2007) and Article 18, Decree

on the Trade Register (*Handelsregisterbesluit* 2008). Neither the church regulations nor the board members of the church communities are registered. Nevertheless, the trade register has an important function: in this way, (new) religious communities which might feel uncertain, in the absence of any official
recognition or registration, about whether they can operate as a church society
(which means, as a legal person), can now be certain of that.

The Chamber of Commerce may refuse registration as a church society if it
discovers that an organization doesn't meet the requirements of Article 2 CC,
and the Act and Decree on the Commercial Register. When a religious community is registered as a church society, it can show a copy of its registration when
opening a bank account or purchasing land. However, in case of a conflict, the
court is still the final judge on whether the organization is a church society or
not.

4   The Involvement of the Government with the Internal Structure of Religious Communities

A very important aspect of the freedom of religion, guaranteed by Article 9 of
the European Convention on Human Rights (ECHR), is that religious communities may design their own organizational structure and appoint their own
officials, if applicable. This is clearly stated by the European Court on Human
rights.[24] In 1968, was decided that legal persons could not appeal against Article 9 of the ECHR.[25] This was revised by the Commission in 1979.[26] The legal
persons that were used by religious communities were accepted by the court
as bearers of the freedom of religion, representing its 'adherents'.[27] In countries
with a state church, the state generally has a say in the organizational structure
and, sometimes, in the appointment (and dismissal) of church officials.[28] On a
local level, the public authorities mostly do not interfere.

When a country uses the system of accepting religious communities as legal
persons as a way of recognizing them, the independence of the religious community is usually also recognized, explicitly or implicitly. They are allowed to
design their own internal structure, and to appoint and dismiss their own Ministers.[29] It is well known that Christian religious communities have very different structures: from very hierarchical (Roman Catholic, Eastern Orthodox)
to very democratic (Pentecostal, Baptist). Strangely enough, several European
countries have legal regulations regarding the internal structure of recognized
religious communities.[30] The appointment of ministers—or other officials—is
mostly not dependent on governmental influence.

The legal regulations around religious communities in *Belgium* (see Section
2.3) seem, in a way, to also disrupt the internal structure of religious communities. The division of property between the ecclesiastical administration (*kerkfabriek*) and the (legal person of the) local community prevents the religious

community from seriously taking its own decisions, and being responsible for them.

As described above (Section 2), in all systems, religious communities may choose, either voluntarily or mandatorily (if they don't meet the criteria of being a recognized religion/religious community), secular legal persons forms like associations and foundations. The situation in England is different, because of its different legal system. I will not go into detail about this. When these secular forms are chosen *voluntarily*, the religious community cannot complain if the chosen form restricts the community's internal structure, compared with its own religiously inspired regulation. In the Dutch situation, religious communities are not forced to take a secular form, thus, if they have chosen such a form, they have to comply with the rules of this form. Raaijmakers, however, argues that religious communities in secular forms have internal freedom as well.[31] In my opinion, this would only be true if a religious community is forced to choose a secular form. This could, for instance, be the case if the religious organization didn't meet the criteria for recognition or registration.

The legal rules on associations, aimed at—a certain—democracy may be very contrary to its—traditional—religious internal structure. The German civil code has regulated a suspension from many rules for religious associations, regarding the internal structure of associations.[32] Generally, the rules regarding the internal organization of foundations are rather limited, and do not cause problems for religious communities. The foundation generally serves, however, not as the legal identity of the religious community as a whole, but as a legal instrument. The relationship between the religious community and the legal person is in that case more complicated than when a religious community receives legal personality as such (see Sections 2.3 and 6).

5 Differentiation of Governmental Facilities Regarding Religious Communities

In this section, we look at the way religious communities are treated by the governments in the countries that were included in the earlier sections, with regard to some specific domains. Generally, all religious communities, irrespective of their legal form, enjoy the collective freedom of religion. The government is, in principle, only obliged to guarantee that religious communities may enjoy their freedom of religion. There are, however, some domains where the government facilitates religious communities in other ways. The freedom of religion doesn't require this. There is much debate about whether such facilitation is compatible with the separation of church and state. In most cases, not all religious communities are facilitated; the question is then whether all religious communities are treated equally, which would be the logical approach of a neutral state.

With regard to the separation between church and state, there are different opinions. The extremes are: a) the state may cooperate with religions and support them, but should treat them—and other worldviews—equally, and b) the state should keep religion outside the public sphere.[33] In most countries, the cooperation-model is used. This is also true for The Netherlands.[34] The most prominent example of the separation-model is France.

Like France, in The Netherlands there are no religious communities that have a special relationship with the government. Therefore, it is within the competence of the religious organizations themselves to set up their own umbrella organizations for their relationship with government and parliament. The oldest of these is—since 1946—the CIO, the contact body for the relationship of Christian and Jewish church societies with the government. Newer are the two umbrella-organizations formed by Muslim organizations, a Hindu organization and a Buddhist Union.

I will mention four domains in which governments facilitate religious communities.

49

a. Direct *religious activities* are made available and *financed* by the government and performed by Ministers of religious communities, in the domain of pastoral care for military personnel, in penitential institutions and in health and youth care institutions. The presence of religion in institutions such as these, where people's freedom is usually very limited, is considered necessary. The provision of pastoral care in these circumstances is seen as being of public interest; it is (also) a way of guaranteeing freedom of religion for the individuals who inhabit the institutions.

Education on religion (or humanism) in public schools can be mentioned here as well. The aim of such education (mostly cultural) and the aims of the religious teachers involved vary widely throughout Europe.[35] In the Netherlands, religious (humanistic) education in public schools has only recently been subsidized by the government, as it is considered an important aspect of education in a pluralistic society. Earlier, such education was provided by volunteers. The subsidies come with quality requirements.

In countries with a state church, such pastoral care and education is performed by the state church, financed by the state.[36] In countries with recognized or registered religious communities, the appointment of a minister (or religious teacher) takes place through mutual collaboration of the religious community and the public institution involved. In case the institution has a private law character—e.g., hospitals and youth institutions in the Netherlands—it hires the minister as an employee, usually in connection with a nearby parish. Which religious denominations are allowed to provide pastoral care in (public) institutions, or provide religious education, is left to be decided by the umbrella organizations (CIO) mentioned in the introduction of Section 5.

b. Another important domain is *tax facilities* for religious organizations and their members or donors. The reason for such tax facilities—for religious and other life philosophy organizations—is that the government appreciates these as being beneficial to a harmonious society. Tax facilities are clearly supportive for donations. Religious organizations enjoy, in most countries, tax exemptions, for instance on gift and inheritance tax, and often on estate tax. The members or donors of the religious organizations enjoy income tax deductions because of their donations.

In some countries, tax facilities regarding donations are only given to state churches, rather than to recognized religions. Denmark is a special case. Here, private religious organizations may ask for a specific recognition by the tax authorities.[37] In Germany, tax benefits are given to all religious communities, regardless of their legal form or status.[38] In The Netherlands, religious communities, regardless of their form, can—like other charitable organizations—request that the tax authorities recognize them as an 'Institution for Public Benefit' (*Algemeen Nut Beogende Instelling*, ANBI).[39] A very substantial number of ANBI's are religious communities.

c. Religious communities may also receive *subsidies* when the government makes subsidies available for certain projects. If religious organizations are able to carry out the project and meet the criteria, the fact that the organization is religious should not hinder the government in granting a subsidy to them, rather than any other—secular—applicant. In the separation-model, this subsidy is impossible or unlikely. This approach to subsidy fits within the cooperation-model. In fact, this should not be viewed as governmental support of religious organizations, but as a sign of equal treatment of religious and other organizations. Subsidies for social work, etcetera, are in most cases provided by local governments. Local religious communities generally have more contact with local government than the national religious communities have with national government. Municipalities have more room for supporting religious communities than the national government.[40]

d. One important area where the interests of the religious communities and the government coincide is *monumental churches* (religious buildings). Because of the cultural value of monuments, the government usually provides religious communities that own such monuments with funds for their renovation and/or maintenance. As such, the funding will not be dependent on the legal form of the religious community, because it is provided to the owner of the monumental building for the building, and not for the worship. That this support is also advantageous for the (worship of the) religious community is a side effect.

6   Conclusions

When we compare the situation of religious communities in The Netherlands to those in other European countries, with regard to the aspects of legal personality and governmental facilities, we can draw some conclusions.
- From the perspective of the separation between church and state, the system in which the state has no involvement in the establishment or legal personality of a religious community, seems optimal.
- As such, a specific legal form for religious communities seems advisable, as the freedom of religion may call for greater internal freedom than is provided for in association law. It would be good, in The Netherlands, to find a better name than 'church society' for the legal persons form of any religious community, regardless of their religion.[41]
- An important advantage of a special legal personality for religious communities is the ability for that community to create, in its regulations, autonomous bodies with legal personality. Such an ability can be seen as a consequence of the recognition by the state of the self-determination of the religious community.[42]
- It is important for religious communities that a formal requirement exists regarding the establishment (existence) of the religious community as a legal person. The Dutch Civil Code lacks such a formal requirement, which causes uncertainty. The statement of the government: that the court has to rule whether a religious community is really a church society or not, doesn't solve the problem.
- It should be possible for a religious community to have no legal personality and not be registered.[43] In The Netherlands, the system is that a religious community is a church society, and therefore automatically a legal person that should be registered.
- Religious communities may also make use of the (secular) forms association and foundation, but the adequacy of this depends of the specificity of the regulations for these forms of legal persons. Especially the association form—with mandatory rights for members and a general assembly—in The Netherlands may often not fit the religious community.
- A religious community may also make use of a secular form (association or foundation) for one or more specific tasks, and not for the religious community as a whole. In that case, the danger may be that the relationship between the legal person and the religious community becomes too weak.
- Because in The Netherlands, there is no division between recognized and non-recognized religious communities, the facilities that the government provides for religious communities—pastoral care in institutions, religious education in public schools, tax facilities, support of (social) activities—is

not related to such a distinction. This seems attractive from the perspective of equal treatment by the state.

Although from the perspective of clear regulation of the legal personality of religious communities, the Dutch system is not optimal, the system has clear advantages from the perspective of the freedom of religion. For legal personality, no governmental involvement is required, and generally, religious communities are equally treated in relation to the facilities provided by the government.

1   Compare Guidelines for Review of Legislation Pertaining to Registration or Belief (OSCE-ODIHR, 2004), 17.

2   Compare ECHR 13 December 2001, nr. 45731/99 (Metropolitan Church of Bessarabia vs. Moldova), par. 101, in which it is stated that a community acts on behalf of its adherents.

3   See L. Friedner, ed., Churches and Other Religious Organizations as Legal Persons (Leuven: Peeters, 2007).

4   S. Ferrari, 'Religious Communities as Legal Persons: an Introduction to the National Reports,' in Friedner, Churches, 3 ff.

5   See N. Doe, Law and Religion in Europe; a Comparative Introduction (Oxford: Oxford University Press 2011) 30-33.

6   See Guidelines, 17-18.

7   Doe, Law and Religion in Europe, 95.

8   Contrary to Doe, Law and Religion in Europe, 98.

9   S. Mükl, 'Religious Communities as Legal Persons—Germany,' in Friedner, Churches, 109.

10 Doe, Law and Religion in Europe, 115-116.

11 S. Motilla, 'Religious Communities as Legal Persons—Spain,' in Friedner, Churches, 209 ff.

12 S. Ferrari, 'Entités Religieuses comme Personnes Juridiques—Italie,' in Friedner, Churches, 143.

13 Ferrari, Entités Religieuses, 145 and 147.

14 Compare R. Torfs, 'Religious Entities as Legal Persons—Belgium,' in Friedner, Churches, 45 ff.

15 Torfs, Religious Entities—Belgium, 45 ff.

16 D. Tamm, 'Religious Entities as Legal Persons—Denmark,' in Friedner, Churches, 61 ff.

17 Doe, Law and Religion in Europe, 97.

18 B. Basdevant-Gaudemet and F. Messner, 'Entités Religieuses comme Personnes Juridiques — France,' in Friedner, Churches, 101 ff.

19 Law of 10 September 1853, Stb. 102.

20 A.H. Santing-Wubs, De positie van kerkgenootschappen in het civiele recht (The position of church societies in civil law), NTKR.nl 2010, 38 ff.

21 T.J. van der Ploeg, De overheid en de rechtspersoonlijkheid van kerkgenootschappen (Government and the Legal Personality of Church Societies), NTKR.nl 2008, 78 ff, esp., 83-85.

22 T.J. van der Ploeg, Registratie van kerkgenootschappen en de vrijheid van godsdienst in historisch en rechtsvergelijkend perspectief, (Registration of Church Societies and the Freedom of Religion in Historical and Juridical-comparative Perspective) NTKR.nl 2009, 28 ff.

23 T.J. van der Ploeg, Past een heilig lichaam in een gewoon bed? De vereniging en stichting als rechtspersoon voor geloofsgemeenschappen, (Does a holy body fit in an ordinary bed? The Association and Foundation as Legal Persons Form for Religious Communities) NTKR.nl 2010, 114 ff.

24 The judgement of October 26, 2000, Hasan and Chaush vs. Bulgaria (App. 30985/96, 2002, 34 EHRR 1339). See also the judgement of this court of December 14, 2001, Metropolitan Church of Bessarabia vs. Moldova (App. 45701/99, 2002, 35 EHRR 306).

25 Decision of the Commission of December 17, 1968, Church of Scientology vs U.K., (App. 3798/68), Decision (1969) 12 Yearbook, 306.

26 Decision of the Commission of May 5, 1979, Pastor X and Church of Scientology vs. Sweden (App. 7805/77); Decision (1979) 22 Yearbook 244, at 250.

27 For instance, EHRM 27-06-2000, Cha'are shalom veTsedek vs. France.Appl. no. 27417/95. Compare: C. Ovey and R. White, *Jacobs and White, The European Convention on Human Rights*, 4th edition, revised and updated by C. Ovey and R. White (Oxford: Oxford University Press, 2006), 302.

28 Doe, *Law and Religion in Europe*, 115-128.

29 Doe, *Law and Religion in Europe*, 123 ff.

30 Doe, *Law and Religion in Europe*, 106 f.

31 M.J.G.C. Raaijmakers, *Kerkgenootschap en stichting; iets over HR 12 mei 2000* (Church Society and Foundation; Some Reflections on the Judgement of the Supreme Court of May 12, 2000), *A-T-D (Van Schilfgaarde-bundel)* (Deventer: Kluwer, 2000), 351.

32 Art. 30 CC (BGB).

33 For further details on these models, see S.V. Monsma and J.C. Soper, *The Challenge of Pluralism; Church and State in Five Democracies* (Lanham MD: Rowman & Littlefield, 1997).

34 Doe, *Law and Religion in Europe*, 39 seems to have another opinion.

35 Doe, *Law and Religion in Europe*, 188-198.

36 Doe, *Law and Religion in Europe*, 203 ff.

37 Doe, *Law and Religion in Europe*, 94, 184-185.

38 Mückl, *Religious Communities—Germany*, 113.

39 See extensively T. van Kooten, 'Kerk en fiscus: de zilveren koorde te nauw aange-haald? (Church and Taxes: Too Tight a Financial Relationship?),' in *Overheid, recht en religie* (Government, Law and Religion), ed. H. Broeksteeg and A. Terlouw (Deventer: Kluwer, 2011), 75-102.

40 The association of Dutch municipalities (VNG) has issued a very interesting report on this issue: *Tweeluik religie en publiek domein* (Diptych Religion and Public Domain), ('s-Gravenhage: VNG, 2009).

41 See Van der Ploeg, *De overheid*.

42 Doe, *Law and Religion in Europe*, 91 f.

43 See *Guidelines, 17 second bullet*.

* 3 *

Religion, Social Capital
and Charity

Ab Klink

54

An important sociologist in the USA, Robert Putnam, conducted research on the involvement of people in voluntary associations and civil projects and examined the impact that this had on individuals and society. One of his books is called *Bowling Alone*.¹ Its title points to the individualization process that we see occurring in the Western world; even in the field of sports, we can see that people choose activities they can do on their own: jogging, bowling, playing video games, etc. Putnam also looked at what people usually do in their spare time. They more and more watch television, are on the internet, and so on.

This individualization has quite a big impact on people's personal lives. They lose networks, have fewer friends, are more depressed, and are less socially and politically involved. They see the state as a 'far away' institution and are not interested in public issues. Loneliness is always a threat for them. Putnam's conclusion is that individualization makes people unhappy, atomistic, isolated, and detached from the common good. Detached people are usually no threat to the authorities, as Tocqueville stated when he wrote about his journey to the USA back in the 19th century.²

But, on the other hand, these people are also detached when public issues are involved such as the environment, solidarity towards the poor, and so on. In another survey Putnam undertook, he found that in specific regions of Italy where people were engaged in associations and voluntary work, they were more prosperous, knew more about solidarity and were more constructive toward government, being less populist and separatist in their attitudes. It also transpired that people who had religious affiliations were less detached and more involved in civil society.³ We see this picture, more or less, in Dutch society. People who go to church spend more of their time doing social work, they participate more frequently in school boards, hospitals etc. This is an important conclusion.

Many people in Western countries see religion as a potential threat to public order. Fundamentalism plays an important role here. In the West, the images of 9/11 had a massive impact; once again a religion had become violent. This time it was Islam, but in the past we had our religious wars between Catholics and Protestants which devastated the European countries in the seventeenth century. It was only after the liberals and secularists took over (the French Revolution) in the 19th century and enforced the freedom of religion, that peace was restored in a stable way.

Which of these approaches is true, or do they both contain an element of truth? Should religion be pushed back to the private sphere of personal convictions and lives? Or is it potentially an important pillar of a cohesive society? Or does it depend upon the specific content of religions, which of course differ a lot on issues like personal responsibility, ethics, the role of the state, etcetera?

Max Weber, for example, is quite critical of Islam in his sociology of religion, although he is very much aware of the differences between the Shia and the Sufis. He also points to the desire of Calvinists to dominate the state, as opposed to other branches of Christianity which favor a neutral state and want to reserve ethical and religious questions to the private sphere. The only thing that the state has to do is to safeguard and respect the freedom of the people and of their religion, under the condition that churches and religious people do not try to use the state as a means of imposing their convictions on other people. I will return to these questions later. But let me now look at the experiences we have had in the Netherlands.

Until the 19th century, we can see that initiatives in the field of health care, the struggle against poverty and education were dominated by the churches. It was part of the mission of Christian people to care for the other; poverty had to be combated, older people had to be given help, and so on. Of course, education and charity also gave the churches the means to dominate the lives of people and to impose their convictions upon them, but nevertheless the church really helped people to survive periods of illness and poverty. They also educated people, and contributed to their independence and respectability.

In the 19th century, government, first at a local level and afterwards at the level of the state, became more important. Social issues also became political issues. Poverty was no longer seen as a private fate or responsibility, but also and foremost as a question of society and power. Marxism and socialism became popular. On the other hand, secular liberals saw the private initiatives of churches and religious people as a way of churches gaining power in society, and of preventing people from being free of indoctrination. And churches had to admit that their initiatives were very much dependent on the gifts of wealthier people. Besides that: their relief of poverty couldn't be perceived as a right. It was a gift.

In the Netherlands, these different perceptions led to fierce combat between liberals and Christians. Nevertheless, one of our most famous and influential statesmen, Rudolf Thorbecke, writer of the 1848 constitution (which promoted all kinds of freedom and political participation rights) once had a debate with a professor in Amsterdam about the freedom of Protestants to found their own primary schools. His opponent stated that this posed a real threat to society and public order. These more or less fundamentalist Protestants would certainly educate their children in all kinds of foolish dogmas, regarding original sin, and the predominant importance of religious convictions. In the end, this could threaten the state. Children would be influenced by ideas that would make their integration into society considerably more difficult. The result, he feared, would be a state within a state.

But Thorbecke, although a secular person and a liberal, wrote a book opposing this view, stating that the very participation of these people in the public realm and field would have an integrating effect and result. By involving themselves in the educational field, they would become aware of broader issues, of questions regarding society, and would become publicly involved. These are exactly the same views as those of Tocqueville. Local communities and voluntary associations predestine people to be good and autonomous citizens, who in the end contribute to the public interest.

Thorbecke formulated the freedom of expression of religion and the educational freedom in the Dutch constitution of 1848. But then the Christian democrats said, well, we do not only want freedom, but we want the same rights as others have. It is good to have the right to create your own schools. But it is another thing to have the financial means to finance these initiatives. And if the state is financing public schools with the money they collect from all the people—also from the Christians—it is unfair to ask from the religious people that they should pay for their own schools. Actually, they would be paying double in that case.

This discussion dominated Dutch politics throughout the nineteenth century. In those days, political parties of Protestants and Catholics emerged. The freedom of religion and the opportunity to express their convictions in the public field dominated the political agenda during these years with Protestants and Catholics trying to get as large a share of the vote as they could in order to change the practices and rules of the state.

In the end these parties won the struggle by democratic and, of course, peaceful means. At the beginning of the twentieth century, their right to create schools of their own religious denomination was adopted, even in the constitution. And it worked: there were no separatist tendencies. Their schools functioned very well and were of high quality. So, in the Netherlands, the government does not only pay for public education, but also for private schools with a religious background, provided they meet certain minimal quality standards.

We have seen the same developments in other fields: the media and broadcasting associations, welfare institutions, health care; in all these fields, religiously inspired organizations appeared. So we see a mix between freedom of organization and religion, and a government which actively supports this freedom, so that it can have a real impact on society.

And it has had a huge impact on society, and also on government and public management. Political and civil elites were recruited from the different religious groups and associations. The Netherlands turned out to be pluralistic as well as homogenous. Different groups respected the freedom of the other. On national issues such as safety, defense, social security but also on defending freedom rights and pluralism they worked together. This freedom of religion, of course, also means that people can change their religion or world view. No one can force them to be member of a church or mosque. Private enforcement or enforcement by a religious community is forbidden by law.

So the Netherlands can be seen as a kind of experimental region in which the advantages of freedom and private non-profit organizations have proven themselves. In the academic literature we see many arguments in favor of non-profit organizations and initiatives:

- these private initiatives offer a higher quality of service because there is a lot of participant involvement. Usually they work on a smaller scale, and are more flexible and adaptive.
- these initiatives have an historical background of charity. So they also focus on have-nots, and have a relatively large sense of social justice.
- they are less costly because they can rely on the help of volunteers and gifts.
- private initiatives can be started by anyone. So these organizations are very flexible and open. They are more innovative than governmental bodies and organizations.
- these institutions are the channels through which people get involved in societal questions and dilemmas. It enhances their citizenship. This was the argument of Tocqueville, Thorbecke and Putnam. Theda Skocpol actually did a survey on this issue that also confirmed this relationship.
- it gives people the opportunity to express their values and enhances pluralism in society.
- the public involvement creates a feeling of belonging and of citizenship in society. Usually, people who are engaged in one field of society also see their responsibility on other issues like environmental questions, charity, and so on.

In the literature three disadvantages are mentioned:

- particularity: the services of these organizations are offered to a small group of people who have the same opinions and convictions. This might lead to separated subgroups and disintegration.
- paternalism: the elites in these subgroups use these institutions to enforce

their opinions upon others: children, the sick and weaker persons, and so on.
- amateurism: because non-profit organizations depend on volunteers, this might lower the professional level of the services.

Social studies in the Netherlands on education, media and health care did not confirm these potential disadvantages. The freedom rights and pluralism created a peaceful society and there were no sectarian tendencies.

Nevertheless, these societal benefits might also be explained by some of the larger social developments taking place in Western countries: the process of individualization and secularism. It might very well be that over the past decades, secularization has undermined the orthodoxy and the solid convictions of religious groups and elites. So, on the one hand, we still have the well known institutions of the past, with their religious names and backgrounds. But, on the other, the former convictions have vanished in such a way that tolerance is now the dominant feature of all these institutions. Particularity and paternalism cannot function in such a climate.

In that case we still have many non profit making charities, a lot of volunteers and many publicly involved people, without the disadvantage of any potential religious cleavages. The best of both worlds, one might say.

Many people think so. Particularly as fierce debates have occurred in Western countries about the possibilities for Muslims to express their identity in the public sphere. Can they wear burkas in public spaces? Should they be offered the possibility of creating their own schools? Should political parties, which want to introduce the sharia in our countries, be tolerated? If Christians have political rights, should they also have the option of doing so? Is Islam not fundamentally different from Christianity and, for example, Buddhism? These are religions that focus on the individual and his or her personal life and not on rules; on obligations, and not on the responsibility of the state to obey holy rules. Islam does not recognize a separation of church and state; is it, therefore, a greater threat to democracy and freedom rights.

Others take the view that Thorbecke once promoted: let these people create their own schools, then they will become involved in public issues. And besides the fact that it is their right to make use of their constitutional rights, this is also the best way to integrate them in society, unless, of course, they promote unconstitutional attitudes. In the end, their organizations will end up just as the Christian institutions did: orthodox attitudes will lose their attraction. Tolerance will prevail. We will once again have the best of both worlds: non-profit organizations; private initiatives but without iron convictions.

So, just one final question remains: can private and public involvement exist without religious conviction? I personally am quite convinced of this. But still there are some dangers. The other side of the coin, secularism and individualism, presents exactly the problems that Putnam mentioned in his studies: a more hedonistic life style, bowling and playing alone, less social investments, more disappointed people, and so on.

I do not think that charity is dependent on religious outlooks or spirituality, but still we find that religious people are relatively over-represented as volunteers. Religious convictions and practices, and belonging to a church, seems to have an empirical correlation with social involvement. But the question remains: is this because of the convictions held by people, or just because these people function in networks that encourage them to be engaged, and could this be achieved just as well by sport clubs? Is this involvement religiously motivated, or is it just a sociological product of social network membership? Or is it, perhaps, both?

1 R.D. Putnam, *Bowling Alone: The Collapse and Revival of American Community* (New York: Simon and Schuster, 2000). See also his earlier article 'Bowling Alone: America's Declining Social Capital,' in: *Journal of Democracy* 6 (1): 65-78, 1995.

2 A. de Tocqueville, *Democracy in America* (Chicago: University of Chicago Press, 2000).

3 R.D. Putnam, *Making Democracy Work: Civic Traditions in Modern Italy* (Princeton: Princeton University Press, 1993).

4

Can a Crusade be Civil? Evangelism
as Social Contribution

Daniëlle Koning

1   Introduction: Evangelism as a Contribution to Civil Society

What constitutes civil society, or what is 'the good society'? Mirroring the phenomenon to which this term points, there are many scholarly voices that address this question in both contrasting and complementary ways. Van der Meulen[1] clarifies and summarizes the complex debate by highlighting four main positions: civil society is the place where free discussion and the formation of rational public opinion is made possible ('communicative rationality'); power bases alternative to the government are formed ('distribution of power'); living in cohesive communities is learned and practiced ('solidarity'); or social networks are formed and utilized ('social capital').

In Van der Meulen's analysis, which serves as an introduction to his empirical study of two modern-day Christian churches in a Dutch suburb, it is observed that the contribution of religion to civil society is contentious. Some scholars suggest that there is a negative relationship between religion and the emergence of solidarity or communicative rationality, and appreciate religion solely for its non-religious (e.g. social and public) functions. However, on the basis of his study, Van der Meulen concludes that it is problematic to locate religion in civil society by delimiting it in this way.

First, he concludes that religious groups are fully part of civil society. Drawing on Taylor, he adopts a definition of civil society that centers on the idea of 'communities of common understanding'. This definition is inclusive of religious organizations, because it does not prescribe what these communities revolve around. Communities of common understanding can be organized around whatever they find important, as long as they are communities, e.g. they connect people with each other and with the public debate. In this definition, religious organizations and their understanding of the good society become a fully legitimate part of civil society.

Secondly, Van der Meulen suggests that it is tricky to separate the 'social' contributions of religious groups from their 'religious' motivations, beliefs and practices. Much research on religion and civil society has isolated 'civil' aspects of religion (e.g. community volunteering, financial giving, political involvement and so on) from their immediate religious context. However, in their lived reality and from the perspective of religious groups themselves, the social contributions of religion cannot be neatly separated from religious aspects of religion.

In this chapter, I want to explore the nature and significance of these conclusions, which Van der Meulen left as a research agenda. For this purpose, I will specifically examine a common expression of religious participation that has rarely been studied in terms of its relationship to civil society: evangelism, or the attempt to convert others to one's religion. I will highlight the ways in which this phenomenon reveals the intersections of 'civil' and 'religious' aspects of religion, and analyze what this means for our understanding of religion and civil society.

My analysis will be based on my research of Christian immigrant churches in the Netherlands.[2] I will start by outlining the global context of these churches illustrating how they express the demographic shifts in world Christianity and its missionary flows. I will then sketch the local setting of these churches in the Netherlands move on to an examination of the religious-civil dynamics of these churches' evangelistic endeavors. I will conclude this analysis by suggesting the importance of understanding religion as religion in civil society.

2   Global Context of Case Study: Shifts in Worldwide Christianity and Missionary Flows

If Christianity ever was a Western religion, it is barely so today. According to Jenkins' famous thesis, Christianity is becoming 'Southernized': its center of gravity is rapidly shifting to the Southern hemisphere of our globe.[3] The largest Christian communities today can be found in Africa and Latin America, and also increasingly in Asia. Jenkins predicts that in 2050, only one in every five Christians will be a non-Hispanic white person, and notes that we should start to visualize a typical contemporary Christian as a 'woman living in a village in Nigeria or in a Brazilian *favela*'.[4]

The Southernisation of Christian adherents, in addition to the strong migration currents all over the globe, are simultaneously Southernizing Christian missionaries. In fact, missiologist Keyes[5] argues that mission from the non-Western world is the 'last age of missions'. Keyes depicts four geographical centers in Christian mission history: 1. The Middle East (until 400 C.E.),

2. Europe (from 400-1800), 3. North America (1800-now), and 4. The Third World (today), referring to the nations of Africa, Asia, Latin America, and Oceania, including their emigrants to the West. He catalogued 472 active missionary-sending agencies from the Third World in the 1980s. In their reports on 'missiometrics' (statistics on global mission and world Christianity), Barrett, Johnson, and Crossing confirm that global evangelistic plans are increasingly initiated and led by Christians from the 'Global South': Africa, Asia and Latin America.[6] The authors show that among the 11 countries which sent out the highest number of missionaries, two are non-Western, namely Brazil and South Korea, and that Europe receives more missionaries today than Africa or Asia does.[7] Although the mission work by Western agencies is still numerically predominant,[8] non-Western 'senders' and Western 'receivers' are on the rise.

Non-Western missionaries are active in non-Western regions. Countries such as Brazil, India, and China have large numbers of national mission workers—India has as many as Germany.[9] Non-Western missionaries also cross national boundaries in non-Western regions. Mwaura,[10] for example, discusses the evangelistic activity and influence of Nigerian Pentecostal churches in Kenya. Kalu refers to Africans leading non-African congregations in Southeast Asia, often on the basis of visions.[11] Others point to other South-South relations such as Brazilian and Ghanaian missions in Southern Africa,[12] and East-East relations such as Korean missionaries in Japan[13] and Russia.[14]

Non-Western missionaries are not only active in non-Western regions, but also in the West. In recent years, a small but growing number of scholars have begun to show interest in this type of mission activity. A most prominent aspect of this is the discussion about 'reversed mission': the idea that non-Westerners are bringing back the gospel to the West; a West which seems to have forgotten what it once preached. Reversed mission is expressed in various modes such as the intentional mission of (affluent) non-Western individuals or organizations in the West, non-Western Christian ministers leading 'indigenous' congregations in the West, partnerships between Western and non-Western churches, and, finally, the work of churches that are formed by immigrants.[15] It is to these immigrant churches,[16] which are an expression of the global shifts in Christianity and the rise of non-Western mission movements, that we will now turn in the context of the Netherlands.

3 Local Context of Case Study: Immigrant Churches in the Netherlands

The religious landscape of the Netherlands today can be described as generally secularized, at least in the sense of institutional Christianity. Though a small group of indigenous churches is growing, the general trend is a decrease in church attendance and membership. In the period 1971-2004/05, the churches that became the PKN (Protestant Church in the Netherlands) lost 51% of their members.[17] However, trends of secularization are mixed with 'sacralization'. Religion has not disappeared, but emerges in different forms, which are often more individualized.[18] Beliefs and practices in the realm of alternative spiritualities, for example, have gradually become popularized, though relatively small numbers of people are active in this realm.[19] An important religious trend in the Netherlands is also Islam, the adherents of which are estimated to be between 850,000 and 950,000 in the country, though within this community there are also tendencies towards secularization.[20]

In this complex context, the Netherlands is also the residence of hundreds of thousands of immigrant Christians. The presence of non-native believers in the country has a long history. For example, French-speaking Protestant refugees from the Southern Netherlands and France established the first Wallonian churches in what is now the Netherlands as early as 1571. There are still 14 Wallonian churches in the Netherlands today. The oldest non-Western church in the country is the Armenian Apostolic Church. Christian Armenians in Amsterdam already had their own priest in 1665 and had their own church built in 1714.[21] Today there are still two Armenian churches in the Netherlands that gather on a regular basis. Immigrant Christians and churches in the Netherlands are thus not a new phenomenon.

However, most immigrant Christians who still have an organized presence in the country today came after the Second World War. These arrivals roughly came in two waves. The first wave was in the 1950s-1970s and mostly included immigrants from former Dutch colonies: Indonesia, the Moluccas, Surinam, and the Dutch Antilles. The second wave started from the late 1980s onward and included immigrants from various African countries and Eastern Europe. A recent estimate brings the total of non-Western immigrant Christians in the Netherlands to over half a million.[22] About 900 immigrant churches and 200 churches with foreign language services[23] are scattered all over the country, particularly in the larger cities. Worshippers speak over 75 different languages and come from lands as varied as Brazil, Turkey, Ghana, and Korea. Theologies range from Nigerian Pentecostal to Serbian Orthodox; even new 'mother churches' have been established by immigrants on Dutch soil.[24] In all their historical, ethnic and religious variety, these churches are active participants in their communities and larger society. Many have a specifically evangelistic outlook. It is to the missionary aspect of these churches that we will now turn.

4   Analysis: Evangelism and its Religious-Civil Dynamics

In this section I will move to an analysis of the evangelistic dimensions of immigrant churches in terms of their religious-civil dynamics. The analysis will be organised in terms of two of the civil society foci that Van der Meulen highlighted: social capital and solidarity.

Evangelism is by nature an act of 'bridging'. On the one hand, the idea of needing to convert the other assumes an element of excluding: 'you are not part of
us' or 'you are not part of the right group'. On the other hand, the missionary
attitude simultaneously translates this othering into an attitude of including:
'you could and even should be part of us/the right group'. The act of evangelism
is based on seeking to connect *because* division is constructed. Warner affirms
this paradox of evangelism. He observes that since evangelizing groups express
a desire to expand the boundaries of their community, they are more 'bridging'
in nature than groups that seek to protect ethnic purity.[25] Moreover, groups
that are evangelistically minded have a *particularly strong potential for bridging capital* because of their religious beliefs and motivations. Other groups that seek to
bridge, i.e. those that seek to meet outsiders' secular needs, are less connective
than evangelizing groups, because the latter take the radically open position
that outsiders can and should become part of their own community.[26]

I will illustrate the high generation of bridging capital in evangelizing
groups by drawing on my case study of immigrant churches in the Netherlands. Firstly, the immigrant churches' motive to 'share Christ with the world'
proved to be a powerful incentive to go through the trials of seeking to *cross
ethnic and racial boundaries*. Most churches were interested in sharing the gospel
with the native Dutch, who were, much to their surprise, not as strong in the
Christian faith as many pastors and members had expected. This prompted or
reinforced Christian immigrants' interest in the Dutch language and culture.
A pastor of an African Pentecostal church, for example, organized evangelistic training courses that addressed the issue of reaching the Dutch in a contextual way. In one of the sessions, he gave his students the following suggestions
to get closer to the 'natives': to talk about the weather (a common and casual
Dutch conservational topic), to sit next to 'whites' in the subway, and to refrain
from judging the Dutch for their relaxed attitude towards prostitution. This
pastor also claimed that he had altered some aspects of how he traditionally
ran church life to better fit Dutch culture: he allowed men and women to sit
next to each other during church services (rather than separating them), and
implemented a liberal dress code (he did not require hair cover for ladies, and
allowed jeans and make-up). For the purposes of effective evangelism, this pastor thus made an explicit effort to link church members and church practices
to elements of Dutch culture.[27] With regard to language, immigrant church
leaders expressed their strong desire to speak the Dutch language. Many pastors already spoke it to a fair degree, and some churches decided to translate
their services into Dutch (one even offered services in the regional language of
West Frisian).[28]

Small quantities of 'white' Dutch attendees were present in almost all of the churches. Some were converts to Christianity or a particular type of Christianity, or experienced a revitalization of a dormant Christian identity through their contact with the churches. In a Ghanaian church, a white Dutch lady was spontaneously baptized during a baptismal service. Another Dutch lady found her spiritual 'destiny' in a Serbian Orthodox church. In some cases, the presence and conversion of Dutch people was related to marital ties (such as in the Japanese and Spanish-speaking churches). In other cases, it was a specific interest in the new type of religiosity these churches bring to the Netherlands (such as in the Russian Orthodox church in Amsterdam, where no less than one third of the attendees is Dutch). New bridges were thus created through religious presence and outreach.

The evangelistic vision of immigrant churches also inspired them to seek to *build bridges with other religious groups* within their ethnic (fellow immigrant) group in the Netherlands. Evangelistic activities were intentionally designed to meet particular needs of and provide a sense of familiarity for these fellow ethnics from other religious traditions. Language, ethnic food and cultural symbols such as flags were deliberately used. For example, the prison ministry of a Spanish-speaking parish sang Spanish songs in Dutch prisons, and the Koreans used the Korean Harvest Festival to invite non-Christian Koreans to church. Issues of concern, such as the importance of national identity to Kurdish and Chinese immigrants, were specifically addressed in evangelistic settings. Church leaders that were active in reaching out to Muslims adjusted religious rituals, the content of studies, the language used, social interaction, personal behavior, and other mission strategies to accommodate Muslim sensibilities.

The response of fellow ethnics from other religious traditions to these evangelistic attempts varied. In many cases it revealed that social, emotional and spiritual needs were met in a significant way. For example, Koreans, Japanese and Kurdish non-Christians found a 'cultural' home-from-home in immigrant churches. Evangelistic outreach also caused socially distinct groups to mingle; Muslims, Buddhists and Hindus attended special church services, concerts, social activities and Christmas celebrations organized by fellow ethnic Christians and, for example, African Muslims joined African Christians in their outdoors fitness training in Amsterdam, which included prayer and singing Christian songs.

A final way in which evangelism served as a bridge to other groups in society was through its radically open nature. Though many churches had particular target groups for their mission (e.g. 'the white Dutch' or 'all Ghanaians in Amsterdam'), they all agreed that *everyone* needs to hear the Word of God. This belief was expressed in public evangelistic activities, such as preaching in Amsterdam's popular red-light district, singing in the crowded, orange-colored streets on Queen's Day, and leaving Christian leaflets in buses and trains. In such settings, immigrants with sometimes marginal positions connected boldly to mainstream society through the mediation of a missionary agenda. On this level, then, as well, evangelism emerged as a phenomenon with a special potential for generating bridging capital.

4.2   Solidarity: Evangelism as Social Action

The second civil society focus that I wish to explore in its relationship to evangelism is solidarity. Evangelism can be related to solidarity, or social action, in various ways. However, 'little research has focused on the connection between spiritual and social outreach, in part because little connection has been imagined to exist'.[29] Rolland Unruh and Sider, in their study of mission orientations, innovatively provide a typology of four different ways in which churches tend to connect evangelism and social action. For my purposes here I will focus specifically on their 'holistic' type, in which evangelism and social action are considered to be dynamically interconnected. The holistic mission orientation assumes a 'connection between spiritual transformation and socioeconomic empowerment'.[30] This means that evangelistic and social programs are both considered necessary to achieve the greatest well-being or the best society. Rolland Unruh and Sider distinguish two sub-types of this holistic approach: 'holistic-complementary' and 'holistic-instrumental'. The former considers evangelism and social action to be part of the same seamless mission, without clearly distinguishing between them. The latter views both evangelism and social action as intrinsically important, but also employs social action as a portal to the priority of winning souls.

The holistic-complementary mission orientation was prevalent among immigrant churches in the Netherlands. A separate use of categories for 'evangelism and social action was constantly challenged by my respondents. For example, in a Ghanaian church, a marriage and family seminar was described as 'evangelistic'. When the seminar was finished, I asked whether it was considered successful. I received the answer 'yes, because now the visitors from the seminar will start coming to our church', but also the answer 'yes, because many family lives have been improved'. The seminar clearly served both evangelistic and social purposes, even though it was described as evangelistic. As another example, a Caribbean church produced a leaflet called '133 ways to evangelize' which encourages believers to 'wear a T-shirt with a religious message' but also to 'help collect funds for the Red Cross'; to 'share tracts with supermarket workers', but also to 'engage in stress seminars'; to 'place a religious sticker on your car', but also to 'organize programs that deal with teenage pregnancy'. Dichotomizing evangelism and social action was impossible—the churches were just doing what they believed to be right, and this included both sharing gospel truth and providing for socio-economic needs.

Many immigrant churches expressed the (closely connected) holistic-instrumental mission orientation as well. Pastors emphasized the importance of meeting needs so as to attract people to church. Outsiders who would not normally attend a church service were expected to come to church events that addressed needs such as finances, health, and raising children. In a Ghanaian church, evangelistic series relating to theological doctrine and Christian lifestyle were always preceded by a practical series that targeted social or economic needs in the community. Another prevalent type of evangelism that fit the holistic-instrumental type was 'friendship evangelism'. Many church leaders advocated this relational type of mission, as they frequently experienced disappointing results in doing more public forms of evangelism. In friendships, needs could be met in an intimate context, building trust relationships that formed the basis for sharing about Christianity later on. In the migration context, newly arrived immigrants often followed the more established immigrants whom they knew. For example, as more established Ghanaian immigrants introduced newcomers to the places where they could get jobs, take Dutch language courses, or get medical treatment without having insurance, they also acted as guides in the local religious market place. Meeting needs on a personal level was the stage for evangelizing on a personal level.

In both the holistic-complementary and holistic-instrumental mission orientations, evangelism revealed itself as a civil practice in the form of promoting different types of solidarity. Moreover, the particularly religious aspects of evangelism were inextricably tied up with its social aspects and could not always be distinguished.

5   Conclusion: Religion 'as Religion' in Civil Society

In this chapter, I have examined the phenomenon of evangelism as a contribution to civil society in the context of immigrant churches in the Netherlands. Following Van der Meulen's analysis, I assumed that religious groups are a fully legitimate part of civil society. It was my particular aim to explore the relationship between religious groups and civil society by looking at the civil nature of *religion as religion* rather than immediately reducing religion to a civil contribution. To this purpose, I examined the intersections of civil and religious aspects of religion.

My findings are twofold. First, the strong social capital generated by evangelist groups can only be understood by taking the religious content of their motivations and beliefs seriously. It is because evangelistic groups have particular theological convictions (e.g., 'Jesus is coming soon', 'Christ is Lord of all', 'Hell should be empty', and so on) that they go to much greater lengths of bridging than most groups aimed at meeting secular needs would tend to do. The difficult quest to connect with groups that are ethnically, racially and religiously different is, to a large extent, ideology-driven. A proper appreciation of the social capital implied in and generated by evangelizing groups therefore requires taking their religious content seriously.

Secondly, the practices of solidarity or social action that evangelistic groups engage in cannot be understood apart from religious motivations and practices. To some churches, the theoretical distinction between 'social' and 'religious' action is blurred in vision and practice. As one pastor put it, to do mission is simply to 'bring about the reign of God', which includes soup kitchens for the homeless as much as door-to-door Bible studies. In other churches, social action is motivated by an evangelistic agenda, making acts of solidarity serve as stepping stones for proclaiming the gospel. Again, a true appreciation of the solidarity that is generated by evangelizing groups needs to take into account the 'religious' elements of religion.

The analysis of the religious phenomenon of evangelizing in the context of immigrant churches in the Netherlands suggests the following. As religious organizations are analytically included as participants in civil society, their forms of participation will be properly understood only when the immediate religious embedding of their goals and activities are observed and taken into account.

1 M. van der Meulen, *Vroom in de Vinex: Kerk en civil society in de Leidsche Rijn* (Maastricht: Shaker, 2006).

2 The research covered a highly diversified set of churches, including: Ghanaian Seventh-day Adventist, Iraqi Chaldean Catholic, Japanese Protestant, Russian Orthodox, Ghanaian Pentecostal, multi-ethnic Evangelical, Indonesian Evangelical, Serbian Orthodox, Ethiopian Evangelical, Cape Verdean Nazarene, Pakistani inter-denominational, Korean Reformed, Iranian Jehovah's Witness, Spanish-speaking Roman Catholic, and multi-ethnic Christian Reformed (including Kurdish, Chinese and African evangelistic ministries).

3 P. Jenkins, *The Next Christendom. The Coming of Global Christianity* (Oxford: Oxford University Press, 2002).

4 Jenkins, *Next Christendom*, 2.

5 L.E., Keyes, *The Last Age of Missions. A Study of Third World Mission Societies* (Pasadena, CA: William Carey Library, 1983).

6 D.B. Barrett, T.M. Johnson and P.F. Crossing, 'Missiometrics 2008: Reality Checks for Christian World Communions,' in: *International Bulletin of Missionary Research* 32/1(2008): 27-30; T.M. Johnson, D.B. Barrett and P.F. Crossing, 'Christianity 2010: A View from the New Atlas of Global Christianity,' in: International Bulletin of Missionary Research 34/1(2010): 29-36.

7 D.B. Barrett, T.M. Johnson and P.F. Crossing, P.F., 'Missiometrics 2007: Creating Your Own Analysis of Global Data,' in: *International Bulletin of Missionary Research* 31/1(2007): 25-32. These 'missio-metrics' are based only on personnel who are employed full-time by churches and mission agencies, and therefore do not capture the less established mission dynamics of most immigrant churches (G. ter Haar, 'African Christians in Europe,' in: S. Spencer, ed., *Mission and Migration* (Calver, Hope Valley: Cliff College Publishing, 2008), 31-52. Mission involvement from the South may thus be even stronger than these numbers suggest.

8 M. Jaffarian, 'Are There More Non-

Western Missionaries than Western Missionaries?,' in: *International Bulletin of Missionary Research* 28/3(2004): 131-132.

9   Johnson et al., *Christianity* 2010, 29–36.

10 P. Mwaura, 'Nigerian Pentecostal Missionary Enterprise in Kenya: Taking the Cross Over,' in: *Mission and Migration*, 53-77.

11 O. Kalu, *African Pentecostalism. An Introduction* (New York: Oxford University Press, 2008), 288.

12 L. van de Kamp and R. van Dijk, 'Pentecostals Moving South-South: Brazilian and Ghanaian Transnationalism in Southern Africa,' in: A. Adogame and J. Spickard, eds., *Religion Crossing Boundaries: Transnational Dynamics in Africa and the New African Diasporic Religions* (Leiden/ Boston: Brill, 2010), 123-142; P. Freston, 'The Universal Church of the Kingdom of God: a Brazilian Church Finds Success in Southern Africa,' in: *Journal of Religion in Africa* 35/1 (2005), 33-65.

13 I. Noguchi, 'Japan: Het verzoenende geloof van de Koreaanse buren,' in: *CV Koers* 6 (2008): 14-15.

14 J.S. Kovalchuk, 'The New Protestant 10/40 Window: Korean Proselytism in the Asian Region of Russia,' in: R.I.J. Hackett, ed., *Proselytization Revisited. Rights Talk, Free Markets and Culture Wars* (London/ Oakville, CT: Equinox, 2008), 389-407.

15 R. Catto, *From the Rest to the West. Exploring Reversal in Christian Mission in Twenty-first Century Britain*. Ph.D. thesis (Exeter: University of Exeter, 2008), 223; Freston, *Universal Church*.

16 I take immigrant churches to refer to those churches that have a 20% or higher first and/or second generation immigrant membership and have been explicitly established for and/or by first and/or second generation immigrants.

17 J. Becker and J. de Hart, *Godsdienstige veranderingen in Nederland. Verschuivingen in de binding met de kerken en de christelijke traditie* (Den Haag: Sociaal en Cultureel Planbureau, 2006).

18 E. Borgman, and A. van Harskamp, 'Tussen secularisering en hernieuwde sacralisering,' in: M. ter Borg et al., eds.,

Handboek Religie in Nederland (Zoetermeer: Meinema, 2008), 14-25.

19 *Godsdienstige veranderingen.*

20 E. Sengers, 'Kwantitatief onderzoek naar religie,' in *Handboek Religie in Nederland*, 67-81.

21 R. Bekius, and W. Ultee, 'De Armeense kolonie in Amsterdam 1600-1800,' *De Gids* 148 3/4 (1985): 216-224.

22 H. Stoffels, 'A Coat of Many Colours: New Immigrant Churches in the Netherlands,' in: M. Jansen and H. Stoffels, eds., *A Moving God. Immigrant Churches in the Netherlands* (Zürich/Münster: Lit Verlag, 2008), 13-29.

23 A.P. van den Broek, *Ieder hoorde in zijn eigen taal* (Amstelveen: Published privately, 2004).

24 G. ter Haar, *Halfway to Paradise. African Christians in Europe* (Fairwater, Cardiff: Cardiff Academic Press, 1998), 30-33.

25 R.S. Warner, 'Religion, Boundaries, and Bridges,' *Sociology of Religion* 58/3 (1997): 217-238, see 230.

26 R.S. Warner, *New Wine in Old Wineskins: Evangelicals and Liberals in a Small Town Church* (Berkeley: University of California Press, 1988), 293.

27 In his study of the Nigerian-initiated Redeemed Christian Church of God in Edinburgh, Obinna observes similar efforts: the church had tried to attract native Scots by serving the 'contextual' soup of hamburgers, tea, and coffee (E. Obinna, 'Contesting the Ambivalence of Reverse or Revised Mission: Redeemed Christian Church of God, Edinburgh,' Paper read at the SOCREL Conference: *The Changing Face of Christianity*, Edinburgh, April 6-8 2010). Währisch-Oblau points out that Pentecostal/charismatic immigrant pastors in Germany recognize that gospel music is attractive to Germans, and accordingly employ it as a mission strategy C. Währisch-Oblau, *The Missionary Self-Perception of Pentecostal/ Charismatic Church Leaders from the Global South in Europe. Bringing Back the Gospel* (Leiden/Boston: Brill, 2009), 234. More generally, she observes that 'it is likely that many migrant pastors, when engaging

with a German context, do indeed tone down their message and manage without rituals that they know would be alienating'. (Währisch-Oblau, *Missionary Self-Perception*, 303.

28 In Germany, Karagiannis and Glick Schiller similarly found that African Pentecostals in the spirit of Christian universalism found it very important to translate church services into German, even if there was only one German visitor present (E. Karagiannis and N. Glick Schiller, '…the land which the LORD your God giveth you': Two Churches Founded by African Migrants in Oststadt, Germany,'in: A. Adogame, R. Gerloff, and K. Hock, *Christianity in Africa and the African Diaspora. The Appropriation of a Scattered Heritage* (London/New York: Continuum, 2008), 265-278.

29 H. Rolland Unruh and R.J. Sider, *Saving Souls, Serving Society. Understanding the Faith Factor in Church-Based Social Ministry* (Oxford: Oxford University Press, 2005), 133.

30 Holland Unruh and Sider, *Saving Souls,* 140.

5

The Rainbow Nation: Reflections on Religion and Culture in the new South Africa

Annette Combrink

1   Prefatory Remarks

In dealing with a discussion of culture and religion, I need at the outset to provide a brief definition of the notions that I will be dealing with and put them into context. I will also provide a brief, stage-setting, outline of South Africa, especially within the context of that much-vaunted and yet now quite tainted notion[1] of the new South Africa, inhabited by the Rainbow Nation of Desmond Tutu's fond imaginings.[2] On a personal level I also have to state that, during the seventies and eighties, I aligned myself strongly with the cause of liberation and the struggle, to the extent of participating in a visit to Lusaka to meet the banned ANC in exile in 1989 although I did not at any time join the ANC.

Culture can be defined in many ways but one might profitably use the definition coined by Cochrane

> my definition of culture here is a broad one, encompassing religious, aesthetic, political and economic arrangements, practices and behaviours which may describe the particularity of a specific group of people. A culture may be permeated by religious symbols, ideas and practices but will be broader than those.[3]

Cilliers adds a proviso to this general list saying that those ideas, beliefs, feelings, values etc. 'are *learnt* … by which a group of people order their lives and interpret their experiences, and which gives them an identity distinct from other groups'.[4]

'Religion, being imbedded in culture, is as difficult to define as culture. Religion is co-determined by the *perspective* of the *religious person* and his or her situation within a *specific culture*. Religion could be defined holistically as the acts, rituals and ideas of individuals and societies in which the relationship between the immanent reality and the transcendent reality become visible through word, image and acts'—religion also harbors within it the dimensions of spirituality[5] and (the search for) meaning. Cilliers develops the notion of religion as embedded within culture using the well-known metaphor of peeling an onion—and he maintains that 'on peeling the South African onion we are taken to another level, which has to do with the collision of a number of paradigms, affecting the very essence of our society,' and he finds at the core that 'godlessness, and the cause of South Africa's ills is directly equated to a disdain for Christ and Christianity.'[6]

South Africa as a country associated with the West has been known since the fifteenth century, when the great explorers Diaz and Da Gama rounded the Cape. The first formal settling of South Africa by white settlers from Europe in the Cape of Good Hope occurred in 1652, with the settlement of a Dutch complement whose role was to provide fresh provisions for sailors voyaging to the East as part of the activities of the Dutch East India Company. They were joined shortly by the French Huguenots[7] in 1688, and in 1820 by the British Settlers.[8] This potpourri from Europe came up against a similar invasion from the north at a later date as the different African tribes migrated to the south in a process called the *difaqane*. The two waves met in what inevitably became a fraught process of opposition and war. The only original inhabitants of the country, the Khoi-san (a unifying name for two ethnic groups, the Khoi, also described as the Hottentots, and the San, also called by some the Bushmen), were almost obliterated over the course of time; the Khoi were assimilated into other population groups and only small remnants of the San still inhabit the arid desert regions of the Kalahari desert. One can see why South Africa is called a country of immigrants of all descriptions, in many senses like the USA, but race, more particularly political policies centering on race, has been a defining and divisive factor in the failure of South Africa to create more of a melting-pot effect as had occurred in the USA.

South Africa's history has been one of several different kinds of colonialism carried out by different colonizing groups; this particular history has huge significance in relation to the multitudinal nature of the present South African population and society. A number of decisive battles between white settlers, both English and Afrikaans/Dutch (known as the Boers), and black tribes created the platform for the colonization of the country in the context of the European colonization of Africa. At the same time the devastating outcome of the Second Anglo-Boer War, from 1899 to 1902, created the platform for the effective colonization by the British of the Afrikaans population of the country.

This had a profound effect on the history of the country because, in the fight to create a space for Afrikaner patriotism and identity, the black population of the country became doubly marginalized and forced to the periphery (with black women, within the discourse of colonization, being marginalized three times over as a result of the patriarchal nature of indigenous African communities).[9] Thus the process of decolonization in South Africa has had a dual thrust emanating from this double focus, with the first wave of decolonization occurring when South Africa became independent of Britain (which had already been partially achieved by the creation of the Union in 1910) and became a Republic (also leaving the Commonwealth—in 1961), thus entrenching white supremacy in the country within the context of the apartheid state. The end of colonialism as Africa knew it (also in South Africa) had the result that emanates from most relevant theories of civil society in relating to the characteristic political product of colonialism in Africa: a bifurcated state and a divided society.

The second effective decolonization occurred with the dawn of the new South Africa—the first democratic election in 1994 and the assumption of power by the African National Congress, a liberation movement that was created in 1912 but which had to go underground in the late fifties as a result of the relentless efforts of the security apparatus of the apartheid state. Many important members of the freedom movements left South Africa to go into exile, many were incarcerated on Robben Island, and many more worked from the inside to effect change in South Africa, to culminate in what had been anticipated in an article in *Newsweek* in the late eighties, viz. 'South Africa is not likely to have a revolution, but rather a bloody evolution'. This evolution was finally effected in 1990 by the lifting of the ban on liberation movements and the engagement in deliberations about a new South Africa by the then President of the country, F. W. de Klerk. De Klerk has been variously hailed as a traitor, a visionary, a savior of the country—my personal assessment has always been that he is politically savvy, a pragmatist who could create a Damascus experience—and who could, to a large extent, make it work.

And now we have a new South Africa, a country that has been described by one of the most influential commentators on South Africa, Archbishop Desmond Tutu, as a rainbow nation.[10] What does this rainbow nation, and the country it inhabits, look like? Some understanding of this is crucial for an understanding of the way in which culture and religion have been approached, used and manipulated during the fraught history of this country. The transition to democracy, played out on a world stage where it was avidly watched, coming as the culmination of a decades-long punitive international process of boycotts and other measures, was experienced by South Africans across the spectrum as cataclysmic, joyous and so forth. What is true is that, in the first days of the new dispensation, there was an air of euphoria that encompassed the larger part of the country and the people; a sense of hope and expectation particularly among the poor, based on wildly implausible notions of an immediate restitution of land and redistribution of wealth.

The new country is a federal state, comprising a national government and nine provincial governments, with a further tier of local government.[11] The legal system is based on Roman-Dutch law, according to which the 1996 Constitution was created.[12] The population of the country, by mid-2011, was around 50 million, of which an estimated three to four million are illegal immigrants from elsewhere in Africa and the East. The country is large in size, covering 1.2 million square kilometers, with agriculture covering 81% of total land area, but with total arable land only being about 12%. The country has three capitals: Pretoria as the administrative capital, Cape Town as the legislative capital and Bloemfontein as the judicial capital. There are nine provinces: Eastern Cape, Western Cape, Northern Cape, Free State, Kwa-Zulu Natal, Mpumalanga, Limpopo, Gauteng and the North-West. The country is considered to be the biggest and strongest economy on the African continent, being one of the world's biggest suppliers of precious metals and diamonds (biggest supplier of platinum and chromium). With this goes the problem, however, that unemployment rates in the country are devastating (officially 26%, unofficially closer to 40%). This is one of the main drivers of the current paralyzing instances of labor unrest in the country, as extreme poverty lies at the one end of the spectrum while huge strides in wealth have been made at the other end by black entrepreneurs. It is daunting to realize that in a statement by the Deputy President Thabo Mbeki in 1998, it was pointed out that South Africa and Brazil shared the dubious honor of having the largest gap between the *haves* and the *have nots*—this lent credence to Mbeki's statement (which was contested at the time) describing South Africa as 'two nations within one South Africa'. And this situation has, if anything, become worse.

It is significant, in terms of the diversity in the country, that there are eleven official languages and six others that enjoy positions of support by government. The eleven languages are the former official languages, Afrikaans and English, isiZulu, isiXhosa, siSwati, seSotho, SePedi, seTswana, isiNdebele, xiTsonga and chiVenda. These languages all have areas of geographical concentration in the country and are provincial official languages in terms of their relative geographical density. Sign language is being promoted as a formal twelfth official language, and other protected languages include Khoi, San, French, German and Gujerati.

Religions in South Africa are predictably distributed, given the varied backgrounds which present-day South Africans come from. Christianity still accounts for almost 80% of the avowed religious persuasions of the country, but this should be seen within the context of the indigenous African religions as well.

Islam came to South Africa very early. The early Dutch settlers needed slaves, who were captured in Indonesia and brought to the Cape, with their dominant religion accompanying them. Hinduism came to South Africa as a first important wave during the 1850s when labor was needed on the sugar plantations in Natal and Indian laborers were imported by the British colonial powers in Natal.

Judaism began to gain a real foothold in South Africa during the gold and diamond rushes of the 1880s and continued strongly until just after the Second World War. An interesting reverse situation has developed with many Jewish families leaving South Africa to settle in Israel, as well as the other popular refuges for South African emigrants, Canada and Australia.

Throughout the colonial history of South Africa religion has played a decisive role. The dominant (Eurocentric) culture of the entire colonial period played the most decisive role, in line with the beliefs and persuasions of the colonial power in charge at the time, but the protestant brand of Christianity espoused by the Dutch, and especially the French Huguenots, has played the single most decisive role in the contested relationship between church and state until the change in South Africa to a new dispensation, which is ostensibly secular, but which, as we will see, is strangely entangled with notions of religion. In view of the fact that the overwhelming majority of South Africans profess to believe in some form of Christianity, reference in this context will be made to Christianity as a broad concept (including the African forms of Christianity).

The invidious impact of the use of religion by the earlier dispensation is succinctly conveyed by Cochrane, who echoes many other commentators:

> Christian thought and tradition was used by the apartheid government morally to justify its policies and defend its integrity. Yet against this same government, we saw a Christian denunciation of its policies and practices, and corresponding theological defense of liberation struggles against its regime.[13]

In the new South Africa this situation has been exacerbated to a certain extent by new complexities—past opponents of apartheid continue to appeal to the theological foundations they laid in the struggle against the apartheid regime, but they struggle to find a new relevance in a transformed political landscape; the easily definable target of the apartheid system gone so their focus has become a lot more diffuse, with a reduced general impact. Cochrane comments that

> at an even deeper level the ambiguity of religion lies in differing understandings of the nature of religious experience, its proper location, and its modal-

ity. These understandings, in turn, do not arrive de novo, but out of historical, cultural and personal experiences which are both synchronic and diachronic, and themselves filled with conflictual dynamics.[14]

In a recent article in the critical newspaper, The Mail and Guardian, on 23 December 2014, there is an interesting reflection on 'why churches dumped the ANC'—a move which has alarmed the ANC and which has profound implications for the ruling party.

2   Secularization

The general trend in South Africa in terms of the public sphere has been a consistent *ostensible* move towards secularization:

> A recent analysis of the representation of Christianity in Parliament has shown that those who appeal overtly to their Christian faith in the political debates of the house, particularly those from the conservative traditions who did not resist apartheid, are often the subject of mockery or barely disguised contempt.[15]

The result of this, increasingly, is that

> neither of these expressions of religion—reactionary or prophetic—demonstrates any comprehensive power to inspire the remaking of polity and society, particularly where that society is pluralist and not constrained by the authority of one particular tradition or sub-tradition (as in some contemporary theocracies such as Iran). These ambiguities are highlighted in a constitutional democracy, such as South Africa now is, where freedom of religion also means that no particular religion may govern the public sphere. The separating out of the spheres of religion and the state has the effect that religion, in the main, must now bow out of political and economic life … religion is reduced to but one source of values among many others, restricted to a rather narrow location of action within a much broader range of civil society institutions and movements. Politics is then defined primarily in terms of state power, exercised through bureaucracies; economics is defined largely in terms of the regulation of markets, themselves usually defined as 'private'.[16]

The issue of religion within education (state education) is also hotly contested—institutions that are explicitly religious-based can have very limited, if any, state support—the Christian basis of the former Potchefstroom University for Christian Higher Education has had to be sacrificed in the new dispensation, and has had to find a new form in order to keep on existing. However, and this is a crucial consideration, Cochrane feels that

> there are good grounds for believing that the notion of civil society may be a fruitful one for re-imagining the place of religion in public life [...] One may note, as one example, that there are no a priori reasons why the churches in South Africa, or other religious groupings for that matter, cannot transform the role they played in the past in resisting apartheid, into one that builds democracy [...] a re-conceptualization of religious institutions in the broadest sense as an expression of civil society should enable us to think through alternative ways of engagement. It should also [...] be possible to find concrete expressions of a positive engagement by religious institutions in the task of democratization.[17]

With religion being a subset of the notion of culture, how is this to be done? Let us go back for the moment to culture as a broad notion, encompassing religious, aesthetic, political and economic arrangements, practices and behaviors which can describe the particularity of a specific group of people within the contexts of other groups of people.

In South Africa it is a truism that there are many and very divergent cultures—all of whom have been thrown together in one country and within one over-arching context. *Diversity* is the word most often used, and *unity* is frequently used plaintively as a proposed way of curing the ills of diversity. A good summary of the current situation was presented by Johan Cilliers: 'South African society is at present not a unity celebrating her diversity in spite of constant political rhetoric reminding us of the rainbow nation, but rather a nation of mobile, industrialized and individualized consumers.'[18] He is referring here to his analysis of South African cultures in which he identifies three crucial components that, to my mind, encapsulate the situation today very well.

In speaking of *paradigms lost*, he speaks of the clash and resultant implosion of divergent paradigms: the phenomenon of so-called Americanism, the African spirit of *ubuntu* and the role of technological mass media.

He describes Americanism in terms of the notion of consumerism, and it is not necessary to amplify this beyond referring to the stupefying way in which American cultural imperialism has invaded and subdued traditional cultures in South Africa (not to mention the western sections of the population!). He makes the telling remark that the whole notion of community which underlies traditional culture across the continent is reduced and trivialized in favor of the individual in the grip of global consumerism.[19] He postulates that this ideology completely contradicts basic African values, such as *ubuntu*, which believes deeply that one is a human being through others (*'I am because you are and you are because I am'*—this is a cultural precept that promotes communalism and interdependence). The erosion of African culture and spirit by American-ism has, for him, left many South Africans and South African communities in a spiritual void, and he ascribes the rise of the African Independent Churches as being, in part, a response to this. He propounds the notion that the shift in the way churches have reacted to the ways and modes in which culture has been communicated throughout history can be located in the so-called eras or spheres of communication proposed by the French philosopher Debray: the logo-sphere (oral tradition), the grapho-sphere (printed media) and the video-sphere (transmission of images via electronic means). He maintains intrigu-ingly that, while the Western world has largely moved through these spheres, South Africa was slowed down in this process, specifically under *apartheid*, and now faces the challenge of processing in a condensed time-frame what certain other countries have achieved under more normal conditions. Africa is seen by some as still arrested in the logo-sphere, while the grapho and the video-spheres have only been integrated in an elitist fashion at corporate and govern-mental level. However, increasingly, the dawn of the video sphere and the rise of mass media has exacerbated the problems associated with this cultural shift, and has had an impact in many ways. One seemingly small but potentially hor-rifying outcome has been the whole phenomenon of upward social mobility[20] which has seen a rejection of traditional African values, and sadly, the virtual demise of African language use in favor of using English as a mode of empow-erment for the young. This is especially true of the new class known as black diamonds, who have become the role models to be emulated enthusiastically by all aspiring captains of industry.

At the present time in South Africa the initial strides made following the first democratic election are being threatened by the sheer force of bad news: the ubiquitous presence of HIV/AIDS and the appalling effect that this scourge has had and still has in South Africa, the increasing levels of unemployment, mass labor actions, the virtual collapse of a large segment of the education sys-tem, the number of universities needing bailouts because of appallingly bad management, the increasing levels of intolerance and bitterness caused by the injudicious application of policies of affirmative action at a variety of levels, the spiraling crime statistics, etc. etc. Add to this the fact that South Africa is con-sidered to have one of the worst records of xenophobia in the world and the picture nears completion.

Suggestions for palliation are made in a number of instances:

1. Cultural assimilation—which inevitably depends on the holder of the power to effect this. The present situation, as outlined above, militates against this very effectively.

2. Multicultural pluralism—where ethnicity and culture would seem to be the driving forces in determining individual and social identity, and a valid question would be whether these emphases will heal our society or prompt a

regression to apartheid. Whilst cultural assimilation stresses unity to the detriment of diversity, multicultural pluralism tends to over-emphasize diversity against unity.

3. Cultural engineering. No—the South African experience of social and cultural engineering that came to be known as *apartheid* will take a long time to be fully expunged from the popular imagination and the political and social awareness of the majority of the people of this country.

What is needed is an approach that ensures cultural openness. The notion of openness can also be described in terms of interculturality. Interculturality emphasizes exchange and in this context religion can play a role. A problem associated with this approach could be the issue of power—in this instance the relative power of the religion in question. Cilliers comments on this angle by saying that

> in this regard religion can make a meaningful contribution—not, as unfortunately happens time and again, functioning as an agent that legitimizes the status quo of cultural boundaries or separateness. Its dimension of spirituality should rather help to safeguard society from that which is temporal into something permanent or eternal, giving that which is transient a rigid, stable value. Religion should serve the movement from stringency to contingency, from status quo to status flux. In this way it can help to counteract dangerous and dehumanizing myths, preventing history from being turned into nature.[21]

The logical outcome is that one needs to find a safe space within which to work on redefining our identity—a space defined by honesty and respect, and where religion, being part of culture, can operate as a definitive and formative space-creator and space-setter within culture.

But before we reach that stage, what we have is encapsulated in the following quotation from a news website which states in a strongly-worded but very accurate assessment what is currently happening in South Africa and the crime waves, the poverty levels, unemployment rates and the general sense of despondency and disillusionment following the euphoria of the advent of the new South Africa:

> Those in the ANC who support Zuma do not do so because he is a superb leader with an impeccable track record and unrivalled integrity. They do so because they are in a faction that benefits from his continued presidency through political power and patronage, and fear the consequences of losing their positions of privilege. It's not as if most of those who oppose Zuma have purer intentions. Many of his detractors are frustrated by not being able to access political and economic resources while Zumanites are in control. They want their turn to control the levers of power.[22]

79

3 Powerful and Depressing Sentiments

Mokong maintains that a 'diversity of cultures, practices and approaches is a reality that cannot be ignored.'[23] This is in line with the idea of cultural defenses that are said to be blocking tendencies towards cultural homogenization as capitalism expands at the global level. In short, culture, in its relationship to, and like other aspects of human society, such as religion, the economic system, the legal system and ideology, constitutes an autonomous force that has a role within the socio-economic life of society. He argues that the claims that *ubuntu* values could have a role to play in the socio-economic development and advancement of post-apartheid South Africa are real and substantial, in light of the diversity presented by the end of apartheid, a system that thrived on the repression of black people's cultures, and in light of the process of globalization.

James Olthuis has engaged with the present-day South African conundrum in a way that suggests a way—but once again *only if the will to engage is there*. He propounds that a focus, the context of the postmodern world, be put on the role of worldview in engaging with the difficulties of the present, and sounds curiously aligned with the principles of *ubuntu* when he says that:

> The first of these features is the embracing of difference as non-oppositional [...] the second is that with a postmodern understanding of the existence of limited rational knowledge and the crucial role of faith, worldviews need to be seen not as conceptual systems [...] but as faith-oriented, sensory expectancy filters [...] the third is the recognition that responsibility to the other rather than freedom from the other needs to be emphasized [...] in our pluralistic, multi-faith global village, the honourable and respectful embrace of difference is the greatest challenge facing our postmodern world. We urgently need to develop a model of non-oppositional difference, an economy of love in which power-over (with its opposition to the other) is replaced by power-with (mutual recognition, attunement and empowerment). Love of the self and the other is not oppositional but correlational. Loving the other enhances the self, hating the other diminishes the self. However, no matter how promising the idea of non-oppositional difference, in our fallen world the ever-present economy of violence makes it extremely difficult, often virtually impossible, to put into practice.[24]

Olthuis continues in this vein by stating that,

> whereas in Modernism, 'freedom from' is the first word, Postmodernism insists that, before anyone says yes or no to the other call of the other, we are already summoned to be responsible to the other. The face of the other, says

Emmanuel Levinas, enjoins us, calling us to responsibility [...] this ethical call to responsibility is not only congenial with the ethos of the Gospel, but it also challenges us to readjust and refocus our worldview formulations.[25]

But for all this to work, there is a long way to go. Olthuis continues:

Whereas Modernism seems fixated on its need to control, dominate and exploit reality with all its attendant oppression and injustice, Postmodernism, with all of the positive features that I have noted above, is nevertheless so impacted by the unspeakable atrocities that afflict us, so mesmerized by the human penchant for evil that, even as it works for and longs for the coming of justice, it seems captive to the fear that, finally, we live only by Chance and, in the end, there is only death.[26]

And he finds the only solution in a renewal of confession by Christians—and the evocation of a Christian post-postmodern worldview, which would enable Christians to assist in the redemption of the world.

Thus we have a sense that renewal is possible through the principles of *ubuntu* and the notion of Christian love in a postmodern context—both of which strive towards the same ideal, but the current depressing reality is that the present political context in South Africa will not accommodate anything as reasonable and ethical as these schools of thought.

Renewal can only work if the will to engage is there.

1   Charles Villa-Vicencio has put it as strongly as the following: 'South Africa is at a crossroads. The poison of xenophobia and blood soaked divisionism will either escalate or we will need to embrace an inclusive identity as Africans and South Africans that can lead us to a future beyond the rigidities of identity and culture that threatens to destroy what we once called the South African miracle'. (C. Villa-Vicencio, *On Being South African: Identity, Religion and Culture* (Beyers Naudé Memorial Lecture: University of Johannesburg, 18 June 2008).

2   It is, of course, a real and constant danger that the circumscribed diversity implied in the metaphoric construct 'rainbow nation' is a strengthened ethnography.

3   J.R. Cochrane, 'Of Religion and Theory in a Civil Society: Readings from the South African Case,' in *Christ in a Postmodern World: Theology in Critical Dialogue* (Grand Rapids, MI: Eerdmans, 2002), 19. Cochrane speaks very persuasively of culture and religion in the context of civil society—it is useful to note that the present manuscript was written immediately after the attack on the twin towers in New York. 'To think again of theology, and religion, in the public place, in the market square, I focus on the lens offered by the idea of civil society, to highlight some important challenges to theology in our time, in dialogue with the African context, and with the work of people such as Mahmood Mamdani, Cohen and Arato, Jürgen Habermas, Jean Bethke Elshtain. Questions about the ecclesia and the believing/acting/responsible human being emerge clearly. I end by claiming that responsible theological reflection seeks to break open new possibilities amidst the

limits of present actualities. It partakes of what is to come, refuses to possess the truth, supports the struggle of human beings to actualize themselves, takes its stand against suffering, and incorporates the other in just institutions and ways of living well together. I argue that it is not difficult to test our thought and our action against criteria, or thereby to grasp the task of religion, or practical faith, in civil society.'

4 J. Cilliers, *Creating Space within the Dynamics of Interculturality: the Impact of Religious and Cultural Transformations in Post-Apartheid South Africa* (International Academy of Practical Theology: Berlin, 30 March 2007).

5 J. Cilliers, *Formations and Movements of Christian Spirituality in Urban African contexts.*
The term 'Religie', used in both Dutch and Afrikaans, is a much more useful one to use to differentiate between this notion of spiritual awareness and formal religion ('godsdiens').

6 Cilliers, *Creating Space*, 4.

7 The French Huguenots came to the Cape following the decimation of the Protes-tants after the revocation of the Edict of Nantes (1685) and the subsequent slaughter of St Bartholomew's night, following which the French Protestants fled to the Netherlands and thence to the Cape of Good Hope, where they played a singularly important role in subse-quent developments of Western religion, especially Protestantism, in the Cape.

8 The British Settlers came to South Africa as a result of the urbanization and the destruction of cottage industries in Britain in the throes of the Industrial Revolution, and they were rather calcu-latedly settled in what is now the Eastern Cape to provide a buffer between warring indigenous tribes and the British colonial powers in the Eastern Cape.

9 The policies by which Black people were disenfranchised in terms of possession of land which had been in operation in the Parliament of the Cape Colony under Cecil Rhodes and others were extended to the rest of the country, and were attacked in eloquent terms by Sol Plaatje, the first Secretary-General of the ANC, in his landmark publication *The Natives' Land Act* of 1913.

10 The term rainbow nation is a significant one, as it resonates with a number of ways in which unity and diversity are dealt with in the course of the discussion.

11 It is a system that lends itself at all levels, but particularly at local level, to unbelievable acts of nepotism, corruption and theft, culminating in a crisis of service delivery that is increasingly paralyzing the country, as the appointment of people, particularly at senior level is done without the least consideration of capacity, both professionally and personally. In recent times fraud associated with claims of qualifications obtained has become rampant.

12 It is instructive to realize that the South African Constitution is considered by many to be a model constitution, and in fact it is, though it is not always adhered to, especially in terms of its spirit.

13 Cochrane, *Of Religion*, 2.

14 Cochrane, *Of Religion*, 2.

15 Cochrane, *Of Religion*, 2.

16 Cochrane, *Of Religion*, 2. He continues: 'Many people argue that Africa generally, South Africa included, does not face a crisis of religion or a mood of seculari-zation. On the contrary, it is argued that religion is deeply rooted and largely holistic, certainly among such groupings as the African Initiated Churches but also among those who practice African traditional religion. Further, Islamic understandings of the sacred and the secular prevent any dualism between them, and the Islamic perspective has significant political presence in South Africa. The same may be said of Judaism and Hinduism, the other major religious groupings in the country.'

17 Cochrane, *Of Religion*, 2.

18 Cilliers, *Creating Space*, 11.

19 Cilliers, *Creating Space*, 6.

20 In this context Mogong speaks of the cultural shame exhibited by some black

Africans. He suggests that the resilience of the culture of *ubuntu* could counter the cultural shame element, but like other desiderata in the South African context this would seem to be something of a tall order.

21 Cilliers, *Creating Space*.
22 R. Munusamy, 'Quote of the week: Zumanites' (*Daily Maverick*, 1 October 2012).
23 S. M. Mokong, 'Culture versus religion: A theoretical analysis of the role of indigenous African culture of Ubuntu in social change and economic development in the post-apartheid South African Society,' *Politics and Religion*, 1/III (2009), 76-96.
24 J. Olthuis, 'A vision of and for love: Towards a Christian post-modern worldview,' *Koers*, 77/4 (2010), 23-31.
25 Olthuis, *Vision*.
26 Olthuis, *Vision*.

PARTL II

CHINA

6

On Promoting Religious Harmony,
and Helping Religion to Play
an Active Role in China

Xunmou Zhang

87

China is a country with many religions, but Buddhism, Daoism, Islam, Catholicism and Protestantism are the five most important ones. According to incomplete statistics, there are more than 100 million religious believers, 360,000 religious personnel, nearly 140,000 sites of religious activities, 5,500 religious bodies and around 100 institutes of religious education in China.

Article 36 of the Constitution stipulates clearly that:

> Citizens of the People's Republic of China enjoy freedom of religious belief. No state organ, public organization or individual may compel citizens to believe in, or not to believe in, any religion; nor may they discriminate against citizens who believe in, or do not believe in, any religion.
> The state protects normal religious activities. No one may make use of religion to engage in activities that disrupt public order, impair the health of citizens or interfere with the educational system of the state.
> Religious bodies and religious affairs are not subject to any foreign domination.

Article 36 sets out the three basic principles of freedom of religious belief, separation of church and state, and autonomy of Chinese religions. Based on these principles, the Chinese government has committed itself to three main tasks when dealing with religious matters, i.e. adhering to the policy of freedom of religious belief, promoting religious harmony, and helping religion to play a positive and active role.

1 Adhering to the Policy of Freedom of Religious Belief

The Chinese government adheres to the policy of freedom of religious belief, and regards it as a basic and long-term one. The policy contains three aspects: (1) both religious and non-religious believers have the freedom to believe in or not to believe in any religion; (2) the separation of church and state; (3) the unity of rights and obligations.

1.1 Safeguarding Citizens' Rights of Freedom of Religious Belief

The Chinese government believes that the freedom of religious belief is one of the fundamental rights of citizens protected by the Constitution. Chinese citizens have the freedom to believe in, or not believe in, any religion, and the freedom to believe in this or that religion. A non-religious person may become follower of a religion and a religious believer may withdraw from a religion. The essence of the freedom of religious belief is to make the issue of religious belief a private issue for citizens and a matter of their own choosing. The core of the policy of the freedom of religious belief is to respect and protect citizens' rights of freedom of religious belief. No organization or individual may compel citizens to believe in, or not believe in, any religion or change their religion, nor may they discriminate against citizens who believe in or do not believe in any religion.

1.2 Adhering to the Separation of Church and State

The separation of church and state is the premise and the basis of freedom of religious belief, and a common value of modern countries. The Chinese Constitution provides the principle of separation of church and state and that of religion and education. The separation of church and state requires that religion should not be eliminated or developed by the state's will and administrative power. That is, on one hand, the state should not interfere in citizens' rights of freedom of religious belief and the internal affairs of religion, and should be impartial to all religions. The state should not use its power to suppress or support any particular religion. All religions are equal before the law. On the other hand, religions should not meddle in the state's administration, jurisdiction and education. Nor should anyone take advantage of religion to do such things or to disturb the social order, or harm other citizens.

1.3 Adhering to the Unity of Rights and Obligations

To adhere to the unity of rights and obligations is a primary principle of modern law. While enjoying rights, one must undertake obligations; this is a basic requirement of modern law and an important guarantee of the freedom of religious belief. China is a secular country, running state affairs according to law. The greatest authority in China is law. All social organizations, including religious organizations, must abide by the Constitution and the law. None of them may go beyond the law, nor may they harm the interests of the state, society and the community, or interfere with the lawful rights of other citizens.

2 Promoting Religious Harmony

Peace, development and cooperation remain the themes of the times; however, the world is far from tranquil. Interactions among religions are increasingly frequent, conflicts concerning religion are scaling up, and all these have an increasingly important impact on international politics and world affairs.

With the migration of population and cultural exchange, people from different religious traditions encounter each other more frequently, and contradictions and conflicts caused by, or related to, religion constantly arise. Therefore, eliminating religious contradictions and conflicts, and promoting religious harmony, has become a new requirement of the era.

Without religious harmony, there will be no social harmony. Without religious harmony, there will be no world harmony. Constructing a harmonious society and building a harmonious world is not possible without religious harmony. Thus, the Chinese government advocates and promotes religious harmony. Promoting religious harmony is to realize social harmony by dealing properly with the relationship between religion and society, between various religions, between religious and non-religious followers, and between citizens who believe in this or that religion, and so forth.

The Chinese government has been making efforts to realize such a goal. It encourages and supports religious dialogue, and keeps exploring the mode of church-state relationship which matches the features of China and can guarantee the freedom of religious belief. Such a relationship aims to promote harmony between church and state by separating them from each other. In order to realize such an aim, the Chinese government established three principles: to respect each other in faith, to unite and cooperate in politics, and to hold on to the supremacy of the law, In this way, the Chinese government is promoting the harmony between Chinese religions and society by promoting the harmony between church and state.

On January 28, 2011, leaders of the national associations of the five main religions of China gathered in Beijing to hold a joint symposium, to support the resolution of the United Nations 65th General Assembly in making the first week of every February 'World Interfaith Harmony Week'. It also released a *Joint Declaration on Promoting Religious Harmony*, which encourages the following five principles: (1) to love the country and love religion; (2) to uphold equity and inclusiveness; (3) to carry forward the concept of harmony; (4) to oppose the willful distortion and utilization of religion; (5) to play an active role.[1]

3 Helping Religion to Play a Positive and Active Role

Since the start of the period of reform and opening-up, the Chinese government has actively guided religion in making adjustments to the socialist society, encouraging and supporting religion to play a positive and active role and Chinese religions have taken an active part in the causes of state construction and public welfare. Delegates from religious bodies can participate in political life in lawful ways. They can, for example, express their social opinions, offer suggestions or evaluations on various affairs through the national people's congress or the provincial, county, district and township people's congresses and political consultative conference. In recent years, the Chinese government has realized more clearly that religious believers, together with the non-religious believers, can also take an active role in building a socialist society with Chinese characteristics. It has, therefore, taken measures to make it easier for religious personnel and religious believers to play a positive role in promoting social harmony, cultural prosperity and social economic development.

3.1 Exploring the Harmonious Resources to Play a Positive Role in Promoting Cultural Prosperity and Social Harmony

A harmonious society needs not only an economical basis and a political guarantee, but also powerful spiritual support and a good cultural basis. The key to building a harmonious culture is to advocate a harmonious ideal and to cultivate a harmonious spirit. Religion possesses enormous harmonious elements. Buddhism, Taoism, Islam, Catholicism and Christianity are all rich in resources of harmonious ideas. The unique role of religion should be played in building a harmonious culture. In order to promote social harmony by promoting religious harmony, Chinese religions have been making great efforts. For example, three World Buddhist forums have been held,[2] and participants have pledged the following six vows to promote the relevant actions:

> May the human heart be genial and kind, treasuring every opportunity to protect life, and practice gratitude;
> May the family be accommodating and happy, reinforcing personal relationships, and practice offering and contribution;
> May social relationships be cordial and smooth, being communicative and helpful, and develop amiable friendship;

May the society be secure and neighborly, everybody getting what they need, and practice tolerance and conciliation;

May civilizations be harmonious, being mutually appreciative, and practice respect;

May the world be peaceful, transforming hatred to friendship, and practice sharing.

A harmonious world begins within our minds. Let us synergize and cooperate our conditions so that we can walk together with common goals and vision.

3.2   Carrying Forward the Fine Tradition of Playing an Active Role in Promoting Social and Economic Development

Chinese religious believers have a fine tradition of loving the country and loving religion, serving society and bringing benefit to the people. In order to have religious believers and the religious masses play an active role in socio-economical development, it is important to encourage and support religious believers in engaging actively in charity and social services. Chinese religions have made great achievements in this field.

According to an incomplete survey, over the past five years, charitable donations from religious circles have reached up to 3 billion RMB. The fields of charity and social services have been expanded, the number of people served has increased, and the level of service has been raised. The attitude towards charity and social services has changed from passive to active. The content of the services provided has expanded from serving only material needs to serving psychological, spiritual and social needs, The mode of providing services has changed from scattered, spontaneous and single to systematic, organized and multiple. We can take the Protestant churches as an example. According to incomplete statistics, they have set up 37 hospitals and clinics, more than 180 homes for the aged, 9 homes for orphans, have donated 200,000 wheelchairs for the disabled, 28 medical vehicles, and have aided the set up of 129 schools and 167 water resource facilities.

On February 12, 2012, six ministries of the central government jointly issued a document *On Encouraging and Regulating Religious Circles Engaging in Charity and Social Services*, setting out the four basic principles of 'active support, equal treatment, administration according to the law and perfect mechanism'.[3] On September 17, 2012, a meeting on the *Exchange of Experiences of Religious Circles Engaged in Charity and Social Services* was held in Wuhan, and a 'Week of Religious Charity' was launched with the theme of 'Loving the world, five main religions walk together'.[4] All these initiatives will push forward the religious circles and encourage them to engage in charity and social services.

1   See http://www.sara.gov.cn/ztzz/
    sjbtxyjhxz/gtxyyw/7843.htm, accessed
    September 14, 2013.
2   In 2006, 2009 and 2012. See http://
    en.wikipedia.org/wiki/World_Buddhist_
    Forum, accessed September 14, 2013;
    http://news.xinhuanet.com/english/2009-
    03/28/content_11087458.htm, accessed
    September 14, 2013; http://china.org.cn/
    china/2012-04/26/content_25242027.htm,
    accessed September 14, 2013.
3   See http://www.chinadaily.com.cn/
    china/2012-03/01/content_14726002.htm
    accessed September 14, 2013.
4   See http://www.ucanews.com/news/
    state-launches-religious-charity-
    campaign/60618, accessed September
    14, 2013.

7

A Threefold Perspective on the Research into the Sinicization of Christianity

Zhigang Zhang

The sinicization of Christianity is a research subject that has both important academic value and realistic significance. Since China started to reform and open up, its government has implemented policies promoting freedom of religious belief. Consequently, all the major religions in China have rebounded and grown. The rapid growth of the number of Christian believers has been the most remarkable. Thus the historical challenge of how best to handle the relations between Christianity and the Chinese culture, the Chinese nation, and contemporary Chinese society in particular, is once again forced onto the horizon of our study.

Substantial research has been performed by scholars both in and outside of China on the problematic of the indigenization, localization, contextualization and sinicization of Christianity. Having looked at the scholarship available, especially after considering, comparing and evaluating a variety of inclinations, opinions and propositions, this author believes that, in order to see real progress in the sinicization of Christianity, a three-fold vision of research which takes into account its 'past, present and future' is vital. That is to say, it is only by taking a thorough approach to investigating the past, present and future of Christianity in China that we will have any chance of representing the major problems that exist in the sinicization process of Christianity, and of arriving at some basic consensus.

1   The Past is not Past: the Necessity of the Sinicization of Christianity

Previous studies have demonstrated that, as a non-native religion, Christianity has only been able to take root in China after four major 'comings': the first coming of Nestorianism during China's Tang dynasty, the second coming as

'Arkagun' during the Yuan dynasty, the China mission of the Catholic Church during the late Ming and early Qing periods and, finally, the new arrivals of Catholicism, Eastern Orthodoxy and Protestantism since around the time of the Opium Wars. Comparatively speaking, scholars both in and outside of China have paid more attention to the latter two processes, although their research orientations, as well as their results, have demonstrated great divergence.

Some scholars, for instance, have tended to focus on the pioneering work of the Christian missionaries who came to China during the late Ming and early Qing periods, and the contributions they made to the cultural exchanges between China and the West, i.e. both *xixuedongjian*, the introduction of Western scholarship to the Far East, and *zhongxuexichuan*, the communication of Chinese culture to the West. In contrast, other scholars argue that the introduction of Western scholarship, especially its modern technology, by the missionaries was just a means of supporting their theology and teachings. Moreover, the scientific and technological knowledge that they brought was not very advanced, and some of it had already become outdated. For the time period starting with the Opium Wars, some scholars argue that the entry of Christianity in China during the mid 19th century was intertwined with the military aggression of Western colonial powers. Hence, Christianity became a tool of invasion used by the imperialist powers, and played an ugly or negative role in the Chinese nation's hundred-year long history of suffering after the Opium Wars. In contrast, some other scholars have focused on studying the many positive works that Christians and missionaries have performed in building the educational system, public health services, charitable institutions, and publishing houses in early modern China.

Although these contrasting approaches do not reflect the whole landscape of previous scholarship, and certainly cannot represent the theoretical positions that seek to combine or balance the two approaches, they at least enable us to be clearly aware of the following two facts: First, while these two periods of Christian mission have attracted the most attention and have been the most contentious, it is only because of their different backgrounds and standpoints that researchers have developed different inclinations and viewpoints. Second, although the two historical periods in question are complex in their details (hence the variety of research perspectives and evaluative propositions) they have become history and the fact remains.

So, will we be able to find any common ground on such key aspects as academic standpoints, theoretical horizons, and the main research topics? From the point of view of this author, building such a basic consensus is not only necessary but is also possible. All researchers, whether they are in academia, in the religious professions or in politics, should take the perspective of the interests of the Chinese nation as a whole. That is, they should prioritize the interests of the people and focus on the cultural tradition of the Chinese nation and the historical process of Chinese society. They should then be able to arrive at rational and objective historical evaluations of the two periods of Christian mission in China, especially of its major cultural influences and social functions.

Experts both in and outside of China tend to agree that, when Catholicism entered China during the late Ming and early Qing periods, this did not mean that the Chinese were encountering yet another foreign religion. If Catholicism can be perceived as the religious and cultural tradition that still played a dominant role in the European societies, its entry into China should be seen as the 'first encounter, collision and breaking-in' between the beliefs and values of the mainstream cultures of China and the West.[1] This deep cultural exchange was initiated by the missionaries, who attempted to accommodate, stretch or revise traditional Confucian thought, while simultaneously proselytizing by introducing Western scholarship in the humanities, science and technology. Yet, as a matter of fact, this latter move played quite a positive role in promoting two-way communication between, and mutual understanding of, Chinese and Western cultural traditions, and especially in facilitating the formation and development of modern science in China. Nevertheless, all this came to a halt due to the Chinese Rites controversy that was started in the China missions. The Chinese Rites controversy and its results exposed, for the first time in history, the differences, incompatibilities and conflicts between the cultural traditions of China and the Christian West.[2] Catholic and Protestant missionaries from Europe and America, following the military triumphs of Western powers during the Opium Wars, poured into China under the protection of a series of unequal treaties. The contradictions and conflicts between Western Christianity and the Chinese nation, Chinese society and its cultural tradition were intensified, to the point that Western Christianity became associated with an invasion of China, with missionary cases, the anti-Christianity movement, and the anti-religious movement, and has become part of the nation's unforgettable memory about its early modern period. Not surprisingly, against this particular historical background, and based on its social roles and cultural impact, phrases such as 'foreign religion,' 'tools of cultural invasion,' 'one more Christian, one less Chinese person,' 'it is not "Chinese Christianity", but "Christianity in China,"' and so forth, became keywords or major themes in the history of Christianity in early modern China. The quiet contributions to Chinese society made by the many missionaries, especially the majority of Chinese Christians, inevitably became a minor theme or was even omitted altogether.

This brief analysis shows that the main historical difficulty in the sinicization of Christianity lies in the incompatibilities and conflicts between Christianity as proselytized by Western missionaries, on the one hand, and Chinese culture, the Chinese nation and Chinese society on the other. At the same time, this is also the fundamental reason why the sinicization of Christianity is necessary in China. However, in order to fully argue this point, we have to take into consideration a prevalent argument put forward by Christian apologetics, which rejects the indigenization, localization, contextualization and in particular sinicization of Christianity on the grounds of the universality of Christianity. In the face of this challenge, we shall follow the principle of consistency between logic and history in our analysis, and shall accordingly engage with the three problems involved, i.e. the concept of universality, the history of world religions, and in particular, the aforementioned historical difficulty of the Christian mission in China.

First of all, with regard to the conceptual meaning, the aforementioned prevalent view is obviously lacking in a dialectic understanding of the concept of universality: if we could agree that what the Christian faith communicates is a universal doctrine or spirituality, this doctrine or spirituality would have to be able to be indigenized, localized, contextualized or sinicized. Should anyone deny this necessity, there would be no universality of the Christian faith to speak of. Or, to explain it with a classical Chinese reference, it would not be able to 'extend over all the ground to the four seas'.

Second, if we look at the history of world religions, it is clear that, for the major world religions to spread far and wide across the world for hundreds and thousands of years, they had to be able to adapt to different cultures, peoples, countries or societies, and thus be able to achieve indigenization, localization, contextualization or nationalization. Ninian Smart points out that, when we investigate the world's many religious traditions, we should never forget that there is a great variety of them. Take Christianity, for instance. In many countries or regions, we find that different cultures have added new features to the same religious tradition. Thus, Catholicism in the Ukraine is different from that in Ireland; the Greek Orthodox Church is different from the Russian Orthodox Church; the German Lutherans differ from the American ones.[3] The account quoted above thus leads right into the question previously raised: if Christianity is as it should be in these other countries or regions, why did it not go through the same process within the Chinese culture and social context?

Finally, to look into the aforementioned historical difficulty and take up this the last question, we may ask why it is that Christian faith, as evangelized by Western missionaries, should have entered into such sharp conflict with Chinese culture, the Chinese people and Chinese society. As mentioned earlier, this historical difficulty started with the Chinese Rites controversy during the late Ming and early Qing periods. Looking back at this historical case, we cannot but reflect on this academic phenomenon: why is it that hundreds of years after the controversy, there is still a multitude of well-known Western scholars who have continued to focus on the issue and voice their opinions? Why is it that this controversy has remained a key research focus or one of the hot topics in such areas as Western Sinology, the history of Chinese religions, and the history of Chinese-Western cultural exchange? All of the above thus indicates, undoubtedly, that this long-lasting controversy had not been caused simply by the conflicts among the missionaries with respect to mission strategies, nor had it ended with the contest of authority between the Pope in Rome and the reigning Chinese emperor. Rather, it has reflected, in a fundamental way, the tensions and conflicts between the religious and cultural traditions and thoughts of China and the West.

Drawing on the recent developments in the study of intercultural dialogue and interreligious dialogue in international academia, in particular, we can again see that there is a deeper reason for the tension and conflicts between the religious and cultural traditions and thoughts of China and the West. Apart from the three concrete issues that previous researchers have paid special attention to (the problems of ancestor worship, the worship of Confucius, and the Chinese translation of the name of God), and apart from the multiple differences between the conflicting parties on the cultural, religious, philosophical, social and political fronts, there was always a deeper reason for these conflicts, which then became value-driven, namely: the Western Christian centrism that was prevalent among the missionaries coming to China, and their strong exclusivist orientation. The reason why this deep-rooted cause of conflict is worth probing is precisely because, being the general mentality, it had enabled missionaries of all orders to perceive themselves as owning the Truth: the Western Christianity that they taught was the only true religion, and only the belief in the Western God (as they interpreted it) was the absolute true faith. In contrast, all the other forms of belief that the Chinese people already had, no matter whether they were native or foreign in origin, or philosophical or religious in nature, were perceived as either containing some legitimate elements, or as being complete idolatry, or even superstition. On this point, based on previous scholarship, we could go even further by arguing that it was precisely because of this holier-than-thou attitude and exclusivist mentality, shared by the majority of the missionaries coming to China since the late Ming and early Qing periods that, at the ideological level, the Chinese Rites controversy, as well as the tensions and conflicts between the religious and cultural traditions and thoughts of China and the West since the Opium Wars, had become a process of historical necessity. Thus, without giving up its Western Christian centrism and exclusivist mentality, Christianity will have little chance of taking root in the soil of Chinese culture, of integrating into its mainstream society, or of achieving indigenization, localization, contextualization, or sinicization.

2   Respect for Reality: the Importance of the Sinicization of Christianity

Since the reform and opening up of China, the rapid growth of Christianity, especially Protestantism, in Mainland China has drawn wide attention from academia, the religious professions, and the political sphere, both in and out-side of China. In particular, a multitude of difficult problems has been brought in front of the researchers. Based on the investigations and discussions around this subject during the recent years, all the difficulties that Christianity is expe-riencing in Chinese society today may be summed up in one key question: what important impact will the rapid growth of Christianity have on the reli-gious, cultural and social realities of China?

Over the last five or six years, scholars all across the world have had intense debates on this key question and given many thought-provoking opinions. For instance, some experts and scholars point out that there is a not insignificant international background or Western backing to the rapid development of Christianity in China. Still aiming at a 'Peaceful Evolution' in China, hostile forces of the West continue to engage in a campaign of Christianizing China, which has become especially obvious in the large presence of underground churches or house churches. The illegitimacy and exclusiveness of these under-ground or house churches not only violates China's principle of running its religious affairs independently, but it also affects the true image of Christianity. What's even more worrying is that, if Christianity became the biggest or even the dominant religion in China, it would surely cause damage to China's reli-gious ecosystem, hurt Chinese culture, both the main body and its plurality, and negatively affect its social harmony and national security.

Looked at objectively and from all sides, the opinion discussed above may not be widely shared by scholars in and outside of China, but it is not unwar-ranted. Comparatively speaking, Buddhism, Christianity and Islam, all the world religions that are present in the Chinese society today, were once imported. Moreover, in recent years, many scholars, based on their own research, have reached the following conclusion: even though Christianity has seen the most rapid growth in the number of its believers since China's reform and opening up, Buddhism is the religion with the greatest overall influence on society, and Islam is the religion with the greatest influence on multiple ethnic groups. It thus begs the question, why have there been so few people in the Chi-nese or international academia, religious professions or political sphere, who emphasize the international background or backing with regard to Chinese Buddhism or Chinese Islam, and yet many believe that there is still a long way to go for the sinicization of Christianity? Does that mean that up until today, Christianity has not relieved itself of the heavy historical burden of being a 'for-eign religion', and thus has yet to integrate into the Chinese culture or the Chi-nese nation as Buddhism and Islam have already done?

While taking full consideration of the opinions mentioned above and acknowledging their legitimacy, this author would prefer to take up the follow-ing questions: should we not focus predominantly on the national situation of contemporary China, especially the great developments that have taken place in

Chinese society during the last three decades since China's reform and opening up, so that we could take seriously the overall reality of Chinese Christianity? By 'taking seriously', I mean we should advance a deep, dialectical methodology and grasp the substantial and the mainstream aspects of Chinese Christianity when observing and considering its overall situation. As part of the reality of Chinese religions, Chinese Christians, just like believers of other major religions, not only enjoy religious freedom as a constitutional right, but they are first and foremost citizens of China, which means that they are undoubtedly going to play important roles in promoting social harmony and the prosperity and progress of the Chinese nation. If the above evaluative proposition matches the overall national situation of China today, we have sufficient reason to believe that the vast majority of China's Christian churches, church organizations and individual believers, no matter whether they are above ground or underground, or whether they belong to the Three Self Church or to the house churches, have been faithful to both their country and their religion. They will be willing, in the way taught by the faith they pursue, to build up a great motherland together with all the people of the country, and to play important and positive roles in numerous areas such as economical development, cultural affairs, social service, charities and public goods, and especially morality and ethics. Naturally, no one can deny the existence of outside forces that have attempted to use Christianity to infiltrate China to promote its 'Peaceful Evolution'. Meanwhile, there have also been a small number of church organizations or individuals who use faith in order to disguise their political motives, and work in collaboration with hostile forces from outside. Nevertheless, none of us can afford to focus our attention on the above-mentioned 'small number' inside China or overseas, and be led to overlook or even deny the substantial and mainstream aspects of China's Christian Church and its vast faith community. It would constitute an attitude of 'looking at the sky through a tube'.

We have argued for focusing on the substantial and mainstream aspects so as to be objective and comprehensive in grasping the overall situation of Chinese Christianity today. That does not mean making only positive judgments and neglecting or avoiding the current inadequacies or problems. Frankly speaking, even though the number of Christian believers has increased rapidly since the reform and opening up of China, it is not only the majority of Chinese people who still lack knowledge or understanding of Christianity, many experts and scholars have also voiced their doubts or worries about the rapid growth of religion in China. An objective phenomenon that cannot be overlooked is that, in contrast with the deep changes that Chinese society has undergone since its reform and opening up, Christian churches in China have obviously not completely adapted to the urgent need that the whole country has felt in a number of areas, such as economic and political system reform, the rule of law and social morality, social services and public good, and cultural development and prosperity. They have not fully played the important and positive social and cultural role that is expected of them. That means that the main problem and challenge that Christianity faces today in Chinese society lies not so much with the number of believers but with the quality of the church, i.e. what exactly can the tens of millions Chinese Christians contribute to the Chinese society. That is exactly why the question as to whether Christianity can fully play its important positive and constructive role in the development and progress of contemporary Chinese society has become of utmost importance.

3 Looking Ahead to the Future: the Importance of the Sinicization of Christianity

Arguably, the theoretical intention of human and social scientific research consists in reflecting on the past, understanding the present, and looking ahead to the future. Thus, our research dedicated to the sinicization of Christianity is a future-oriented, constructive project, the goal being to help Chinese Christianity to overcome the major difficulties it is facing, and to proactively integrate it into Chinese culture, the Chinese nation and especially contemporary Chinese society. No doubt this is a research project that demands long and hard work, and its success will depend on the collective wisdom and joint efforts of many experts and scholars both in and outside of China, be they Christian or non-Christian. For starters, I am willing to make the following three points in the hope of generating more discussion.

3.1 Sinicization of Christianity: a Contribution of Chinese Wisdom for Building a Theology for Intercultural Dialogue

In order for Christianity to become Chinese too, a theological system with Chinese characteristics needs to be developed, first and foremost, for theology as the discourse of the church can obviously provide conceptual orientation and theoretical support for the indigenization, localization, contextualization or sinicization of Christianity. Thus, amid the current positive atmosphere in Chinese society, where efforts are dedicated to properly managing religious relations, and where religious professionals and members of faith communities are urged to contribute to social harmony and cultural prosperity, how can we develop a more original approach to exploring a theological system with Chinese characteristics? In my opinion, both the comparative method and the concept of dialogue, as promoted in the international field of religious studies, can help to update our ideas and broaden our views on this project of theological construction. The comparative method, arguably the fundamental methodology of contemporary religious studies, aims at breaking the isolation and exclusivity of all religions, and urging them to conduct comparative research and arrive at the 'double knowledge', that is, the knowledge of the other, and the knowledge of ourselves. The notion of dialogue on the other hand, is not only a theoretical extension or a recent trend in the comparative study of religion, but also a practical idea for managing religious relations in the era of globalization. Urging all religions to engage in sincere cross-cultural or cross-denominational dialogue helps to resolve religious disputes and promote mutual understanding, friendly cooperation, and collaboration between the religions in response to the many difficulties, crises or challenges of the global age. If we really understand the academic developments mentioned above, couldn't we also think that Chinese culture—with its long history, its rich variety of Chinese religions, and especially its cultural and religious traditions which stress inclusiveness and integration, harmony but not uniformity—would not only provide particularly favorable objective conditions for comparative studies and dialogues, but also for building up the potential for a theological construction of China's Christian Church. And, with the help of Chinese cultural wisdom, such a Church could make a contribution to the exploration of a theology of intercultural dialogue which accords with the reality of the religious plurality of our world today.

For instance, Christianity borrowed a lot from ancient Greek philosophy in forming its own theological system; by integrating theories of ontology with that of a belief in God, it provided the intellectual foundation for an externally oriented quest for transcendence. In contrast, classical Chinese philosophical traditions have integrated the best teachings of Confucianism, Buddhism and Daoism, and have developed a faith orientation that focuses on internal cultivation. Obviously, these two different forms of faith can potentially inspire and complete each other. If we are able to integrate the two and innovate on that basis, not only will the theories of mind in classical Chinese philosophy be deepened again (as they were once deepened by Chan Buddhism), but China's contemporary study of philosophy will also become enriched and strengthened in its ontological awareness of the theory of the transcendent. In this way it will be possible to create a theory of belief and practice, which, by integrating external transcendence and internal cultivation, will complement and complete the cultural traditions of China.

3.2 Sinicization of Christianity as a Positive Contribution to Solving Major Problems

Over the last three decades there has been a new move in the international field of religious studies, which is to orient religious dialogues toward moral practices, and to call for collaboration between all religions to rebuild world ethics and share social responsibilities, in response to the numerous difficulties, crises and challenges that humankind is facing. Thus, if Christianity in China is to develop into a religion which is characteristic of Chinese ethics, i.e. with a strong emphasis on morality and social contribution, it will be both in accordance with the developmental trends of world religions and with meeting the real needs of Chinese society.

For instance, recent years have seen a lot of attention focused on the debate about the moral bottom line of our society, frauds in manufacturing, commerce and finance, and even credibility crises within organizations dedicated to social welfare and charity. If the Chinese Christian churches could work extensively with the other religions and academics to help build a moral and ethical code that suits the national situation, both the theoretical and practical value and significance of Christianity would be fully on display. Or take the instance of the global ecological and environmental crisis. If the Chinese Christian Church can enter into deep dialogue with Daoist and Buddhist circles on their visions of the universe and of nature, the theological construction of Chinese Christianity is bound to achieve the kind of theoretical results that will have an international impact. Or take yet another instance, the escalating national and religious conflicts in some countries or religions since the end of the Cold War. If the Chinese Christian church could benefit from the profound Chinese cultural tradition that promotes tolerance and integration, it will undoubtedly be able to make a contribution, by means of a theological wisdom with Chinese characteristics, to the project of building a harmonious society and a harmonious world.

3.3 Sinicization of Christianity as the Bridge for Expanding Friendly Cultural Exchanges between China and the World

As Bertrand Russell once said, a review of history shows that encounters between civilizations often prove to be landmark events in terms of human progress. For instance, the Greeks learned from the Egyptians, the Romans from the Greeks, the Arabs from the Roman Empire, Medieval Europe from the Arabs, and Renaissance Europe from Byzantium. In all cases, the later encounters proved to become even more remarkable than the previous ones.[4] Besides this 'mutual learning' that Russell commented on, in light of the plurality and variety of human civilizations or cultural traditions, we should also insist on borrowing from and inspiring and complementing each other. In a word, we should seek to absorb and benefit from all reasonable elements of other civilizations or cultural traditions.

According to a Chinese expert, the history of Sino-foreign cultural exchange shows that, surprisingly, the three major world religions have played bridging roles in this very process. For instance, Buddhism, which originated in the Indian civilization, was brought to China during its Han dynasty. For nearly two thousand years, it has undergone assimilation and transformation, during which it has not only become an integral part of the ethnic cultures in regions such as Tibet and Mongolia, but has also played a bridging role in the cultural exchanges between China and regions such as South Asia, Southeast Asia and Central Asia. Islam, as the cultural foundation of the Arabic-Persian world, was brought to China during its Tang dynasty. For more than a thousand years, it has gone through assimilation and transformation, and has become not only the cultural component of many ethnic groups such as Hui, Uygur, Kazak, Kirgiz, Tajic, Tatar, Salar, Dongxiang and Bao'an, but also a channel for cultural exchanges between China and the Persian-Arabic world. Christianity, the symbol of Greco-Roman civilization, first came to China during the Tang dynasty, and has since gone through multiple periods of breaking in. In the process, it has also become a part of Chinese national culture, and a bridge for cultural exchange between China and the West.[5]

Based on the current status of the world religions, Christianity, with Catholicism, Protestantism and Eastern Orthodoxy taken as a whole, is arguably the world's largest religion. According to a recent estimate, there are nearly 2.3 billion Christians all over the world, which is about a third of the world's population. These include about 1.2 billion Catholics, about 700 million Protestants, and nearly 300 million Orthodox Christians, all of whom live in as many as 251 countries and regions across the world. In light of this, we could perhaps say that, just as a market economy is essentially neither capitalist nor socialist, Christian faith in its true sense should be perceived as neither Western nor Chinese. The heart of the matter is that, if we can truly bring about the sinicization of Christianity, we will have built one more golden bridge for cultural exchange and dialogue between China and the world.[6]

1   Just as Jacques Gernet points out, the divergence between the civilizations of China and the West is an extremely meaningful subject for research, and the best starting point is perhaps to investigate their earliest contact and respective reactions during the late Ming dynasty. It is because the first dispatch of Jesuit missionaries arrived in China around this time and established a relationship with its most cultured class. This enabled Europe and Asia, the two societies that had developed relatively independent of each other, to come into real contact for the first time in the history. (See J. Gernet, 'Preface to the Chinese Translation', in *China and the Christian Impact* (Shanghai: Shanghai Classics Publishing House, 1991).

2   The Chinese Rites controversy was a dispute amongCatholic missionaries over the religiosity of Confucianism and Chinese rituals during the 17th and 18th centuries. They debated whether the Chinese ritual practices of honoring family ancestors and other formal Confucian and Chinese imperial rites qualified as religious rites, and should thus be considered as incompatible with Catholic belief. The Jesuits argued that these Chinese rites were secular rituals that, within certain limits, were compatible with Christianity, and should thus be tolerated. The Dominicans and Franciscans argued otherwise and reported the issue to Rome.

3   N. Smart, 'Introduction', in *The World's Religions* (Beijing: Beijing University Press, 2004).

4 B. Russell, *The Problem of China* (Shanghai: Xuelin Publishing House, 2009), 147.

5 Geng Sheng, 'A Word from the Translator,' in Jacques Gernet, *China and the Christian Impact* (Shanghai: Shanghai Classics Publishing House, 1991), 5.

6 This is a condensed paper. For a detailed argument by this author, please refer to the article, 'Three-fold Thinking on the Sinicization of Christianity,' *Studies in World Religions* 2 (2012).

8

From Northwest to Southeast: Islam in Contemporary Chinese Society

Yujie Wang

Even by the most conservative calculation, the religion of Islam has existed in China for over a thousand years and has obtained many distinctive Chinese characteristics during its continuous interaction with Chinese native society in the course of history, becoming an important constituent of the Chinese cultural configuration of plurality and unity. During the process of great social change which has taken place in Chinese society since the late twentieth century, Muslims living from northwestern to southeastern China have been confronted with a similar problem to that facing a number of other groups of Chinese people. Meanwhile, similar social changes have had different effects on Muslims in different regions, and also on the future direction of Chinese Islam.

1 History

The precise time that Islam was first introduced into China is still under debate in academic circle. According to historical documents recorded in *Jiu Tang Shu* (*The Old Book of the Tang Dynasty*), Arabian diplomats and merchants came to Chang'an, the capital of Tang China as early as the second year of Emperor Gaozong (651 C.E.) since that time. From then on a large number of Muslims came to China for permanent residence, some of whom became very wealthy and consequently enjoyed high social status. However, these Muslims tended not to do missionary work among Chinese in general, and Islam 'remained a religion exclusively of Muslim emigrants.'[1] The situation did not change until the Mongolian westward expansion in the thirteenth century during which large numbers of Muslims from Central Asia and Persia settled in China, and Muslims were no longer grouped primarily in the capital and treaty ports; *Hui Hui* (Muslims in China) were, in fact, everywhere throughout the country. They were generically known as *semu* (people with colored eyes), enjoying higher political and economic positions, and some even took control of the central and regional governments. By that time Muslims had taken root in China, and had begun to spread Islam throughout the land.

In the *Yuan* dynasty, after the development of *Tang* and *Song* dynasties, *Hui Hui* who were living across the country became the major population of Chinese Muslims replacing the overseas merchants, being an important constituent of Chinese society. Muslims were no longer considered to be 'uncultivated people' while the overwhelming majority of adherents of Islam were Chinese who scattered right across the country; the spread of Islam was now multi-regional and multi-ethnic.

During its introduction, Islam obtained a couple of special features that are unique to China.

First of all, China has a history of a separation of religion from politics. In other words, the country is not run according to any religious laws, and religious authority never exceeds secular power. With such a background provided, although there were conflicts between religious and imperial powers at times, Islam in inland China had quite a limited influence upon politics, and thus failed to develop into a distinct political power.

Islam's introduction into China and its process of development and expansion was characterized by a slow dispersal; it did not have any intense impact on the original Chinese culture, and did not aim to conquer the latter. Islam, therefore, has never become the dominant ideology throughout Chinese history. On the contrary, the tolerant nature of traditional Chinese culture which embraces diverse foreign cultures impelled Muslims to become involved in Chinese political institutions. In the *Yuan* dynasty, Muslim officials prayed to Allah asking that the non-Muslim Mongol emperors' life be prolonged, and the dual-loyalty idea of being 'obedient to God while loyal to the earthly ruler' began to take shape. Muslim communities gradually became engaged in Chinese society instead of forming a distinct group which could exert an impact on politics.

After hundred years of contact with Chinese society, Islam's political principle of caesaropapism had become marginal; there were some politicization activities of Islam in various regions of China, but these were mainly manipulated by a local religious authority or foreign political power. In other words, in Chinese history, Islam did not have any severe or inevitable confrontations with the central government, but it did not unite with any political institutions either.

Second, the restrictions that *sharia*, the Islamic moral code and religious law imposed on Chinese Muslims changed to a certain extent. There are two primary sources of *sharia* law: the precepts set forth in the Quran, and the example set by the Islamic prophet Muhammad in the *Sunnah*, which is considered sacred. Islamic law for the Muslims who came to inland China, had never had an exclusive impact on their life. Since the Tang dynasty, Muslims have been bound not only by *sharia*, but also by Chinese law and regulations when they engage in the Chinese society. In the Yuan dynasty, *Hui Hui* who broke the criminal law were sent to the regional judicial authorities. The power of *Qadis* who had jurisdiction over all legal matters was removed by the central government, and *sharia* was conducted merely in the direction of Muslim's religious life and some aspects of personal life. As a matter of fact, the pattern of the relationship between *sharia* and Chinese law was finally settled. From the Ming dynasty onwards, this pattern of judicial power belonging to the central government has been maintained; the position of *Qadi* was no longer established across the country, and imams only had the right to lead the worship.

Since the Qing government unified Xinjiang in the middle of the eighteenth century, the judicial powers of the border areas have been gradually taken back by central government, and the application range of *sharia* has been reduced. When Xinjiang was established as a province of the Qing dynasty in 1884, not only were imams prohibited from interfering in the judicial process, but the local leaders were not allowed to judge civil or criminal cases in accordance with Quran either. Although there were still religious courts run by religious figures, these were merely allowed to deal with lawsuits about the inheritance of property, marriage and family, *zakat*, and some cases submitted by the local government. Furthermore, during the democratic reform of religions held after the foundation of the People's Republic of China, the limited power of religious figures was taken over by the government, and the influence of Islamic law was completely withdrawn from the public sphere, only supervising people's private life.

Whether in the border areas or inland China, the relationship between *sharia* and Chinese secular law has been established after hundreds of years of adjustment. Besides interpreting the core belief of Islam, *sharia* usually plays a role as local customary law, dealing with daily affairs such as diet, funeral customs, marriage and wedding, etc. Even in these fields, *sharia* has obtained the color of specific ethnic groups. Meanwhile, from the perspective of traditional Chinese law, the matters that could be regulated by *sharia* mainly depend on Confucian ethics and common regulations and the restrictions exerted by *sharia* on Muslim's daily life do not conflict with state laws.

When mentioning 'the plurality and unity in the configuration of the Chinese nationality', the famous Chinese anthropologist Fei Xiaotong said:

> its mainstream came into being through the contact, connection and emergence of many scattered but isolated ethnic units. They at the same time split and died out, and consequently formed a unity with unique characteristics, which is likely to be the formation process of all ethnic groups across the world.[2]

Therefore, the theory of 'the plurality and unity in the configuration of the Chinese nationality' refers not merely to the state of the multi-ethnic groups' co-existence, but to the plurality within any community which is considered to be an ethnic group. Experiencing the long history of China and the influence of regional features, Chinese Islam has been an essential part of the configuration of Chinese culture. Meanwhile, it shows varied characteristics from the Northwest to the Southeast.

Today, Chinese Muslims live all over the country, but are concentrated mainly in the northwestern region. Compared to the economically developed southeastern provinces, Muslim communities in the Northwest have several special features. First, the absolute number of Muslims is large. Currently the total Muslim population in China is around 23 million, and 75% live in five northwestern provinces, namely Shaanxi, Gansu, Ningxia, Qinghai and Xinjiang. Second, there are multiple branches in each sect and *menhuan*.[3] The sects and their branches of Chinese Islam such as Qadim, Ikhwan and Salafiyyah and the four major *menhuans* all originate from and flourish in the Northwest, and each of them has a huge number of adherents. Third, there are many religious places, not only the mosques that can be seen everywhere, but also *tariqs* and *qubbas*. Besides, because people belong to various sects or *menhuans*, there is usually more than one mosque in a small area. Last and most important, Muslims of the Northwest are keen on religious practices in a pious atmosphere.

As a matter of fact, the Southeast is the earliest region of China which embraced Islam. Despite this, however, Islam exerts much less impact here than in the Northwest. It is undeniable that the first *fan fangs* (foreign settlements) were established in the coastal areas of the Southeast. The Islamic architectural remains and inscriptions found in southeastern cities such as Guangzhou, Yangzhou and Quanzhou are the best proof of Islam's introduction and successful development in these areas. Nevertheless, the number of Muslims living in the Southeast is quite small today. Although it is commonly considered that the ten ethnic minority peoples including *Hui* are predominantly Muslim, there are many people in southeastern regions who recognize that they are Hui yet are unclear as to what Islam is and how a Muslim should behave. Mosques may be built in many cities, but although imams lead the services of worship Muslims who attend religious activities are mainly migrant workers from the Northwest. Local *Hui* people seldom enter mosques, and do not have enough religious knowledge or the will to serve as professional religious personnel.

2 Challenges

Like other religions, Islam faces new challenges brought about by the great changes which have occurred in China during the latter half of the twentieth century. However, in the vast land from the Northwest to the Southeast, the same challenge has brought about different changes to different Muslim communities. Some are confronted with real challenges, while others see them as opportunities. It will be analyzed here from three aspects: economic development, urbanization and the increase in external communication.

With the development of the economy, believer's voluntary donations to religious organizations have gradually increased, and thus the latter's economic power continues to grow. Northwestern Muslims built and extended a large number of mosques, with the expense of several millions, or even tens of millions, and the condition of religious places has been greatly enhanced. Nevertheless, the income increase led to frequent conflict caused by economic interests within *menhuans*; in some areas this even resulted in new branches splitting off. Besides, with economic interests challenging the pattern of traditional religious education, and fewer and fewer *manlas* tending to finish mosque education, some eminent imams also start to conduct businesses. The traditional talent-training method has been severely challenged. In some *menhuans*, the succession of leaders has met many problems, or even conflicts.

In the Southeast, the results of economic development contradict those of the Northwest. Religion and economic development have interacted soundly. The local governments in some regions introduced a series of preferential policies which indirectly prompted the development of religion; people who were not conscious of their ethnic identity began to re-consider themselves as *Hui*, and return to their predecessors' religious beliefs. Meanwhile, in some cities where there were only a few Muslims, new Muslim communities arose as a result of the development of international business. In a few words, 'marketization reform is a process of radical secularization on one hand; it provides possibilities for religious extension on the other.'[4]

Similarly, the process of urbanization also brings new challenge to Chinese Islam, in both in the Northwest or Southeast, Muslims have the tradition of living in the neighborhood of a mosque, forming small concentric communities around them. These are called *Jiaofangs* (*Jama'at*) by Chinese Muslims. A mosque serves not only as a religious place, but a center for Muslim cultural life and social communication. With the acceleration of urbanization and urban reform, the traditional residence pattern has come up against great challenges especially in the big cities. Muslims live alongside non-Muslims, and previously introverted Muslim communities open up to the public. The traditional mosque-and-imam-centered method of maintaining religious identity has weakened. This is certainly a result of the acceleration of urbanization, and northwestern Muslims continuously coming to middle and southeastern cities where there were few Muslims or only withered Muslim communities. The trend gradually attracts new converts and impels Muslims to return to their innate religious beliefs, which to some degree expands the influence of Islam.

Meanwhile, more Muslims are increasingly leaving the Northwest and moving across the whole country; in recent years some are even going abroad. Among these a large portion are leaving to conduct businesses while others attend religious schools. Therefore, Chinese Muslims have been influenced by various ideas from the Islamic world. For instance, the *wahhabi* ideas that originated in Saudi Arabia were introduced into China in the late nineteenth and early twentieth century, which gave birth to some new sects such as the *Ikhwani* school. In recent years, with the increase of foreign exchange, the *wahhabi* ideas have become even stronger. One group of Muslims, for example, strongly criticize some of traditional religious customs which have Chinese features, such as the *Qadim* (old sect)'s commemoration of the dead, the *menhuan*'s visiting of tombs (*Ziyarah al-Qubaa*) and the *Amal* activities. They consider these activities violations of *sharia*, and call upon Muslims to obey the Quran and stop these practices. Under its influence, a number of *menhuan* and *Qadim* adherents converted to the teachings of *Ikhwan* or other sects, which has led to a decrease in the numbers of *menhuan* and *Qadim* followers, which causes conflicts among them.

Unlike the situation in the Northwest, the increase of foreign contact has diluted sectarian differences among southeastern Muslim communities. Chinese and oversea Muslims worship together, and the tension and conflicts among Muslims of varied sects seldom occur. 'People with different group features bring about influences in different regions,' and consequently change the culture of the Muslim community, which is quite unlike the relatively stable northwestern communities where sectarian differences were easily generated.

In the face of social changes of multiple kinds, there are two elements that are likely to have great influence upon the future of Chinese Islam.

The first is the relationship between religious belief and national identity. As mentioned above, the overwhelming majority of Chinese Muslims are from the ten ethnic minorities, and Islam once played an essential role in the formation of those people. It is difficult to draw a clear distinction between their national attribute and religious belief, which is largely different from the situation of other religions in China such as Buddhism, Daoism and Christianity. Thus, there has been a lot debate among Chinese Muslims on whether 'to open or not to open'; these arguments are usually based on the following topics: Is Islam a religion revealed to certain specific peoples? Will Islam be introduced to other people? Can members of non-Muslim people convert to Islam? Although the debate has been held for several ages, the consensus has not yet formed on the relationship between people and religion. Today, the Chinese are free to choose their own beliefs from the various religions and sects, and the gates of temples and churches are wide open in order to attract new adherents. Undoubtedly, the choice of whether 'to open or not to open' is of primary importance for the future development of Chinese Islam.

The second element is the increasing mobility of Chinese Muslims. It is estimated that the floating population of Chinese Muslims is around 3 million. A large number of Muslims have moved from the Northwest to the middle, eastern and southeastern areas where there had been only a small number of Muslims. With increasing mobility, the social formation of both Muslim and non-Muslim regions is changing. The Muslims who migrate to non-Muslim areas find themselves unable to adjust into the local religious environment. They consider local Muslims impious, and can hardly find religious places in the neighborhood or around their workplace, not to mention satisfactory religious personnel. Moreover, according to the principle of local administration, migrant Muslims prefer not to engage in the management of local mosques. In this case, some Muslims start to organize religious activities outside mosques on their own, which breaks the traditional pattern of religious activities that are held in mosques and centered on imams. This change is not merely the future direction of development of the Chinese Muslims, but represents a real challenge for the management of religious affairs in present-day China as a whole.

3 Conclusion

From the Northwest to the Southeast, Chinese Islam has presented a wide range of colorful diversity. These differences are not going to disappear but are likely to increase as social change continues to take place in China today. However, Chinese Islam is, and will remain, an important constituent in the configuration of the Chinese culture of plurality and unity, and its adherents will be confronted with the same huge challenges that all the citizens living in China face during this period of rapid development.[5]

1 Z. Xiefan and S. Qiuzhen, *Islam in China*, (Beijing: Huawen Press, 2002), 53.

2 F. Xiaotong, 'Plurality and Unity in the Configuration of the Chinese Nationality,' in: *Collections of Fei Xiaotong(1987-1989)*, vol.11 (Beijing: Qunyan Press, 1999).

3 *Menhuan* is a term for a Chinese-style Sufi order. Briefly, *menhuan* is a religious organization which arrived when the various branches of Sufi orders were introduced from foreign lands into Gansu, Ningxia and Qinghai. It has some special characteristics of traditional Chinese society.

4 W. Hui, 'Orientalism, Regional Ethnic Autonomy and Dignified Politics: Some Thoughts on the Tibetan Issue', *Tianya*, vol. 4, 2008.

5 This article was translated from the Chinese by Li Xiaotong, Ph.D. Candidate, Graduate School of Chinese Academy of Social Sciences.

9

Contemporary Buddhism in China:
The Little Courtyard in
Shanxi Province

Caifang Zhu

112

The Buddhist practice which is examined in this article originated in a little courtyard in Datong, a city in Shanxi province of Northern China. The core of the religious practice under scrutiny is highlighted by a seven-day Ksitigarbha retreat, which involves six types of rigorous and devotional activities. The phenomenon was described in a documentary entitled *A Little Courtyard in Shanxi* and been the focus of a considerable amount of attention across China since its inception in 2002. It has also caused a degree of controversy because of its highly ritualized and overtly devotional practice which has converted large numbers of people and entire extended families.

This paper attempts to interpret the phenomenon within a context of humanistic Buddhism and the international revival of religion. Examining how 'the Little Courtyard phenomenon' is related or unrelated to humanistic Buddhism and religious fundamentalism, the paper concludes that the phenomenon of the Little Courtyard in Shanxi seems to be relevant to both humanistic Buddhism and religious fundamentalism. The paper closes by proposing that the practice should be viewed as a health and healing oriented type of Buddhism.

The chief method of study has been to view the documentary, analyze the data and discuss the phenomenon in the context of Chinese Buddhism and religious fundamentalism across the world.

1   The Phenomenon of the Little Courtyard in Shanxi

A little courtyard in Datong, Shanxi province of Northern China has become well known in contemporary Buddhist practice since the turn of the millennium. Over the past decade or so, people from different parts of China have gone there to practice a highly devotional type of Buddhism. The practice is epitomized by a seven-day retreat known as the Ksitigarbha Retreat during which participants learn worshipping practices in order to invoke assistance from Ksitigarbha Bodhisattva, one of the four best known Bodhisattvas in Chinese Buddhism. One of the most frequently quoted sayings of Ksitigarbha Bodhisattva is: 'I vow not to attain Buddhahood until the hells are emptied'. Ksitigarbha Bodhisattva is, therefore, called the Bodhisattva of Great Vows. In the case of the Little Courtyard in Shanxi, the practitioners, most of whom are suffering from severe illnesses, invoke the name of Ksitigarbha Bodhisattva or chant the *Ksitigarbha Sutra*,[1] asking the Bodhisattva to help deliver the spirit or ghost that is believed to be haunting them.

In the beginning, people only went to the Little Courtyard in Shanxi sporadically, and most of these were from the vicinity of the city of Datong. Many of them probably heard about it by word of mouth. But, gradually, as the place and practice became better known, it became more organized, and finally it became as regimented and ritualized as it is today.

During the seven-day Ksitigarbha retreat, 6 main activities are offered, which are performed collectively by all the attendees. These six activities are:

1. having a vegetarian diet
2. chanting the *Sutra of Bodhisattva Ksitigarbha's Vow* or the *Ksitigarbha Sutra*
3. worshiping and repenting
4. buying and freeing animals in captivity
5. performing good deeds
6. invoking Amitabha to be reborn in the Pure Land

The *A Little Courtyard in Shanxi*[2] documentary has six parts. Each lasts about an hour, and consists of several testimonials given by practitioners of this type of Buddhism. Presumably, these people have also trained in the seven-day Ksitigarbha retreat, and have no doubt practiced at the Little Courtyard. In Figure 1 below there is a chart of some of the key information from the first five of the six parts of the documentary which is now available on the internet for free downloading.

Serial No.	No. of Testimonials	Male/Female	Age ratio	Average Range	Testimonial length Age
1	6	2:5	28-65	46	3-7 minutes
2	9	1:8	7-68	46.7	1-8 min
3	7	1:6	36-63	47.3	2-9.5 min
4	6	2:4	24-60	47	4-10 min
5	7	0:7	50-83	61.7	2-12 min
Total	36	6:30	7-83	49.7	1-12 min

Figure 1.

Although the age range seems vast, most of the people attending the retreat can be clustered in their thirties (six), forties (five), fifties (ten) and sixties (ten). The youngest one was only 7 years old and the oldest 83. There were two people in their twenties. Among the total of 36 testimonials, 9 were below 40 years of age, so only 25%. That is to say, 75% of them were above 40 years of age, and 58% were above 50. With regard to gender, the ratio of male to female was 6 to 30.

The length of testimonials for serial number 4 and 5 is based on incomplete information. The recorded time range thereof comes from only two speakers from each of the two serials. It should be noted that following one or two testimonials in a given serial there is a brief didactic episode, or Buddhist sermon known as 'dharma talk', given by the venerable Jing Kong (b. 1927). A widely revered but also highly controversial Buddhist teacher in the Chinese Buddhist community in China and around the world, Jing Kong is devoted to promoting the Pure Land School of Buddhism, which emphasizes reliance on the power of Amitabha and Avalokiteshvara Bodhisattva. His dharma talks, inserted by the documentary director, do not always seem to be closely related to the testimonial that preceded them.

According to venerable Jing Kong's dharma talk in the second of the six-part series, there are three kinds of illnesses that people suffer from: the first is physical illness that can be cured by seeing a medical doctor, the second is caused by the deceased people whom the patient has hurt such as family members, relatives and others to whom the patient is indebted. According to Jing Kong, there is no medication to cure an illness such as this other than by delivering the spirits or ghosts of the deceased people which have been 'bothering' the patient. The third kind of illness is called karmic illness (*yezhang bing*). In this type of illness it is the bad karma, resulting from the unwholesome deeds that one has performed, that causes the illness. The cure, therefore, consists in genuine repentance. Virtually all the testimonials in the documentary are narrations by individuals recounting how they had their illness cured by following the second and/or the third method, that is, by chanting sutras such as the *Ksitigarbha Sutra* and invoking Amitabha to deliver the haunting spirit or ghost, and repenting.

Let us now take a close look at the second of the six-part series of the documentary (a random choice) and examine this healing and cure. All the testimonials, except for the last one (a seven year old girl) are from lay Buddhists.

2 Humanistic Buddhism

The basic Buddhist tenets include the three dharma seals (impermanence, no-self and nirvana), the fourfold noble truth (suffering, the cause of suffering, the cessation of suffering and the way to end suffering), the eightfold path[3] and

No.	Gender	Age	Illness type	Way of healing and cure
1	Female	52	Breast cancer	Cured by chanting *Ksitigarbha Sutra* and invoking Avalokitesvara and Amitabha
2	Male	32	Headache at 3pm everyday	Cured by chanting *Ksitigarbha Sutra*
3	Female	68	Hydrocephaly	Cured by chanting *Ksitigarbha Sutra* and *The Sutra of Immeasurable Life*[5]
4	Female	50	Heart problem	Cured by chanting *Ksitigarbha Sutra*
5	Female	65	Gastrointestinal disease	Cured by chanting *Ksitigarbha Sutra* and *The Sutra of Immeasurable Life*
6	Female	65	Hyperosteogeny	Relieved by chanting *The Sutra of Immeasurable Life*
7	Female	32	Anxiety	Relieved by reciting *Ksitigarbha Sutra*
8	Female	49	Gall stones; breast cancer hysteromyoma;	Cured by chanting *Ksitigarbha Sutra*
9	Female	7	Glue 101 mistakenly used instead of eye drops	Recovered by mother's prayers to Bodhisattva

Figure 2.

the twelve-linked chain of causality[4]. These teachings are primarily what Buddhists in South and Southeast Asian countries follow (the so-called Hinayana or Theravada traditions), although they constitute an important component in the teachings of Mahayana Buddhism as well. What highlights Mahayana Buddhism is such teachings as the six *paramitas* (six perfections)[6] and the Bodhisattva's path of compassion and service.

Despite the fact that Chinese Buddhism was clearly in the Mahayana tradition in general, from the Ming dynasty (1368-1644) onward, Buddhism in China started to become preoccupied with life after death, and the service to the dead and the dying. In the early 1900s, the venerable Taixu (1889-1947) became very vocal in advocating what he called humanistic Buddhism (*rensheng fojiao*) that aimed to engage life, the society and the world in Buddhism, and to shift the emphasis from overwhelmingly serving the dead and dying to paying more attention to the development of the wholesome human character and personality.[7] Taixu defined humanistic Buddhism as follows:

Although Buddhism is for all sentient beings, it should center around human beings and develop in conformity with modern culture. Although Buddhism does not distinguish life from death, existence from extinction, it should center around 'human existence and development' in order to adapt to the modern life of reality. This is the first dimension of humanistic Buddhism.

Although Buddhism includes Hinayana, which results in individual liberation or selflessness, modern community life calls for a Buddhism of great compassion and wisdom that can serve the masses. This is what Taixu called the second dimension of humanistic Buddhism:

> Mahayana Buddhism seeks the complete perfection of enabling all sentient beings to attain Buddhahood. There is both a gradual approach and a sudden realization approach to achieving complete perfection. In our modern scientific age that values empirical studies, order and procedure, and evidence, we should center around the gradual approach to Mahayana Buddhism. This is the third dimension of humanistic Buddhism.[8]

So, humanistic Buddhism by and large suspends 'the realm of ghosts'. It cleanses the superstitions related to the teachings of the realm of hungry ghosts and to some extent the realm of heaven (it is incompatible with Heaven in Christianity). It realizes the potentials of life and moves toward higher forms of life. Based on the modern concept of life, the masses and science, humanistic Buddhism will be developed into a Mahayana Buddhism that looks to unsurpassed complete awakening, which can be realized through both the gradual and sudden approaches.[9]

As mentioned earlier, Buddhism in China has long been mistaken to a large extent for the 'Buddhism of death' and the 'Buddhism of ghosts'. It has long been taken for granted that practicing Buddhism serves the purpose of enabling the individual to have a good death while dying, and have a good life after death. But this is not the truth of Buddhism. It is just a result of its problematic evolution through transmissions, Taixu argued. What Taixu called 'humanistic Buddhism' is a reaction to the two deeply-rooted tendencies mentioned above, and leans toward improving life and connecting directly to perfection and luminosity in the dharma realm. In other words, humanistic Buddhism, as proposed today, emphasizes the improvement of human life. Those who stand out while practicing humanistic Buddhism can proceed to attain *bodhi* (liberation), and the fruition of the path of Mahayana Buddhism.[10] The movement of humanistic Buddhism, following Taixu, has been carried on in China and Taiwan up to the present day. Among its leaders are Yinshun (1906-2005),

Shengyan (1930-2009), Jinghui (1933-2013), Xingyun (b. 1927) and Zhengyan (b. 1937).

3 Global Revival of Religion and Alert of Fundamentalism

Since the 9/11 tragedy in the USA in 2001, the public interest in the study of religion has increased globally. The fall of 2001 was the first semester of my three years at Harvard Divinity School. I remember that at the *Religion in Global Politics* class offered by Samuel Huntington, David Little and Jessica Stern in fall 2003—open to all Harvard students—the first meeting was so crammed that it had to be moved to a larger venue. At her regular Morning Prayer address to begin the academic year in September 2012, Harvard President Drew Faust said, 'Four decades ago, widespread scholarly and popular opinion anticipated the waning or even the disappearance of religion as modernity advanced across the globe. And yet, just the opposite has occurred'.[11] China too has witnessed a steady revival of interest in religion over the past three decades, and the Little Courtyard in Shanxi is just one such example.

From a social-psychological perspective of religion, research by McIntosh, Newton and Poulin shows that religion functions with two components (social and psychological) and three variables (social support, the search for meaning and cognitive processing or appraisal). Their survey of Christian adults found that 'those who believed in a combination of control by the self and a deity reported fewer physical symptoms. Interestingly, there was no association between illness and the belief in internal control or God control alone.'[12] The research by Tsang on the 'benefits of forgiveness' presented three types of benefits: (1) Psychological: decreases in depression; (2) Physiological: lowered blood pressure and heart rate; decrease in stress response as manifested in EMG and skin conductance; (3) Interpersonal: enhancing marital satisfaction as well as positive benefits in other relationships.[13] McCullough and Worthington found a discrepancy between religion and forgiveness: religious people give more value to forgiveness than they actually forgive specific transgressions. Religious people do not differ in forgiveness levels from non-religious people when specific events are measured.[14]

The aforementioned resurrection of religion has been accompanied in some way by the fear of the rise of fundamentalism, notably in Islamic fundamentalism. According to the *Oxford Dictionary*, fundamentalism is 'a form of a religion, especially Islam or Protestant Christianity, that upholds belief in the strict, literal interpretation of scripture'.[15] It is 'the demand for a strict adherence to specific theological doctrines usually understood as a reaction against modernist theology, primarily to promote continuity and accuracy.'[16] Christian fundamentalism in USA has over time been distilled to 'five fundamentals':

The inspiration of the Bible and the inerrancy of scripture as a result of this.
The virgin birth of Christ.
The belief that Christ's death was the atonement for sin.
The bodily resurrection of Christ
The historical reality of Christ miracles[17]
How, then, can the rise of fundamentalism possibly be related to Buddhism, especially the Little Courtyard phenomenon?

4   The Status of the Little Courtyard in an International Context

Despite the fact that the term 'fundamentalism' has been widely accepted in academic, political, religious and media circles and that it has been applied to Protestant Christianity, Islam, Judaism and even Hinduism, there is hardly any discussion of Buddhist fundamentalism. The reason for this is perhaps, that there has not been a strong enough modernist movement within Buddhism to provoke a reaction to it. Why didn't modernism or modernist philosophy constitute a major challenge to Buddhism?

The reason is that the core teachings of Buddhism such as the three dharma seals, the fourfold noble truth, the eightfold path, and their inter-dependent origination, among others, don't seem to be at odds with science and modernist views. In fact, they appear so Eastern that they might even constitute a post-modernist philosophy or world view. Carl Jung is right to say, 'There is no conflict between religion and science in the East, because no science is there based on the passion for facts, no religion upon mere faith; there is religious cognition and cognitive religion'.[18]

Another reason is that in Buddhism, canonization of the sort that occurred in Christianity, Judaism and Islam, has never happened. Consequently, the Pali Canon, the Chinese Canon and the Tibetan Canon have all been circulating without any efforts being made to crystallize the thousands of texts into one book, the size of the Bible or the Koran. Among the numerous texts that have accumulated, from the sermons by Shakyamuni Buddha to the teachings of medieval Chinese, Tibetan and Japanese masters, one can always find teachings with which to respond to various problems and challenges.

The humanistic Buddhism that Taixu spearheaded in the first half of the twentieth century was indeed a welcome response to the modern spirit of the times, characterized by the scientific world view. Though Taixu did not use the label of fundamentalism for the conservative belief and practices of Chinese Buddhism in his time, we can extrapolate that that is just what he meant, especially when he called for a 'change in interpreting Buddhist doctrines'[19]. Unfortunately, Taixu's revolutionary proposal and his efforts have not met with much success in mainland China, although the theory of humanistic Buddhism has been generally accepted.

The interviewees in the testimonials contained in the *Little Courtyard in Shanxi* appear to adopt a strict and literal interpretation of the meanings of the texts when they chant or recite *the Kṣitigarbha Sutra, the Sutra of Immeasurable Life* and so forth. In this sense, the documentary seems to be in line with the equivalent of Buddhist fundamentalism. On the other hand, the *Little Courtyard* appears to be embodying some values of humanistic Buddhism, in that it emphasizes the living rather than the dying, death or life-after-death.

'Curing illnesses, saving people and eradicating the misfortunate' is the overarching slogan that always accompanies the *Little Courtyard*. This is not only humanistic, but also in line with the research results of social and psychological perspectives of religion which were presented earlier (psycho-physiological healing, search for the meaning of life, and the social support provided by the community). This is, in some way, also a result of the Chinese administration's policy on religions over the past thirty years. The central communist administration has, for the last thirty years, allowed considerable freedom for individuals to practice religions in officially registered sites. Still, the administration keeps 'guiding' the direction of religious belief and practice. Contributions from religion to social harmony, patriotism, the reconstruction of morality and individual healing (physical and psycho-spiritual) are among the major expectations of the Chinese government. Overall, in view of the complexity of the nature of the Little Courtyard, we may look at the phenomenon of the Little Courtyard in Shanxi as a religious practice, a health-oriented new type of Buddhist practice.

5   Conclusion

This paper described the phenomena of the *Little Courtyard in Shanxi*, a six-part documentary based on selected testimonials of a health and healing-oriented type of Buddhist practice. All the individuals making the testimonials give their personal experience of how they have had their chronic, acute or terminal diseases magically cured or relieved by following the instructions of the course taught in the Little Courtyard in Shanxi. No cases of failure have been included in the documentary which could have offered a wider picture of the practice. Viewed within the international context of religion, especially the revival of religion after the 9/11 tragedy, the Little Courtyard phenomenon appears to have combined elements of humanistic Buddhism and fundamentalism with a focus on healing efficacy. It is a health-oriented new practice of Buddhism. The phenomenon also reflects some aspects of the current Chinese policy of religion: considerable freedom to practice, with some expectations from the state with regard to contributing to social harmony, patriotism, the reconstruction of morality and individual healing.

1 *Ksitigarbha Sutra*, www.cbeta.org/result/normal/T13/0412_001.htm, accessed April 29, 2013.

2 *A Little Courtyard in Shanxi* is a documentary in Chinese, www.rushiwowen.org/vod/10680001.jsp

3 The *Sutra of Immeasurable Life* (*wuliang shou jing*) is one of the three major sutras for Pure Land Buddhism in China and the rest of East Asia. It contains the 48 vows of a monk named Fazang, who had been a king and who would become Amitabha later. Fazang vowed to take aspirants to the Pure Land at the end of their life if they chant the sutra, or he would not seek to attain liberation and enlightenment. www.cbeta.org/result/normal/T12/0360_001.htm through www.cbeta.org/result/normal/T12/0360_002.htm, accessed April 29, 2013.

4 Right view, right thought, right speech, right action, right livelihood, right effort, right concentration and right wisdom.

5 Ignorance (*avidya*), action (*samskara*),consciousness (*vijnana*), name and form (*nama-rupa*), six sense organs (*shad-ayatana*), contact (*sparsha*), sensation (*vedana*), desire (*trishna*), attachment (*upadana*); existence (*bhava*); birth (*jati*); aging and death (*jara-marana*).

6 Giving alms, tolerance, precepts, right effort, meditation and wisdom.

7 B. Chen, L. Yin, T-B. Luo and Y-H. Wang, eds., *Humanistic Buddhism* (Shijiazhuang: Hebei Buddhist Association, 2001).

8 Taixu (1928), *Illustrations on Humanistic Buddhism*. Retrieved on April 27, 2013 from http://www.hhfg.org/rjfj/f4.html

9 Taixu, ed., *The Journal of Hai Chao Yin* 9/6 (1929).

10 Taixu, ed., *The Journal of Hai Chao Yin* 26/1 (1945).

11 *Harvard Gazette*, September 4, 2012.

12 D. McIntosh, T. Newton and M.J. Poulin, 'Religion and Spirituality in Midst of Stress and Trauma,' in *2012 China-US Psychology of Religion Conference Proceedings* (Beijing: Renmin, 2012), 15.

13 J-A. Tsang, 'Benefits of Forgiveness,' in *2012 China-US*.

14 M. E. McCullough and E.L. Worthington, Jr., 'Models of interpersonal forgiveness and their applications to counseling: Review and critique,' *Counseling and Values* 39 (1994), 2-14.

15 http://oxforddictionaries.com/definition/english/fundamentalism

16 http://en.wikipedia.org/wiki/Fundamentalism, accessed April 29, 2013.

17 http://en.wikipedia.org/wiki/Fundamentalism, accessed April 29, 2013.

18 C.G. Jung, *Psychology and Religion: West and East* (New Haven, CT: Princeton University Press, 1969), par. 768.

19 Chen et al., *Humanistic Buddhism*, 131.

10

Popular Religion in Modern and Contemporary China

Yongsi Liu

1 Introduction

During the Late Qing Dynasty and the Republican Period, the Chinese state endeavored to construct a new style of government. In the modernization scheme of the whole state, the reform of religions was one of the important and indispensable components. The state sacrifice was abolished: the Confucian, Buddhist and Daoist temples, which used to be supported by the empire during Late Imperial China, were consciously reconstructed into schools or buildings for other public organizations (e.g., local police stations). This attempt to confiscate temples had already begun during The Hundred Days of Reform in China (also known as the Wuxu Reform) in 1898, although it had limited immediate effect.[1] The separation of the temples from the state, as a principle, was gradually established, and strengthened in the following twentieth century. Religion became a component which was separate from politics, while the state controlled the authority to decide which 'faith' could be classified under the category of 'religion'. The state even granted some privileges to certain religious organizations, allowing them to organize and manage their own priests, adherents, temples (churches) educational institutes, and so on.

For China, the twentieth century has been a remarkable period of great change and transformation, going through a long process of simultaneous economic, cultural and social revolution. The transitions became even faster after 1978, with the implementation of the 'Reform and Opening up' Policy.[2] As a result, Chinese society has experienced unprecedented growth thereafter. The transformation from a Soviet-style planned economy, where production decisions were made by the state, to a market-oriented system, has led to a further increase in social development. During this long process, many aspects of Chinese religions[3] have been transformed. For example, the Buddhist and Daoist monasteries, like most Chinese state-owned enterprises, can no longer depend on financial support from the government, but have to be financially responsible for their own profits and losses.[4] And, more notably, Chinese popular religion has experienced a remarkable resurgence in the recent three decades following the 'Reform and Opening up', with the Fujian Province often taking the lead. The revival and prosperity of Popular Religion in Southeast China is closely related to the investment made by Chinese people living overseas who brought back the faiths in local deities to their native places, like the famous goddess Mazu, when investing in their hometowns.

In fact, both the discourse of Chinese religions and their situation has changed a great deal. Therefore, in the following sections, this paper first looks at the various discourses concerning the classification of Chinese religions, and discusses their internal structure. It continues with a further outline of the typology of Chinese popular religion, according to different styles in the dimension of social organization. Finally, it explores and summarizes the revival mechanism of popular religion in contemporary China.

2   The Discourses on Chinese Popular Religion

The terminology of 'religion' was imported into China from post-Renaissance Europe via Japan, no earlier than the end of the nineteenth-century. In the Western definition of what a religion is, canonical texts, transcendent pursuits, institutional organizations, and professional clergies play an indispensable role. The normative prototype of 'religion' is Christianity, which represents a kind of Eurocentric value.[5] Such criteria cannot be applied directly to describe the landscape of Chinese religion. Though C. K. Yang has tried to use the paradigms of institutional religion and diffused religion[6] to smooth over the difficulties encountered when applying the Western definition of 'religion' to the Chinese case, such refinement is still unsatisfactory.

Similarly, 'popular religion' is also a foreign term of Western origin, juxtaposing popular and official religion. However, in traditional Chinese society, none of the members of the imperial court, officials, literati, local elites or religious leaders used this term to describe the thoughts, rituals and symbolic systems of ordinary Chinese people. In late imperial China, Confucianism, Buddhism and Daoism, the 'Three Teachings' (sanjiao),[7]—which means, three kinds of positive teachings given by the sages—were legal institutional components of the Chinese religious system. Sacrifice was of such great significance that the imperial court classified it into two categories: 'proper sacrifice' (zhengsi) which was legal, and 'improper[8] sacrifice' (yinsi) which was illegal.

There was another term, 'heterodoxy' (xiejiao), during late imperial China, which may be used to describe beliefs that differ from strictly orthodox views in the Roman Catholic and Eastern Orthodox churches. In China, this term first appeared in some Chinese translations of Buddhist scriptures,[9] and was frequently used thereafter by Buddhists and Daoists alike in the debates against each other, both attacking the opposing side as 'heterodoxy'. Hence, the usage of the term 'heterodoxy' was not merely official. In official usage, it usually referred to the sects or cults that could potentially threaten imperial political authority and the social order.

In fact, the Song government had created some strict bans against sectarian groups whose members gathered at night and dispersed at dawn (*yeju xiaosan*). During the reign of Emperor Gao Zong (1131-1162), a new kind of heterodoxy was emphasized: 'eating vegetables and serving the devils' (*chicai shimo*), which was aimed against Manicheism in particular. These criteria were passed down and followed by governments in later generations.

After the Yuan Dynasty, the 'White Lotus Teachings' (*bailian jiao*)[10] gradually became an official synonym for 'heterodoxy'[11] and, in late imperial China, the official criteria to judge whether a religious teaching was 'White Lotus' or not included: (1) gathering at night and dispersing at dawn; (2) men and women intermingling indiscriminately (*nannu hunza*); (3) eating vegetables and serving the devils. However, most of the religious organizations labeled as 'White Lotus' by the officials were barely related to the real White Lotus teachings which prospered during the Yuan Dynasty.

The structure of traditional Chinese religions during the imperial period generally consisted of three components (see Figure 1). The Three Teachings, which were advocated by the state, represented one extreme, while heterodox cults, usually attacked and banned by the state, represented the other. Between

Figure 1. The Structure of Traditional Chinese Religions.

these two extremes, there were hundreds of thousands of popular (or 'folk') religious faiths and practices in China, which were closely connected to the daily lives of the overwhelming majority of Chinese people,[12] even though they were neither promoted nor banned by the imperial state. Most of these folk religious faiths and practices were financially self-dependent, and labeled as 'improper sacrifice,' while some of them were incorporated into the official list of 'proper sacrifice.' How they managed to upgrade from 'improper' to 'proper' is complicated. Sometimes the imperial court wanted to gain support from the inhabitants of remote areas, by means of 'governing through cults and civilizing the realm through the gods' (*shendao shejiao*).

Some deities in Chinese popular religion were so important in certain districts that their miracle stories, in which the deities either helped local inhabitants to survive droughts or plagues, or aided the imperial army to quash rebellions, were reported to the imperial court by magistrates. After going through strict censorship by the Ministry of Rites, some of them were granted honorary titles by the emperor,[13] or were endowed with horizontally inscribed boards by local magistrates or the emperor, which would be hung in the main hall of the temple devoted to the deity involved.

These stories date from before 1898. Since the twentieth century, it has become more difficult, or even barely possible, for ordinary Chinese people to gain official acceptance and recognition of their religious faiths and practices in such a way. The state has made efforts to move forward towards constructing a 'modern' state, which is totally different from a 'feudal' one. In the process of China's modernization, a new discourse of 'feudal superstition' (*fengjian mixin*), as opposed to 'science', has been applied to indicate Chinese popular religion. Therefore, in order to make Chinese religions compatible with the state's progress towards modernization, the main task of religious policy in modern China has been to redefine the boundaries between those that could be accepted and labeled orthodox 'religion', and those that should be rejected and labeled heterodox 'superstition.'[14]

The paradigm of 'religion and superstition' contributed a great deal to the Chinese modernization scheme. Those faiths, whether native or foreign, which could help shape China's modern character, and make Chinese people more adaptable to the modern state, were recognized as 'religion', and were allowed to remain and develop, whereas those faiths which failed to cultivate the scientific and democratic nature of Chinese people, or even made them go against the state's goal of modernization, were categorized as 'superstition', and were subjected to attack and abolition. Across the twentieth century, this paradigm promoted the modernization of Chinese traditional religions and the contextualization of foreign religions introduced into China.

The term 'popular religion', as used in this paper, not only refers to those sectarian cults that are disapproved of by the state, but also to popular religious faiths and practices that are involved with the daily life of ordinary Chinese people. In other words, by 'popular religion', I refer to part of the 'proper sacrifices', and all of the 'improper sacrifices' and 'heterodoxical faiths' (from the perspective of the traditional Chinese religions); that is, 'feudal superstition' from the modern perspective on Chinese religions. However, please note that the Chinese themselves have never used the terminologies of 'popular religion' or 'superstition' to describe their own faiths.

3   Typology of Contemporary Chinese Popular Religion

The situation of popular religion in China is quite complicated. Both Chinese Buddhism and Daoism have always been closely related to it. Even some 'foreign' religions drew inspiration from the experience of Chinese popular religion. For example, the al-Tariqah (*menhuan*) system, which is a unique organizational system of Chinese Muslims, has drawn some elements from Chinese popular religion into their own organization, and their practices of religious cultivation. And the organization of Christianity in rural China has become more and more similar to that of popular religion.

Popular religion in contemporary China can be classified into three categories: sectarian groups, liturgical tradition groups, and communal religious groups, according to their different styles of social organization.

3.1   *Sectarian Groups*

The patriarch of this type of popular religion is worshipped as a god. And most of these groups are organized through an intense hierarchical system, in which the clergy is entitled to control its adherents, with one headquarters (*zongtang*) and several sub-branches (*fentang*). This type of popular religion was often associated with the 'heterodoxy' label, and some of them were subjected to official suppression in the political movement to stamp out 'reactionary sects and secret societies' (*fandong huidaomen*) after 1949. However, their potential threat to social harmony has diminished a great deal. One of the important reasons for this is that the sub-branches and their headquarters are independent from each other in both financial and personnel arrangements; the latter only keeps its leadership in name. Hence, the scope of influence of this type of popular religion has become small. Some of them even have gained recognition as legal religious groups in Hong Kong, Taiwan and some districts in Southeast Asia.

Examples of this type are the 'Three in One Teaching'(*sanyi jiao*), which was developed in the Ming Dynasty; 'Pervasive Truth' (*yiguan dao*) and the 'Teachings of Abiding Principle' (*zaili jiao*), which were developed during the Republican Period. The 'Three in One Teaching' is a particularly successful sectarian tradition, which attempts to assimilate selected teachings of Buddhism and Daoism into an idiosyncratic version of Confucianism. The founder of this tradition, Lin Zhao'en, is worshipped as a god. Today, there remain five active subbranches confined to the Xinghua region near Putian, Fujian Province,[15] where a special administrative institution, the 'Association of Three in One' (sanyijiao xiehui), was established to regulate and supervise the affairs of the temples affiliated with the Three in One.

3.2 Liturgical Tradition Groups

Popular religions of this type have their own nominal patriarchs, but no actual leaders. Their clergy is organized tightly through master-disciple relationships, territorial or lineage connections, and has no control over its followers. Usually, when the followers need a certain ritual service, they will pay and employ the clergy, or rather, ritual specialists, to perform the ritual for them at the home of a follower, or at their lineage hall, or at temples devoted to local deities. Although such groups used to be suppressed as 'feudal superstition', in recent years they are being conserved as 'Intangible Cultural Heritage,' because the music and dance involved in their ritual performances is considered to be a dying traditional art.

Examples of this type are the Lvshan liturgical tradition, which prevails in Southeast China, the Meishan liturgical tradition and the Acharya liturgical tradition, which are popular in Southwest China, and the Pu'an liturgical tradition of the Hakka districts. Most of the clergy in these liturgical traditions get married, and live as peasants who work on their farm land when they aren't offering ritual services. Their skills to perform the rituals, and the instruments and scriptures used during the ritual, are usually inherited from their parents and passed on to their lineal descendants.

3.3 Communal Religious Groups

This type of popular religion has the greatest influence throughout China. Most of these groups do not have a patriarch, or a hierarchical system among clergy and followers. They are organized around the worship of a shared deity and often gather in territorial temple festivals. As local economies have prospered in recent years, large lineages and local entrepreneurs have been involved in the organization of communal religious groups, mostly by fundraising for local temple festivals. But groups such as these have little influential impact on China's nationwide religious situation, as they are focused more on local affairs, such as the development of the local economy and the construction of local infrastructure, rather than on national issues.

4 The Revitalization of Chinese Popular Religion since the 1980s

Chinese popular religion has experienced a remarkable revival since the 1980s; take Fujian Province, for example. According to data released by the Fujian Provincial Department of Ethnic and Religious Affairs in 2007, there are over 100,000 registered popular religious temples, 26,000 of which cover an area of more than 10 square meters, 852 of which are under the administration of the religious bureau, and 328 of which have been conserved as cultural heritage sites.[216]

Shortly after the founding of the People's Republic of China in 1949, the religious policies of Chinese government were favorable for popular religion, especially those in rural China. After the People's Commune Movement was launched in the 1950s, popular religion began to be attacked. But shortly after the Great Chinese Famine, also known as the Great Leap Forward Disaster, occurred in China during 1959-61,[17] religious policy became less harsh. This situation lasted for a period of time until 1964, which allowed the revitalization of popular religion in rural China, and this revitalization made it possible for popular religion to revive and develop in the 1980s, since most of the contemporary elder religious specialists obtained their professional trainings during the early 1960s, so the liturgical tradition did not lose its experts who could pass their knowledge and skills on to a new generation.

Since the 1980s, Chinese popular religion has gradually left the underground and come into the public arena in the form of folk custom, traditional culture, cultural festivals, intangible cultural heritage, and so on. Its impact on Chinese society should not be underestimated. The lineage sacrifice and the temple festival are two important kinds of manifestation that show the vitality of Chinese popular religion in its social organization. Fieldwork studies done by anthropologists, experts in folklore studies and religious studies, after 1979, show that similar religious activities have been revived since the 1980s. As long as there is no potential fire damage, or danger to public security, lineage sacrifices and temple festivals are allowed by the local government, particularly in remote areas. The control on traditional ritual performance is extremely tight in urban areas, while rather loose in suburban ones. The renovation of a lineage hall in a county site, though not impossible, would still run into troubles of various kinds, unless it was a historic site, which is able to attract tourists and thereby contribute to the development of the local economy. Building a temple or lineage hall in a small village far from the county town is generally allowed.[18]

As has been noted by scholars, the revitalization and development of Chinese popular religion has been accompanied by Chinese urbanization, as a result of the transformation and opening up of Chinese society. However, in fact, the size and structure of the temple festivals in Chinese villages has changed, because of the increasing outflow of young labor towards the cities.

Many temple festivals, which used to be flourishing and of vast influence, have become cheerless, since the participants, especially young male participants, have decreased sharply. The roles they played, for example, in dragon dance and lion dance performance, are taken up by older female participants in some areas. Even some of the religious specialists in remote areas have left home to work in the factories of the Pearl River Delta or the Yangtze River Delta, because they can earn more money in a factory as a blue collar worker than being a respectable religious specialist in their hometown. While in large and medium-sized cities, the potential for popular religion to develop and flourish is quite limited, except when local governments support certain temples and faiths in local deities, in order to propagate the local culture, or stimulate the development of the local economy. It is much easier, therefore, for city inhabitants to get in touch with the five major religions (Buddhism, Daoism, Catholicism, Protestantism and Islam) than it is for them to be members of a popular religion. Though the revitalization and development of popular religion among different areas is uneven, we should still admit it did show its vitality after the 1980s from a nationwide perspective.

When we discuss the revitalization and development of Chinese popular religion since the 1980s, we should analyze it from two aspects.

One aspect in point is the revitalization and development of collective activity of popular religion, which requires three essential conditions: a) the positive support or at least acquiescence of local government for the purposes of economical development or the promotion of traditional local culture; b) the strong power of local lineage organization; c) a well-developed local economy. The approval of local government is an important precondition. And a powerful lineage guarantees the smooth operation of collective religious activities, especially in the current context of high population mobility, which reduces the cohesion of local communities in rural areas. Without an influential lineage, collective religious activities based on a certain community are barely possible. Last but not least, a well-developed local economy provides not only a robust financial backup for large religious activities, but also stable local participants, who are able to earn a living in local society, which further makes it possible to continue local religious traditions.

The other is the revitalization and development of personal activity of popular religion. It is not easy to fulfill the above three conditions to hold collective activities related to popular religion. According to fieldwork experience in South China, the collective religious events of rural areas, which used to be organized by a certain community and involve all of its members, are now controlled by some spirit mediums, and are participated in mostly by females. These two groups are the main force to promote the renovation and rebuilding of local temples. However, this does not mean that the major Chinese people are no longer enthusiastic about popular religion. Instead, it shows that the ways of participation in popular religious activities by the majority have been changed. In some areas, the number of spirit medium (especially female spirit medium) has been increased, and several belief networks of different sizes have been built around them. The followers turn to a spirit medium to counsel or pray for personal affairs. This no longer concerns the collective well-being of a lineage or a village, but focuses more on the benefit of a person or his or her family. Such kind of personal activity, though different from those traditional collective activities based on territorial or kinship relationship, still has the potential to be developed into an organized network.

In certain respects, the revitalization and development of Chinese popular religion since the 1980s indicates its vitality, and its capacity for adaptation to social transformations towards modernization. And it may present an even more colorful diversity in the future.

1   V. Goossaert, '1898: The Beginning of the End for Chinese Religion?,' *The Journal of Asian Studies*, 65/2 (2006), 307-335.

2   For more details on this policy, see Dwight H. Perkins, 'China's economic policy and performance,' in Roderick MacFarquhar and John K. Fairbank, eds., *The Cambridge History of China*, Vol.15 (Cambridge: Cambridge University Press, 1991), 475-539.

3   In this paper, the term 'Chinese religions' refers to Chinese Buddhism, Daoism, Confucianism and Popular religion.

4   Y. Der-Ruey provides an excellent discussion on the training of Daoist priests and the revival of Daoist ritual economy in suburban Shanghai: Y. Der-Ruey, 'The Changing Economy of Temple Daoism in Shanghai,' in *The State, the Market, and Religions in Contemporary China*, eds. J. Tamney and F. Yang (Leiden: Brill, 113-148).

5   J. Paper, *The Spirits are Drunk: Comparative Approaches to Chinese Religion* (Albany, NY: State University of New York Press, 1995).

6   C.K. Yang, *Religion in Chinese Society: A Study of Contemporary Social Functions of Religion and Some of Their Historical Factors* (Berkeley: University of California Press, 1961).

7   The term 'Three Teachings' had already been in existence in the South and North Dynasty.

8   'Improper' means that one performs a sacrifice beyond one's qualification, or worships unauthorized deities.

9   For example, the Aṣṭasāhasrikā Prajñāpāramitā Sūtra (*daming du wuji jing*), translated by Zhiqian at the end of the Han Dynasty an d under the Wei, and the Śṛgālavāda Sūtra (*foshuo shansheng*) translated by Zhi Fadu in the Western Jin Dynasty.

10 Ter Haar has a wonderful book on the White Lotus Teachings, see B.J. ter Haar, *The White Lotus Teachings in Chinese Religious History* (Leiden/New York: Brill, 1992).

11 The emperors during the Ming Dynasty believed that all sectarian groups acted substantially in accordance with the teachings of the 'White Lotus Sect', though they put a taboo on using its name, see *Veritable Records of Ming Shenzong* (*Ming Shenzong Shilu*), Vol. 533.

12 K. Dean, 'China's Second Government: Regional Ritual Systems in Southeast China,' in *Collected Papers From the International Conference on Social, Ethnic and Cultural Transformation* (Taipei: Centre for Chinese Studies, 2001), 77-109.

13 C.f. J. Watson, 'Standardizing the Gods: the Promotion of T'ien Hou along the South China Coast,' in *Popular Culture in Late Imperial China*, ed. D. Johnson (Berkeley: University of California Press, 1985), 292-324.

14 V. Goossaert, 'State and Religion in Modern China: Religious Policies and

Scholarly Paradigms.' Paper presented at the International Conference on the 50th Anniversary of the Institute of Modern History (Taipei, Academia Sinica, 2005).

15 K. Dean, *Lord of the Three in One: The Spread of a Cult in Southeast China* (Princeton, N.J.: Princeton University Press, 1998), 227.

16 http://www.fjmzzj.gov.cn/View_News.asp?news_type=43&id=742, accessed September 12, 2012.

17 For more information about the People's Commune Movement, the Great Leap Forward and the Great Chinese Famine, see MacFarquhar and Fairbank, *Cambridge History of China*, 293-538.

18 W. L. Tam, 'Local Religion in Contemporary China,' in *Chinese Religions in Contemporary Societies*, ed. J. Miller (Santa Barbara, California: ABC-CLIO, 2006).

11

The Autistic Worldview:
A Case Study of
China

Cindy De Clerck

1 Introduction

What I want to present in this paper might be a little different from the other articles published in the field of religion as it is not, strictly speaking, a religious study but one which developed from medical anthropological research. In this study, we focus on a certain group of people, with a certain demand on society, and examine how religion might function within this community.

I did research on Chinese families with an autistic child, visiting NGOs in the main, to get an overview of how this community functions in society, and how they strategize being in the world. Religion definitely also has a 'of this-world' function, that will be addressed in this article, as it occupied a prominent place in my field research.

I will first give an overview of the study that has been conducted. After that, I will discuss the research methodology that is used. Because this is anthropological research, it is important to understand its methodology. Thirdly, I will present some of the results of the study, placing an emphasis on religion and belief systems. I will end by making some preliminary conclusions.

This study is actually PhD research in progress with a working title: 'Autism in China: An Anthropological Inquiry'. All the elements needed to explain this study are contained in the title. We are looking at China and, within China, we are looking at a particular phenomenon: autism. Below, I will focus on these two elements, and connect them. This is necessary if I am to be able to relate religion—or the notion of a 'worldview'—to autism in China.

2   Autism

Autism is medically seen as a developmental disability. Children do not reach their developmental milestones on time, and this continues throughout their life span. Therefore we also speak of a 'pervasive developmental disorder'.[1] The core aspects of this disability are: problems in communication, problems in social development, and having routine behaviors and fixed schedules.[2].

Autism is now diagnosed all over the world, in every culture and subculture.[3] So this essay will not deal with how many children are autistic in China, or how the autism of a Chinese child differs from that of a Western child. However, it is perceivable that children with autism (and their families) are treated differently in different cultures. My interest lies in how autism and culture link together in China. With this focus in mind, I am not interested in what we can learn about autism through China, but rather what we can learn about China through autism.

How autism is viewed in a socio-cultural environment, depends on what is viewed as normal and abnormal in a certain culture. Also, the way in which autistic symptoms are perceived, whether they are seen as testing the boundaries or not, and whether one sees an autistic child as marginal, depends on a specific culture.[4] I am interested in looking at autism from a cultural (and social) perspective. Is this different from a medical perspective? It is currently believed that autism cannot be seen as a solely cultural phenomenon, and this article will not contest this idea. Every disorder can be seen as either culturally diverse, absolute, or as a universal concept.[5] When one perceives autism as an absolute disorder, autism should have a biological marker. Autism occurs anywhere in the world, and due to this biological marker, autism can be seen as similar everywhere, either in cause, symptoms, or outcome. Since the biological etiology of autism has not been proven yet, this is not a valid approach.[6]

On the other hand, if autism was culturally diverse, autism would be linked to certain cultures and not others. Sanua has described autism as being part of industrial countries, and could not find any evidence of it in developing countries, like China.[7] Even so, this idea has been seen as out-dated. In the middle, one perceives autism as a universal concept; a belief that has been used throughout this research. Autism as a universal concept explains autism as a disorder with the same symptoms all over the world (medical notion), and sees autism as occurring everywhere. However, the way symptoms are problematic, and what symptoms are viewed important and more harmful might be culturally probed. Therefore, an autistic child in an American culture and in a Chinese culture have the same core problems, however, Chinese culture might be more introvert, and therefore views avoiding eye contact and being less assertive as not being a problem in young children, while American culture might.

The thought of autism as a universal concept, with cultural differences in coping and managing the disorder might have some implications in terms of research. This means that the current focus on medical elements might not deal with the whole picture. Since autism can also be seen from a cultural perspective, future research should be more sensitive towards the treatment and coping issues in different cultures. It seems, for now, that parents are culturally sensitive and are already employing this in their coping strategies. In the literature that deals with autism as a cultural concept, one finds proof for this, both in the medical and the social world.

In the medical world, the level of communication with parents has been shown to be culturally sensitive. For India, for instance, it has been shown that medical practitioners are reluctant to label a child as autistic, since they view parents as not being able to handle it, and autism as too harsh a category with few exit points.[8] In Korea, many autism cases are first labeled Reactive Attachment Disorder (RAD),[9] which is basically seen as an unloved child. If the child does not improve, he or she might be re-diagnosed as being autistic.[10] Also in the US, many diagnoses are done with Medicaid wavers and insurance policies in mind.[11] These examples show that having the label of being autistic is already culturally sensitive. A medical practitioner might take more into account than just the diagnostic categories. The way policies and institutions are constructed provide further information about how a certain disability is viewed. In China, there is hardly any governmental institutional help for children with autism, and everything is provided by NGOs.[12]

When a child is labeled as autistic, it goes back into the family where they have to care for it, and answer more profound, internal questions like 'why me?' Anthropological literature has shown that this is also dealt with in a cultural context. There has been a study made on the religious place of autistic children in an ultra-orthodox Jewish community.[13] Shaked paints a picture of an illness narrative where parents view their child as being disabled and unable to perform certain religious rituals as they are supposed to do. But on the other hand, they also view their children as being so pure that they do not need to perform such rituals. Therefore, the cultural concept of autism in this community gives the child a certain status. This is strengthened by the use of facilitated communication (FC) where a facilitator types the words a child moves him to. For this community, language has become very spiritual.[14] In South Asian Muslim societies, the birth of an autistic child is seen as a test from Allah. Therefore, parents do not ask why they have this kind of child with them, but find a way to care for the child in a basic but loving way. Autism is seen in these communities as the last rebirth.[15]

Apart from studies like Shaked's, most studies on autism in the family have concentrated on parental attitudes and coping behaviors. In Taiwan, for instance, studies on parental behaviors show both a discrepancy between mothering and fathering, and a distance from the mother.[16] Studies on coping behaviors show more stress in parents with an autistic child.[17] These studies may not differ so much from Western studies on the subject,[18] but are psychological in nature. Anthropological studies on parenting and parental views are rare. One of the exceptions is the study of Hispanic parents made by Moreno[19] in which she paints a picture of parents talking about their child's diagnosis and future prospects.

3   China

In China the history of disabilities in general and autism in particular is rather short. Autism has only been diagnosed since 1982 (in comparison to 1944 in the West) and has only been recognized as a disability since 2005.[20] Therefore, the knowledge on autism, and the stigma surrounding autism are still very particular.

For my research, it was not enough to speak about autism in the context of China. Very early on, I noticed that autism could have different meanings throughout my research, so I divided it into four different categories. Firstly, autism can be seen as a medical category. This is the one spoken about the most, also in China. It deals with diagnoses and manuals and sees autism as a collection of symptoms that can be tackled by therapy. This form of autism is not particular to China though. We now know that autism as a medical category exists all over and that the symptoms are all similar.

The second category, therefore, takes autism as a socio-cultural category. Here, autism is seen as occurring in a certain environment with a certain background. For China, its particular culture and social structure, but also its history defines how autism is perceived. Language is also an issue here, as there are two words for autism in Chinese and each of these words is linked to a different way of looking at autism, what causes it, and how to manage it.

The third category is seen as a way of perceiving the world. How does one perceive the world when one is autistic or has an autistic child? This too is different in China than it is in other regions, because its particular socio-cultural background defines what the boundaries are for someone with autism or with an autistic child. I have enlisted strategies in my research that are seen as ways of playing with these boundaries and of finding ways of being in the world of an autistic child.

Fourthly, I have created a category linked to values and norms. In China, having an autistic child is linked to feelings of guilt and shame. Parents felt that they had pressured their child too much, or that they had not given it enough attention, and that this had led to the child being autistic.

4 Methodology

An anthropological study, like this one, usually consists of a part where one does fieldwork. This study consists of two separate methods. On the one hand, I connected with families of children with an autistic child, and on the other, I contacted families on the internet.

For the first part (connecting with families in real life), I spent two years in Beijing. Since disclosing that your child has autism is still difficult, it was impossible to just have a list of names of families in Beijing that I could visit. Therefore, I got in contact with NGOs who provide services to children and their families with autism and spent time in a couple of NGOs working as a volunteer. Through this experience, I was able to get in touch with families, follow them, and interview them.

I discovered that there was a huge amount of parent-to-parent support on the internet and so logged on to some websites on the internet and followed the parent-to-parent discussions that went on there.

It is important to note that this research is about the parents and not the children. The reason for this is quite simple. Because autism was only diagnosed in China in 1982 for the first time, there are not very many autistic adults identified in China, therefore, I worked with families of smaller children (usually six years or younger).

5 Results

During the fieldwork it became apparent that autism, as it is presented in most literature, was not enough to explain everything that I witnessed. Autism is usually seen as a medical condition, but I saw that there were also different categories at work. Apart from the medical properties of autism, every family lives in a socio-cultural environment, that defines the way disability is viewed, and that defines how we think about it. Also, autism is perceived in different ways because of our belief system and feelings of, for instance, guilt and shame that become linked to a diagnosis.

We, therefore, create different world views, like those parents who convert to Christianity, for example, because they could not find answers within their own belief system. This is important to notice, since parents need to create a sense of belonging and becoming, and the way they view themselves, and their child, is important in that regard.

These different world views are, therefore, linked to different perceptions. Perceptions about what the properties of autism are, how to care for a child with autism, and how to care for the entire family. Also, one has to break through certain cultural boundaries, to make sure the entire family has a place in the world.

Therefore, the properties of autism change, according to the goal of a certain family over a certain time. Also, when a family crosses boundaries, by for instance converting, their view on autism can also change. This crossing of boundaries has a particular purpose however. One can see that parents are crossing boundaries to fit into the culture they still feel they belong to. To give an example, parents will think about registering for a second child, because they need insurance for themselves when they grow old, and care for the elderly is still a family business in China. Another example would be parents who get a divorce because one parent feels the other parent is not interested in the child at home, and the child is therefore deprived of a future.

Another example, one that I want to explore further, concerns the people who convert to Christianity to be able to accept their child's disability. A few of the families observed did openly state that they had converted to Christianity because they could not get the right answers to their questions on how their child got to be the way it was. By converting to Christianity they felt more open about talking about how their feelings and that there was more conceptual space to do so.

Christianity was also linked with solidarity. Parents felt that Christians were more supportive and less judgmental. One reason for this could be that being Christian was somehow related to having a more 'foreign' attitude. Since autistic children were associated with being foreign this might have reflected on their parent's vision of being in the world.

6   Discussion

In this article I have concentrated on ways of identifying and defining autism and have taken various characteristics into account:
- The nature of the disorder
- The nature of the society one lives in or the one to which one belongs
- The way one puts oneself in the world because of the autism of a family member
- The underlying feelings linked to raising a child with autism

I used these characteristics in order to construct an understanding of the topic 'autism in China'. In my analysis of Chinese families with an autistic child, I felt these mechanisms were useful because they helped me understand what kind of layers there were while working with this type of families. Through this understanding, I was able to provide a thick description of family dynamics and explain why they had come about.

The categories as they are presented here might seem separate, but this is actually not the case. In order to understand why families act the way that they do when caring for a child with autism, one has to link these categories. The underlying notions I presented need to be interpreted as key words that trigger certain functions.

When one is confronted with a child who acts in a way that might not be considered as 'normal' according to the mainstream culture, one is confronted with both socio-cultural and medical properties. The socio-cultural beliefs concerning disability (is disability medical in nature or is it caused by a previous sin in the family?) but also family (what will happen when we have to raise a child with a disability?), parenting and belief systems will guide the search towards an answer as to why this child acts as it does. For the Chinese case, there will also be a medical approach, since disability is mostly dealt with in a medical model of disability in urban China.[21] This medical model will lead someone to a hospital and to medical practitioners, and maybe also towards interventions and therapies. While looking at autism in a medical way, one can never omit cultural and social characteristics. Indeed, the way an intervention is carried out, and what kind of intervention is seen as appropriate, is linked to the culture and the social infrastructure of a region.

During all these interactions between medical and socio-cultural phenomena, one sees some characteristics at work which can be described as norms and values. Again, these cannot be seen as separate from socio-cultural images. They are important to identify, however, because whether a family feels ashamed, guilty or may actually be proud of their child, will determine— together with medical and socio-cultural aspects—how a family will perceive itself in the world, and how the individual members will perceive themselves. Therefore, the perception of autism is actually the sum of all the other categories.

Through this way of looking at autism, and being in the world while having a family member with autism, we can look at how the worldview of these families is constructed. The fact that some families changed religion, or felt they could not get the answers from their traditional ways of looking at the world, is very telling in this regard. It heightens the feeling that parents have to break out of their culture to be a part of this same culture.

1   U. Frith, *Autisme: Verklaringen van het raadsel* (Berchem: EPO, 2003).
2   Frith, *Autisme*.
3   R. R. Grinker, *Unstrange Minds: Remapping the World of Autism* (New York: Basic Books, 2007).
4   H. U. Kim, 'Autism Across Cultures: Rethinking Autism,' *Disability & Society* 27:4 (2012), 535-545.
5   T. C. Daley, 'The Need for Cross-Cultural Research on the Pervasive Developmental Disorders,' *Transcultural Psychiatry* 39 (2002), 531-550; T. T. Dyches, L. K. Wilder, R. R. Sudweeks, F. E. Obiakor and B. Algozzine, 'Multicultural Issues in Autism,' *Journal of Autism Developmental Disorders* 34:2 (2004), 211-222.
6   J. W. Weru, *Cultural Influences on the Behavioral Symptoms of Autism in Kenya and the United States of America* (PhD dissertation: University of Texas, 2005).
7   V. D. Sanua, 'Is Infantile Autism a Universal Phenomenon? An Open

Question,' *International Journal of Social Psychiatry* 30 (1984), 163-177.

8   T. C. Daley, 'From Symptom Recognition to Diagnosis: Children with Autism in Urban India,' *Social Science and Medicine* 58 (2004), 1323-1335.

9   Kim, *Rethinking Autism*.

10   Grinker, *Unstrange Minds*.

11   H. Kutchins and S. A. Kirk, *Making Us Crazy: DSM, the Psychiatric Bible and the Creation of Mental Disorders* (London: Constable, 1997).

12   K. R. Fisher, J. Li and L. Fan, 'Barriers to the Supply of Non-Government Disability Services in China,' *Journal of Social Policy* 41:1 (2012), 161-182.

13   M. Shaked, 'The Social Trajectory of Illness: Autism in the Ultraorthodox Community in Israel,' *Social Science & Medicine* 61 (2005), 2190-2200; M. Shaked and Y. Bilu, 'Grappling with Affliction: Autism in the Jewish Ultraorthodox Community in Israel,' *Culture, Medicine and Psychiatry* 30 (2006), 1-27.

14   Y. Bilu and Y. C. Goodman, 'What Does the Soul Say?: Metaphysical Uses of Facilitated Communication in the Jewish Ultraorthodox Community,' *Ethos* 25:4 (1997), 375-407.

15   B. Jegatheesan, P. J. Miller and S. A. Fowler, 'Autism from a Religious Perspective: A Study of Parental Beliefs in South Asian Muslim Immigrant Families,' *Focus on Autism and Other Developmental Disabilities* 25 (2010), 98-109.

16   S. S-F. Gau, M-C Chou, J-C Lee, C-C Wong, W-J Chou, M-F Chen, W-T Soong and Y-Y Wu, 'Behavioural Problems and Parenting Style among Taiwanese Children with Autism and their Siblings,' *Psychiatry and Clinical Neurosciences* 64 (2010), 70-78.

17   X. Huang, R. Song and Y. Xing, '71 li zibizheng ertong de jiating xuqiu ji fazhan zhichi jiaocha' [71 Autistic Children, Their Families Needs and Developmental Needs], *Zhongguo teshu jiaoyu* 11 (2009), 43-47; P. Wang, C. A. Michaels and M. S. Day, 'Stresses and Coping Strategies of Chinese Families with Children with Autism and Other Developmental Disabilities,' *Journal of Autism and Developmental Disorders* 41 (2011), 783-795.

18   Gau et al., *Behavioural problems*.

19   C. L. Moreno, *Understanding 'El autismo': A Qualitative Study of the Parental Interpretation of autism: A Hispanic Perspective* (PhD dissertation: Ohio State University, 1995).

20   T. Guotai, *Rang guduzheng ertong zouchu gudu* [Let Autistic Children Walk Away from Loneliness], (Beijing: Zhongguo funü chubanshe, 2005).

21   M. Kohrman, *Bodies of Difference: Experiences of Disability and Institutional Advocacy in the Making of Modern China*, (Berkeley/Los Angeles/London: University of California Press, 2005).

PART III

MEETING BETWEEN

CULTURES

12

Islam and Pluralism: Religious-cultural Identity and Multiculturalism

Yaser Ellethy

1   Introduction

Both the issue of 'Otherness' in Islam and the Muslim perception of the 'Other' are embedded in core theological and historical Islamic contexts. Yet, the way a Muslim experiences his own identity within the worldly and mundane range of diversity and differences determines his or her reflection on the notions of pluralism and multiculturalism. This can be partly attributed to the significant role that religion still plays in the social and political domains in the Muslim world, but mostly to the fact that Islam itself is comprised of a rigorous fabric of spiritual and ritual aspects that permeates the Muslim identity.

This article is an attempt to explain, on the one hand, the role of religion in the formation of Muslim identity and on the other, the impact that this role, and the eventual tensions it can create, on ethno-cultural parameters which also constitute important elements in the Muslim identity. This is important for the analysis of whether an Islamic 'sameness' can be monocultural or multicultural in a context of 'Otherness'. Furthermore, the question of religious identity, especially within Islam, is strictly linked to the issues of affiliation and loyalty. Whether a Muslim is more loyal to his own spatio-temporal context or to his transnational and trans-temporal identity, as a member of an *ummah*, and the consequences of this self-consciousness on his cultural and socio-political involvement, is another core problematic dimension in the issue of pluralism. I will, therefore, discuss two main aspects of the Muslim identity: the religious and the cultural, and their pluralistic implications. I start by examining the particular and the individual, and end by looking at the general and the collective. I shall present a survey of a particular image of Muslim religious identity and its major components then illustrate the cultural diversity and parameters within this particular identity and the various manifestations it can produce.

2   Religious Identity

Especially in the case of religious affiliation, the question of 'who is a "…"?' does not only relate to the descriptive aspect of an identity but goes far beyond this and determines the way an adherent of a certain religious tradition perceives the world and acts in his private and social life.[1] In the case of Islam this question has a significant relationship to the notion of pluralism. This is because Islamic traditionalism, as a cultural impetus, is constantly and dynamically active in various aspects and levels of Muslim societies and communities all over the world. The way a Muslim conceives his own identity emerges partially from a number of cognitive elements about Islam as a faith and a tradition, and partially from the surrounding socio-cultural and political circumstances. As a result, this identification of 'Muslimness'[2] has a crucial effect on the ways Muslims see themselves in a broader context. In this section, I focus on some features of the identity of a Muslim as these might emerge from the Quran, the Sunnah and the Islamic tradition. This may help to construct a foundational commonality between the majority of Muslims and the identification of an Islamic religious identity. Consequently, a better understanding of the Muslim identity with all its variations would enable us to assess the pluralistic nature of Muslims in a multicultural and globalized society.[3]

It goes without saying that the Quran, as the divine address to humans implemented by the Prophet, constitutes how a Muslim should know God, the essence of his existence, his position in this world and relation to others (family, neighbors, society, state, *ummah*, world, etc.). The Quranic formation of a Muslim identity can be deduced from a plethora of verses. But it is difficult to restrict the definition of Muslim to certain verses, as the Quran as a whole is meant to frame the character of a Muslim. Nevertheless, we can use some examples which describe a number of features of how a Muslim should be, as these comprise the major characteristics of a Muslim religious identity.

The term Muslim means someone who submits and surrenders wholly to God, the Quran expresses this in many verses, like:

Nay! whoever submits his whole self to Allah and is a doer of good, He will get his reward with his Lord; on such shall be no fear, nor shall they grieve[4]

Who can be better in religion than one who submits his whole self to Allah, does good, and follows the way of Abraham the true in Faith?[5]

This 'Islam', as it is depicted in these verses, requires a whole-hearted and complete commitment to the divine guidance in a quest for success in this world and the Hereafter. The Quran calls upon a Muslim to realize that true acceptance is the acceptance of the entirety of Allah's guidance:

> O you who believe! Enter into Islam perfectly and wholly; and follow not the footsteps of the Satan; for he is to you an avowed enemy.[6]

In this verse, we see that the 'addressed' are those who already believe. Nevertheless, they are asked to enter into Islam. This, perfectly and wholly (kāffa), entrance in (fi) Islam implies that Islam is likely to be a structure which a Muslim should enter and, in doing so, benefit from all its parts. It also implies that a Muslim should not take one part of Islam and leave another, but should instead accept and obey all the rules and regulations as they are inextricable part of the divine guidance.[7] This is one of the differences between Imān (belief/faith), Islam (submission) and 'Islam' as a label,[8] which the following verse touches on:

> The Nomads (wandering Arabs) say: We believe. Say: You do not believe but say, We submit; and faith has not yet entered into your hearts; and if you obey Allah and His Messenger, He will not diminish aught of your deeds; surely Allah is Forgiving, Merciful.[9]

The verse refers to a group of Bedouins (Banu Asad) who claimed Islam outwardly but not inwardly. To speak the shahāda out of the tongue is 'Islam', but imān is to speak it out of the heart and to confirm this with deeds; to submit really to God's guidance.[10] Whoever follows this guidance, which God promised to send to Adam and all his progeny, will never go astray or fall into distress and misery. Adversely, whoever turns away from this guidance will have a straitened life, full of hardship, and will be raised up in blindness, as he could not see God's signs and revelations in his mundane life:

> He (Allah) said: Go down hence, both of you, one of you a foe unto the other. But when there come unto you from Me a guidance, then who so follows My guidance, he will not go astray nor come to grief. But he who turns away from My Remembrance, his will be a narrow life, and I shall bring him blind to the assembly on the Day of Resurrection. He will say: My Lord! Wherefore have You gathered me (hither) blind, when I was wont to see? He will say: So (it must be). Our revelations came unto you but you did forget them. In like manner you are forgotten this Day.[11]

Another verse shows this full submission and compliance of a Muslim with the guidance he received from God. The verse is frequently used by Muslim scholars and preachers to promote a Muslim's complete devotion to the divine guidance embodied in His last message to humankind:

> Say: Verily, my Lord has guided me to a way that is straight,- a right religion, the religion of Abraham the true monotheism, and he (certainly) joined not gods with Allah. Say: Truly, my prayer and my service of sacrifice, my life and my death, are (all) for Allah, the Lord of the worlds. No partner has He: this am I commanded, and I am the first of Muslims.[12]

These indicative Quranic examples, among many other verses, stamp the identity of a Muslim with features related to his self-consciousness as a holder and follower of a divine message and a revealed system that differentiates him from other adherents of mundane worldviews. Moreover, the authority of the Quran in the life of Muslims is not only legislative and constitutional but plays a tremendous formative pedagogic and educational role in the life of Muslims. *Ḥifẓ* (memorization) and *tajwīd* (professional recitation) of the whole Quranic text are two honorable diplomas that many Muslim families strive to obtain for their children at a very early age. Quranic schools and private charitable institutes are exclusively devoted to the memorization and recitation of the Quran. Worldwide competitions are held and generous prizes are awarded for the *ḥuffāẓ*. Most of the famed Muslim scholars across the world ornament their biographies by describing the privilege of having memorized the Quran at an early age in one of the private Quranic schools (*kuttāb/madrasa*). The pedagogic aspect of the Quran in the lives of Muslims comprises a significant factor in the formation of both their individual and collective identities.[13]

It is a fact that Muslims know about the Prophet's life in more details than perhaps any other historical figure. These details include his prenatal period, genealogical line, prophetic and political career and personal life and extend to elaborated information about the very particular features of his physical, ethical, familial and behavioral attributes.[15] His tradition, embodied in the *hadith*'s nar-

If we turn to the second primary source of Islam, the Sunnah, the paradigm of the Prophet will emerge as the archetype of 'Muslimness'. The Prophet as an example to be followed (*uswa*, *qudwa*)[14] represents, in the life of Muslims, the embodiment and personification of this divine address in all aspects of human life. Hence, 'Sunnah' is linguistically a *Way* and technically every spoken word, done act, a tacit or expressed confirmation (*taqrīr*) of the Prophet, and even his physical and moral characteristics. These aspects of the Prophetic tradition form for Muslims, after the Quran, not only the second primary source of Islam but also a substantial *par excellence* human pattern of their identity. In sociological terms, Muhammad represents the *sociometric star* of all Muslims, as his charismatic personality is repeatedly and vehemently inspired in different religious, social and political situations.

rations, presents a primary source for the ethical and behavioral code of Muslims. In a famous authentic *hadith* the Archangel Gabriel teaches Muslims the tenets of their faith through the Prophet who appeared to him in human form in the presence of his companions and asked him about the tenets of Islam:

> [Gabriel] said: 'O Muhammad, tell me about Islam' The Messenger of Allah *(pbuh)* said: *'Islam is to testify that there is none worthy of worship except Allah and that Muhammad is the Messenger of Allah, to establish the prayers, to pay the zakā, to fast [in the month of] Ramadan, and to make the pilgrimage to the House if you have the means to do so'. He said: 'You have spoken truthfully'. We were amazed that he asked the question and then he claimed that he had spoken truthfully. He said: 'Tell me about Imān (faith)'. He [the Prophet] said: 'It is to believe in Allah, His angels, His books, His messengers, the Last Day and to believe in Fate, both the good and the evil thereof'. He said: 'You have spoken truthfully.' He said: 'Tell me about al-iḥsān (goodness/perfection/excellence).' He [the Prophet] said 'iḥsān is to worship God as though you see Him, and while you cannot see Him, indeed He sees you.'*[16]

Based on this *hadith*, it can be said that there are three levels of 'faith' or 'religiousness': *Islam* (submission), *imān* (faith) and *iḥsān* (perfection).[17] The concept of *iḥsān*, which is difficult to translate, approximates to the meaning of perfection as it is a continuous struggle to reach the best (*aḥsan*) in everything; to excel. The interpretation of the Prophet is a scale against which the behavior of every Muslim can be measured. To worship God under this criterion 'while you cannot see God, God indeed sees *you*' is a significant condition which determines the character of a Muslim. In this status of religiousness:

> He will 'feel' and 'experience' Allah always around him and with him. To make a worldly analogy, he will behave as if his most beloved companion is right next to him and he fears that he may do anything to hurt his feelings or bring him harm. Thus, every action is weighed and considered beforehand.[18]

As regulated in the aforementioned *hadith*, another decisive factor in the formation of the Muslim identity should be sought in both its cohesive doctrinal and cumulative ritual systems. The five pillars of Islam are combined in a maximal and formative way which can produce a Muslim who is constantly aware of his religious identity. The testimony of faith (*shahāda*) symbolizes the pact of *submission* between a Muslim and his God. A pact expressed twice in the Quran as '*uruwa wuthqa* (firmest handhold)[19] which should be tightly grasped. The Quranic verb *istamsaka* (grasp), used in the two verses is more expressive than *amsaka* (catch, hold). The augmentation of a word structure in an addition to its meaning (*ziādat al-mabna ziāda fi al-ma'ana*) is a Quranic linguistic and exegetic rule. *Istamsaka* indicates a continuous struggle to grasp and keep this firm handhold with God. It necessitates faith (*imān*) in the Oneness of God (*tawḥīd*), His Angels, Books, Messengers, the Hereafter and Fate (*qadar*) whether good or bad; altogether comprising the six pillars of Islamic faith.

Faith in the Transcendent God and the Unseen (*ghayb*) requires a struggle of the spiritually sublime foresight against the materially tangible awareness of the senses. It also entails a manifestation of this 'submission', hence, the acts of devotion (*'ibādāt*) aimed at keeping a Muslim regularly in full compliance with the Divine guidance. To be in persistent contact five times a day, preferably in groups and in a mosque, reciting the Quran, kneeling and prostrating to God in a spiritual experience supposed to isolate a Muslim from all the preoccupations of the mundane life, is a renewing stamp of religious identity. A prayer proceeded by a well-ordered ablution (*wuḍū'*), pure intention (*niyya*) and freedom from insincerity (*riyā'*) and other prerequisites, means more than a ritual to a Muslim. It comprises a daily affirmation and practice of the identity of *'abd* (servant) before his Lord, on the one hand, and, on the other, a declaration of the commitment to the behavioral code it involves before the other *'ibād* (servants) counterparts in His creation.

To attend once a week the congregational (*jumu'a*) Friday-prayer is a weekly socio-religious reunion which renews the self-consciousness of a collective identity in the micro social scale of the mosque, neighborhood, and religious communal brotherhood.[20] A yearly fast (*ṣawm*) for a period of one month (*ramaḍān*) aims at the re-emergence of the spiritual ego of a Muslim. He builds up his spiritual strength in an intensive one-month course which combines all the ritual and moral virtues of Islam as abstention (*imsāk*) from all worldly pleasures and malicious ethics and turning the heart's compass towards the spiritual and the good to achieve righteousness and piety (*taqwa*).

Increasing (*zakā*) in the form of giving charity to the poor once a year reminds a Muslim of the divine grace he has and the moral obligation that he has to take care of the needy. It is a yearly purification (*taṭhīr-tazkiya*) from ego-centrism to solidarity and altruism with the 'Other', and a reminder of the meaning of sharing.[21]

The quest to visit (*haj*) the Inviolable-Sacred House (*Al-Bayt Al-Ḥarām*) once in a lifetime is a reinforcement of the unity of all Muslim believers in the orientation towards the One and Only God. The repetition of *talbiya* (response to a call)[22] represents the abstinence from worldly life, a reminder of the greater response in the Day of Judgment.

The word mention/remembrance (*dhikr*) is the common denominator in all religious activities of a Muslim, and is even an attribute given to the Quran; a word which has linguistic connotations with reminder and remembrance (*tadhakkur, tadhkira*). A Muslim is both intensively and intentionally reminded of his religious identity through obligatory and voluntary acts of devotion on a daily, weekly, yearly and lifetime basis. This spiritual and behavioral realm is ordained within a cohesive and elaborate legislative system which covers even the most specific details of life.

A cornerstone in the religious identity of a Muslim is his submission as a servant (*'abd*) to Allah. This is crucial in his relationship with his Creator and His creatures. Man is the most honorable creation of God, but he is still God's servant. This characteristic, seen by some non-Muslim as a mere subjugation and humiliation of the human toward the Divine, is for Muslims a title of honor.[23] Being inwardly a servant of the One and Unique God implies being outwardly free from everything and everyone else. It implies exclusive worship (*'ibāda*) of Allah, and what early Muslims perpetuated in their dictum about Islam as a message to turn people from the worshipping of servants (*'ibādat al-'ibād*) to the worshipping of the Lord of all servants (*'ibādat Rab al-'ibād*). This is a feeling described in Muslim tradition in another classical dictum of the early ascetic Ibrahim Ibn Adham (100-c.165): 'if the kings and the sons of the kings know the happiness and paradise we live in they would fight us for it.'[24] Moreover Ibn Qayyim Al-Jawziyya, in his commentary on the first part of verse 5 in the first Sura Al-Fātiḥa (*iyyaka na'budu*; 'You we do worship') distinguishes two kinds of this servitude. The first is general: the servitude of forced subjugation (*'ubūdiyyat qahr*) which characterizes all God's creation. Willing or not, everything in His creation is subjugated to His Will and Might. The second is private, or what we can call volitional subjugation (*'ubūdiyyat ikhtiyār*): the servitude of obedience and love, which characterizes the believers who chose voluntarily to submit themselves to their Creator.[25]

Finally, one can claim that the most dominant characteristic of a Muslim identity is the reference to the Hereafter and the accountability of all that he believes, says, does and achieves in this mundane life. A Muslim is ordered to live a proper mortal life with his eyes set on his immortal life in the Hereafter. It is not for nothing that the last revealed verse of the Quran is:

> And guard yourselves against a day in which you shall be returned to Allah; then every soul shall be paid back in full what it has earned, and they shall not be dealt with unjustly.[26]

To conclude, as we have seen, 'Muslimness' as a religious identity constitutes a deep distinctive component of the Muslim ego. Sociologically it determines not only his self-consciousness, but also his belonging to a certain group, the in-group in comparison with the out-group, and his intergroup behavioral code, as he sees things from his Muslim-group perspective. As a social identity this will be translated in what sociologists of identity theory define as 'self-categorization or identification', through which an identity is formed. In this theory:

The core of an identity is the categorization of the self as an occupant of a role, and the incorporation, into the self, of the meanings and expectations associated with that role and its performance [...]. These expectations and meanings form a set of standards that guide behavior[27]

Self-identification is what a Muslim and a non-Muslim encounter is all about. 'Muslimness' and 'Otherness' is a reciprocal relationship where both sides determine the conditions of the interaction with the out-group from their own perspective. For the Muslim, that 'Muslimness' becomes psychologically activated in some situations; what social identity theorists term as identity 'salience'.[28] This is also to be related to a process of depersonalization, where a Muslim defines himself as an embodiment of his in-group prototypes. Similarly, this process is also involved in seeing the 'Other' as an embodiment of an out-group.[29] In light of these social identity processes, we can conclude that 'Muslimness' refers to an Islam-centric identity which characterizes a Muslim and determines his behavior in various contexts. However, this religious identity should not constitute an impediment against pluralistic coexistence in a multicultural context, whether on a global or regional level. Religiousness can get along with interreligious and multicultural pluralistic coexistence, not in syncretistic terms but, rather, in being convinced that the 'common' is not essentially the 'true' for the 'Other'. In other words, humans should learn how to live diversity as their One Creator willed it to be. In the Muslim case, diversity should be approached as the pluralistic norm, especially when it emanates from the intra-Islamic religious-cultural fabric. This is what I analyze in the following part.

3 Cultural Identity

Having explored the religious Muslim identity we need to pose a question here about the pluralistic implications of this 'Muslimness', as a cultural identity, and whether it is monocultural or multicultural. This question is directly related to the peculiarities which this identity may present in a multicultural democratic society, inside or outside the Muslim context. What I intend to show, in this section, is the intra-Islamic cultural identity and its diverse nature, which should be the basic premise of pluralistic coexistence. Furthermore, an understanding of a Muslim culture is significant for a proper conception of the conditions and attitudes that this culture may present within a multicultural context.[30] First of all, we have to pay attention to the fact that the term multiculturalism is still a confused buzzword in the postmodern glossary. It circumscribes different cases and multitude of meanings such as: 1) the social ethno-demographic change of a homogenous society into a heterogeneous one; 2) recognition of this change as in the case of immigration; 3) showing tolerance toward others (like immigrants); 4) an interpretation of the concept *culture* as there is no 'pure' or 'original' culture; 5) the attitude of looking upon some aspects of the 'Other's' culture as an enrichment of 'our' culture 6) the political-constitutional principle for the reinforcement of pluralism against acculturation or assimilation; and finally 7) an illusory concept which overlooks the necessity for a common culture to enable integration and stability within one unified and homogenized nation-state.[31] Therefore, in the present discussion, which focuses on the pluralistic implications of 'Muslimness', some of the aforementioned cases of multiculturalism, especially the fourth, the fifth and the sixth, would fit in this respect. Multiculturalism, thus, will be defined in our discussion as: *an interpretation of the concept 'culture' in pluralistic terms, as a reinforcement of the sociopolitical attitude of looking upon some aspects of the 'Other's' culture as an enrichment of 'our' culture.*

Within a few years of the emergence of the call of Islam, the first Muslims experienced the notion of multiculturalism at different religious, social, cultural, linguistic and political levels. The first Muslims lived as immigrants in Christian Abyssinia for about 15 years. Afterwards, they emigrated from the Quraishite nomad commerce-centered Mecca to the more settled and agrarian Yathrib (later Medina). Medina remained the political, cultural and religious center of the Muslim state, second only to Mecca. With the expansions and the opening (*fatḥ*) of new geographies and cultures, Islam acquired a wide spectrum of globalized and multicultural civilization. From Mecca to Medina, Kufa, Damascus, Baghdad, Nishabur, Taj Mahal, Cordoba, Cairo, Constantinople, just to name a few examples, Islam interacted with many cultural spheres. Thus, from its beginnings and throughout its long history, Islam knew different ethno-cultural identities which all became politically Islamized although the social particularities were utilized and not assimilated. What we call 'Islamic civilization' is the production of a multicultural contribution which could have never been possible unless under pluralistic political conditions.[32]

In the broader context of the nexus between religion and culture, exploring the different human religious experiences, there are very few examples of the formation of a religious culture which has remained on the margins of the scriptural core. In the history of religions, no single case can be traced where the 'scriptural' fundamentals remained the unique source of faith's expression or religiosity. Interpretations, hermeneutics, clear and allegorical, text and context, religion and culture, are all parameters involved in the process of religious evolution. If this was not the case, why would we permanently need preachers, missionaries and religious reformers?[33] In the case of Islam, the interpretative tradition has presented a diversity of readings of the Islamic *sacra scriptura*. The Quran and the Sunnah have always remained immutable 'sources', while the various interpretations represent different human modalities of understanding them as 'resources'. This has resulted diachronically in the standardization of a methodology of exegesis (*usūl al-tafsīr*) to organize the relationship between the human intellect and the Divine logos. The difference between Islam, the scriptural tradition, and its cultural manifestations is that between a religion and a religious culture, with all the diverse aspects of the latter. The intra-Islamic cultural diversity presented a great mosaic of Muslim multiculturalism early in Islamic history. Both sectarian and doctrinal differences were exhibited as divergences from the pivotal and pristine religious example of the Prophet.

This is also clear in popular religion, where 'alien' elements overwhelm even some doctrinal religious tenets. That cultural identities affect religious identity has always been the impulse behind the emergence of sectarianism and intra-religious schisms. We can trace the echoes of this conflict between culture and religion in many classical Islamic works. For example, Al-Ghazali, in his less renowned philosophical work *al-Qistās al-Mustaqīm* (The Correct Balance), classifies people, or rather believers, into three main categories:

> Common people, who are the safe [sound) people, the dull-witted, the people of the Garden; and the elite [privileged], who are the men of insight and special intelligence; and there is formed between them a group who are the contentious wranglers, they follow the ambiguous part [of the Book], desiring dissention[34]

Al-Ghazali, who was designated by the Abbasid Caliph Al-Mustazhir Billah (Caliphate 1094-1118) to rebut the heretical teachings of some Muslim sects, was mainly concerned about the mass believers, who are always subject to the influence of different cultural, philosophical trends.[35]

On the epistemological level, the recognition and respect of cultural differences and regional particularities has even touched the Islamic scriptural methodology. In the *tafsīr* methodology (*usūl al-tafsīr*) a significant chapter is dedicated to the so-called *isrā'iliyyāt*, which refers to exegetic modes using traditions of the People of the Book, primarily Jewish, in interpreting some Quranic texts. In the *Hadith* methodology, ('*ilm mustalah/usūl al-Hadīth*) the regional cultural particularities are taken seriously into account even in the consideration of the most strict conditions of criticism concerning the narrators/transmitters (*ruwāt/rijāl al-hadīth*): the '*adāla* (uprightness/probity) criterion. For the scholars of *Hadith*, '*adāla* is to be assessed by two major sub-features: *taqwa* (piety, righteousness) and *murū'a* (humanness, gentlemanness).[36] Technically, *murū'a* is the quality of being free from some lowly affairs and defects which are contrary to the requisite of high ambition and virtue. As Kamali explains in the usage of the Arabs, 'it is associated with manliness and courage as well as avoidance of demeaning behaviour that compromises personal honor and is socially humiliating'. The '*adāla* (uprightness), together with *dabt* (precision, accurateness), of the narrators determine the acceptability and degree of authenticity of the second primary source of Islam, the *Hadith*-Sunnah narrations. When Muslim classical *uṣūl* scholars discuss the quality of *murū'a*, they refer to every avoidance of profanities or lowly acts like urinating in a public way, stealing trivial things, association with lowly characters or people of sordid professions, or, even, eating in public thoroughfares and walking bare headed. However, the scholars refer to the prevailing custom and culture which differs from place to place, time to time and people to people. What is seen as trivial, lowly, sordid or shameful in a society and a culture may not be so in another. Thus, what a religious criterion like *murū'a* actually means is often defined by reference to the prevailing culture and custom.[37] Also in Islamic jurisprudence, a famous aphorism grants what is known as *'urf* (custom), be it universal or local, the validity of legal norms: *al-ma'rūf 'urfan k'al-mashrūṭ sharṭan* (what is known by custom is as binding as a contractual stipulation).[38] Imam Al-Shafi'i (d. 820), founder of the known Islamic school of *fiqh*, is another example of taking locality and culture into consideration. His jurisprudential *ijtihād* underwent a remarkable shift after he moved to Egypt; ask for Al-Shafi'i opinion on a juristic matter, and one can receive two different answers; one from his Iraqi scholarship and another from his Egyptian.[39] Cultural Muslim geography is also manifest in the variety of the provenance of Muslim scholars. To give just a few examples from a very long list of names and ethnicites: Al-Bukhari (Bukhara-Khurasan (Uzbekistan)), Moslim Al-Nisaburi (Nishapur-Iran), Al-Ṭaḥawy (Ṭaḥa-Egypt) Al-Tabari (Tabaristan), Al-Qurtubi (Cordoba), Al-Khaṭīb Al-Baghdadi (Baghdad), Al-Mubarakphuri (Mubarakpur-India), Al-Albani (Albania).

As we see, culture may present juxtapositions with religion, but it may also show amazing attitudes of ambivalence towards religiousness. One can find a telling example in the Tuareg, the Berber Maliki Muslim nomad tribes in North and Western Africa. For a Tuareg man, wearing a veil (*tagelmoust/cheche*) which should cover his face excluding the eyes is a must, once he reaches maturity, something that a Tuareg woman, who enjoys great independence, does not do. The veil, here, is the 'traditional-cultural' veil and not the 'Islamic' one. Regional and environmental elements are behind this tradition. The shift from the religious to the cultural is clear. Accordingly, Muslim culture is what a Muslim carries, along with his Muslimness, from ethnic, linguistic, social and doctrinal characteristics that distinguishes him not only from a non-Muslim but also from another Muslim. The only collective element in this cultural variant identity is the reference to the religion of Islam. The parameters include a very complicated fabric of notions and socio-cultural norms which sometimes contradict the very fundamentals of Islam. Honor killings, vendetta, forced marriage and the abuse of women are some examples among many other phenomena which can be charged to one's 'Muslimness'.

Political factors are also predominant in the interaction between religious and cultural identities. The Western dictum *cuius regio, eius religio* has its Arabic-

Islamic equivalent: *al-nās 'ala dīn mulukihim* (people follow the religion of their rulers), but in a different context to that of the Peace of Augsburg (1555). At Muslim-Muslim level, for example, love and reverence of *ahl/āl al-bayt* (members of the Prophetic household) is a common element of piety. Nevertheless, traditional Sunnism is more reluctant about overlooking doctrinal restrictions against exaggeration in honoring them, while traditional Shiism is based on the concepts of their *imāma* (religious-political leadership) and *'isma* (infallibility and sinlessness). This is one of the distinctive doctrinal points between Sunnism and Shiism. Adversely, an aphorism, ascribed to the leader of the Iranian revolution Al-Khomeyni, says that Egypt has a Sunni *madhhab* and a Shiite tendency/passion (*hawā*). This description actually circumscribes the popular religious tradition in a country where the 'official' adopted Islamic doctrine is the Sunni-Shafi'i, but the solemnities and high esteem of *āl al-bayt* belong somehow to the Shiite tradition.[40] Historically, the Shiite Ismaili dynasty of the Fatimids ruled Egypt for two centuries (969-1171). Many of the religious-cultural manifestations today are attributed to that period. One can, indicatively, distinguish religious festivities during Ramadan, birthday celebrations of historical religious figures (*mawlid/mūlid*), visiting mausoleums, shrines and many other religious-cultural manifestations. Even the name of the worldly most renowned and ancient Islamic 'Sunni' University of Al-Azhar is derived from *Al-Zahrā'*, the nickname of the youngest daughter of the Prophet, Fātimah, whereof the name of the whole dynasty of the Fatimids was taken.

At the Muslim-non-Muslim level, we find that another characteristic of the cultural identity, in general, and 'Muslimness', in particular, is the changeability and the transformations which it may go through. Political factors are always documented. Lila Abu Lughod refers, for example, to the striking similarities between the Jewish community of the Tunisian island Djerba and the Muslim neighbors with whom they had co-existed since at least the Middle Ages. Their status changed fundamentally with the establishment of the modern Tunisian state; they became marginalized in terms of a 'minority' within a dominant nation-state and the sense of 'difference' was hardened. Moreover, with the Arab-Israeli War in 1967, polarization with nation-states of the region added more hardening to the pluralistic situation. The political transformation of the region and the emergence of modern nation-states changed even the religious identities.[41] This is also valid for any analysis of most Muslim enthusiastic reactions and uprisings against Western, American, Zionist or other non-Muslim 'out-groups'. The *salience* of the religious identity in these cases is always interwoven with a dominant historical, one may add, culture of an 'unfair Other'. The more political extremism is present, the more religious extremism is activated; a culture of good 'sameness' against evil 'otherness' is salient and many 'scriptural' justifications can be easily recalled. This is because identity is always defined through three main factors:

1. difference from something/someone else;
2. The aspects of identity that are most relevant or salient depend on the context;
3. Identities can be, and constantly are being, given new meanings and mobilized for political purposes [...] all people have multiple identities. The identity that will be most salient or relevant will depend on the context[42]

Muslim cultural identity, in interaction with religious identity, is then, dynamic and not static. Some scholars questioned the homogeneity in what we generally categorize as 'Muslims'. In Modood's words:

> Muslims are not, however, a homogenous group. Some Muslims are devout but apolitical; some are political but do not see their politics as being 'Islamic' (indeed, may even be anti-Islamic). Some identify more with a nationality of origin, such as Turkish; others with the nationality of settlement and perhaps citizenship, such as French. Some prioritise fundraising for mosques, other campaign against discrimination, unemployment or Zionism. For some, Ayatollah Khomeini is a hero and Osama bin Laden an inspiration; for others, the same may be said of Kemal Ataturk or Margaret Thatcher, who created a swathe of Asian millionaires in Britain, brought in Arab capital and was one of the first to call for NATO action to protect Muslims in Kosovo. The category 'Muslim', then, is as internally diverse as 'Christian' or 'Belgian' or 'middle-class', or any other category[43]

This intra-Islamic heterogeneity is compounded with a cultural diversity which determines the different characteristics and modes of Muslim groups in different situations and contexts. Intra-Muslim multiculturalism is lucidly distinguishable in the diaspora. Muslim immigrants, excepting their Muslimness, do not share the same cultural characteristics. Furthermore, religious identity is sometimes defined in cultural terms. Even the most characteristic aspects of ritual devotion carry the cultural particularities of the migrant Muslims. For example, to decide to go for the Friday prayers to the Turkish, Moroccan, Egyptian, Pakistani or Indonesian mosque is to be determined through ethnic, cultural, linguistic and even political factors. On another level, I decide, as a Muslim, to visit the mosque where my doctrinal affiliations are most closely expressed. A Sunni, Shiite, Salafi, Sufi, radical or *moderate* imam are all decisive elements in the choice of my 'in-group group'. What a Muslim 'knows' in relation to his ethno-cultural identity will define his views and judgments. This is why cognitive affiliation is another diverging factor in this intra-Islamic heterogeneity. Average Muslims tend to adapt to a cultural system which their cognitive sphere will/can absorb. Mostly, the more a Muslim gets profound knowledge of his creed and religion the more his religious identity is salient, as well as his cultural selectiveness being activated and specified. Both the High and Low 'Islams' are to be recognized and identified in a 'High Islamic culture' and a 'Low Islamic culture', a *scriptural* Islam and a Muslim popular culture.[44] A Muslim moves from the religious toward the cultural, from the private to the collective, from the monocultural to the multicultural according to a certain conception he has of Islam and the proper role of a Muslim in this world. This cultural variation and dynamism in the conceptions about a certain worldview from an Islamic perspective is what forms the social category *Muslim*. Hopkins, Kwan and Aitchison stress the significance of the 'geography' of the Islamic world in the way Muslim identities can be defined:

> Muslim identities are influenced by global processes, national politics and regional development strategies, as well as by the ways in which everyday spaces, such as the street, home and mosque, are experienced in a range of emotional, spiritual, inclusive and exclusionary ways. Clearly, geography matters to the construction and contestation of Muslim identities, and this collection exemplifies this through a series of insights into specific local, regional and national contexts all of which emphasise the importance of place and time as significant influences over how Islam is experienced, lived out and practiced on an everyday basis[45]

To recap, what one can make out of this intra-Islamic diversity is that Islam, both as a religion and a civilization, is inherently multicultural.[46] Islam established its trans-ethnic and intercultural structure by stressing the universality of its message. Islamic civilization evolved and flourished by achieving a balance between Islamization and acculturation. The success of this civilization, in my view, lies in the reconciliation between what is religiously obligatory and what is culturally profitable. This reconciliation formed an Islamic multicultural experience which enabled prominent companions (*ṣaḥāba*) like Amro Ibn Al-'Aās, leader of the Muslim conquest of Egypt in 640, to establish mosques leaving the remnants of an obsolete paganism undamaged. In new encounters with other cultures and civilizations, early Muslims often knew how to preserve a religious identity which perceives the diversity in every mundane being and reconciles with it, as long as the tenets of faith are safeguarded. The reinforcement of the notion of multiculturalism is generated from the Quran in a verse repeatedly cited by Muslims as a common statement in every discourse on pluralism:

> O humankind! We have created you from a single (pair) of a male and a female, and made you into nations and tribes, that you may know each other (not that you may despise (each other). Verily the most honored of you in

the sight of Allah is (he who is) the most righteous of you. And Allah has full knowledge and is well acquainted (with all things).[47]

The verse begins with a call addressed to 'humankind' and not to the 'believers', as this is not a religiously exclusive assignment, but rather a statement of a human multicultural code. The verse expresses the goal of encounter as 'knowing' each other. The Arabic word *ta'ārafū* is a reflexive verb which presupposes reciprocal action on both parts. Surely, it has never implied terms and conditions for this encounter like 'melt or get out of the pot'. It recognizes instead the profit of 'knowing each other' at a personal and peoples' level, because this is for their collective interest.

> Life circumstances will oblige them to need each other. God apportioned the sources of His graciousness among His creatures. Through this diversity in the divine graciousness, people are supposed to cooperate and support each other, so that the one supplements the defects of the other. Thus, this is a diversity which leads to complementation and not to conflict.[48]

155

It is a fact that 'Muslimness' is fundamentally dependent on a civilizational and cultural status. In times of civilizational stagnation both political and economic factors transform, if not deform, human identity. However, it is through this Islamic concept of pluralism and diversity, which should lead to complementation and not to conflict, that many problems of the contemporary Muslim world can be solved. The 'Other' is often part of an *ego* that 'we' aspire to beyond the status quo, embodying elements that would supplement, enrich or, even, reform our culture, and should not necessarily strip us of the core aspects of our identity that we cherish. In this respect, the Quranic address to 'know each other' is also an incentive to 'supplement each other' and an enforcement of a multicultural and pluralistic coexistence in quest of a balanced relationship between 'Muslimness' and 'Otherness'. It is the tension between the fear of the depersonalization of 'Muslimness' and the struggle to preserve it that shapes the pluralistic attitude of a Muslim. Nevertheless, we should be always reminded that the Islamic tradition has produced such a wide array of cultural diversity that provided historical circumstances under which both religious and cultural identities were not at odds with pluralistic values. This is why a revival of these pluralistic values in the modern context should be considered as a significant prerequisite of any Islamic reform today.[49]

1 See L. Abu-Lughod, 'Thinking about Identity,' in H. Greenberg, *Spotlights on the Middle East: Issues of Identity*, (The American Forum for Global Education, 2004 (revised)), retrieved from: http://www.globaled.org/musmideastid04.pdf, p. 5. She argues that 'The concept of "identity" is a useful starting point for cross-cultural understandings of human experience because it begins with the individual. Thinking about personal identity means asking how people define or think about themselves. This will always be related to how others define them and what options are open to them.'

2 Speaking about identity I use the term 'Muslimness' anthropologically to refer to the individual and collective identity of Muslims as a product of an adherence to Islam and the different socio-cultural and political contexts.

3 This is not an essentialist position on how Muslims are or should be. What I intend to analyze here are some general key features which should not be ignored when one approaches the Muslim juxta-position between multiculturalism and pluralism.

4 Al-Baqara, 2:112. I use the Quran translation of Yusuf Ali, *The Holy Quran: English Translation of the Meanings and Commentary* (Madinah: King Fahd Complex for the Printing of the Holy Qur'an, 1410 A.H.). Minor modifications occur of course where necessary; especially when the translation is closer to the original meaning in Arabic.

5 Al-Nisā', 4:1215.

6 Al-Baqara, 2: 208.

7 Al-Tabari, *Jāmi' al-Bayān 'an Ta'wīl Āyy Al-Qur'ān* [The Eloquent Sententious on the Interpretation of the Quranic Verses] (Cairo: Dar Al-Salam, 2008), vol. II: 1118-1122; Ibn Kathir, *Tafsīr Al-Qur'ān al-'Azīm* [Interpretation of the Glorious Quran] (Cairo: Dar Al-Hadith, 2003), vol. I: 308-309; Al-Shaarawi M., *Tafsīr Al-Shaarawi* (Cairo: Dar Akhbar Al-Youm, 1991), vol. II: 877-884. Other opinions interpret kāffa as 'all together', in indication to the believers, which is not reasonable. The interpre-

tation we give is according to Ibn Kathir the proper one.

8 See Al-Ghazali, *Ihyā 'Ulūm al-Dīn* [Revival of the Religious Sciences] (Cairo: Dar Al-Salam, 2007), vol. I: 136 ff.

9 Al-Hujurāt, 49:14.

10 See Al-Qurtubi, *al-Jāmi' li Ahkām Al-Qur'ān* [The Sententious of the Rulings of the Quran] (Beirut: Mu'ssasat Al-Risala, 2006), vol. 19: 420-421; Al-Zamakhshari, *al-Kashshaf* [The Revealer] (Riyadh: Al-Ubaykan, 1998), vol. V: 587-588.

11 Tāha, 20:123-126.

12 Al-An'aām, 161-163.

13 For this role see for example A. Basfar, 'Hifz al-Sighar li Al-Qur'ān wa Atharuh fi Hifz al-Huwiyya al-Islamiyya' [Kids' Memorization of the Quran and its Influence on Preserving Islamic Identity], paper presented at the 27th Conference of the Muslim League in Sweden: Islamic identity: Constants and Parameters, 29-31/12/2007, retrieved from: *www.albasaer.net/1Offers/hifzq.pdf*.

14 Al-Ahzāb, 33:21: 'Certainly you have in the Messenger of Allah an excellent exemplar for him who hopes in Allah and the latter day and remembers Allah much'. See also F. Okumuş, 'The Prophet as Example', *Studies in Interreligious Dialogue* 18/1 (2008), 82-95.

15 A collection of these attributes can be found in special classical works. See for example Al-Tirmidhi, *al-Shamā'il al-Muhammadiyya* [The Muhammedan Characteristics] (Beirut: Dar Al-Hadith, 1988³); Al-Mubarakfuri, *al-Rahīq al-Makhtūm* [The Sealed Nectar] (Qatar: Ministry of Endowments and Islamic Affairs, 2007); See also the encyclopedic work (12 volumes): Ben Humayd & Ben Mallouh (ed.), *Nadrat al-Na'īm fi Makārim Akhlāq al-Rasūl al-Karīm* [The Radiance of Delight on the Character of the Noble Messenger] (Jeddah: Al-Wasila, 1998).

16 Moslim, *Sahīh Moslim* [The Authentic [collection of hadiths] of Moslim] (Beirut: Dar Al-Marefah, 2007), Kitab al-Iman, hadith 8.; Cf. Al-Bukhari, *Sahīh Al-Bukhari* [The Authentic [collection of hadiths] of Al-Bukhari] (Beirut: Dar Al-Marefah,

2007), Kitab al-Imān, hadith 50.

17   Zarabozo J., *What is Islam?* (Riyadh: The Under-Secretariat of Publications and Research, Ministry of Islamic Affairs and Endowments, Da'wah and Guidance, 2005), 125.

18   Ibid, 141.

19   Al-Baqara, 2:256: 'And he who rejects false deities and believes in Allah has grasped indeed the firmest handhold which will never break. Allah is Hearer, Knower'; Luqman, 31:22: 'Whoever submits his whole self to Allah, and is a doer of good, has grasped indeed the firmest hand-hold: and with Allah rests the End and Decision of (all) affairs'. See Al-Shaarawi, op. cit., vol. II, 1116-1117.

20   Al-Jumu'a, 62:9-10: 'O you who believe! When the call is proclaimed to prayer on Friday, hasten earnestly to the Remembrance of Allah, and leave off business (and traffic): That is best for you if you but knew. And when the Prayer is finished, then may you disperse through the land, and seek of the Bounty of Allah: and celebrate the Praises of Allah often (and without stint): that ye may prosper.'

21   Al-Tawba, 9:103: 'Take alms out of their property, you would cleanse them and purify them thereby'.

22   'Here I am O Allah, (in response to Your call), here I am. Here I am, You have no partner, here I am. Verily all praise, grace and sovereignty belong to You. You have no partner'.

23   All widespread Muslim names beginning with Abd- and ending in one of the Names-Attributes of God (Abdullah: Abd-u-Allah; Abdulrahman: Abd-u-Al-Rahman…etc.) mean generally 'Servant of God.'

24   Al-Bayhaqi, *al-Zuhd al-Kabīr* [The Great Asceticism] (Beirut: Dar Al-Jinan-Mu'assasat Al-Kutub Al-Thaqafiyya, 1987), 81.

25   *al-Muhadhdhab min Madārij al-Salikīn* [The Refined from the Ranks of the Seekers] (Damascus: Dar Al-Qalam, 2005): 46-47.

26   Al-Baqara, 2:281.

27   J. Stets and P. Burke, 'Identity Theory and Social Identity Theory', *Social Psychology Quarterly*, 63/3 (2000), 224f.

28   See Stets and Burke, *Identity*, 229.

29   See Stets and Burke, *Identity*, 231, where depersonalization is defined as 'a cognitive representation of the social category containing the meanings and norms that the person associates with the social category'.

30   See C. Aitchison, M. Kwan and P. Hopkins, *Geographies of Muslim Identities: Diaspora, Gender and Belonging* (Ashgate Publishing Limited: Hampshire, 2007), 2: 'The places where Muslim identities are negotiated, celebrated or resisted matter to how these identities are experienced by Muslims and non-Muslims alike. The geographies of Muslim identities be they based around neighbourhood connections, national affiliations or regional associations, are important to the ways in which these identities are experienced in everyday lives'.

31   F. Heckman, 'Multiculturalism Defined in Seven Ways,' *The Social Contract*, vol. 3, n. 4, summer 1993: 245-246; See also C. Rosado, *Toward a Definition of Multiculturalism* (Rosado Consulting for Change in Human Systems, 1997), 2, www.rosado.net/pdf/Def_of_Multiculturalism.pdf: 'Multiculturalism is a system of beliefs and behaviors that recognizes and respects the presence of all of the diverse groups in an organization or society, acknowledges and values their socio-cultural differences, and encourages and enables their continued contribution within an inclusive cultural context which empowers all within the organization or society'.

32   See B. Lawrence, Multiculturalism in Classical Islamic Civilization, *Footnotes, Foreign Policy Research Institute Bulletin*, vol. 5, n. 9, October 1999, retrieved from: http://www.fpri.org/footnotes/059.199810.lawrence.multiculturalisminclassicalislamiccivilization.html. He argues that: 'Within Islamic civilization are subsumed multiple cultures—Arab, Persian, Turkish, Bengali, Punjabi, Sindhi, Maghribi (North African), West African, Central Asian, Southeast Asian, just to mention a few'.

33 Y. Ellethy, Geloven buiten de Tekst, over Islamitische Volksreligie, *Tussenruimte: Oecumenisch Tijdschrift voor Interculturele Theologie* 2, Juni 2010: 16.

34 Al-Ghazali, Majmūʿat Rasāʾil al-Imām Al-Ghazali (A Collection of the Treatises of Imam Al-Ghazali), ed. Mohammad I., Al-Maktaba Al-Tawfiqiyya, Cairo, 2002, p. 218; The translation is quoted from R. McCarthy, *Freedom and Fulfillment: An Annotated Translation of Al-Ghazālīs Al-Munqidh min Al-Dalal and Other Relevant Works of Al-Ghazali* (Boston: Twayne, 1980), 318.

35 Ellethy, *Geloven*, 16.

36 The term is so difficult to translate from Arabic into foreign languages. It is usually translated as manliness, integrity, decorum. It generally indicates all the qualities that are associated with a 'gentleman'. See M. Kamali, *A Textbook of Hadith Studies* (The Islamic Foundation: Leicestershire 2009), 188.

37 Kamali, op. cit.: 189; Al-Jawabi M., *Al-Jarhwa al-Taʿadīl bayna al-Mutashaddidīn wa al-Mutasahilīn* [Disqualification and Amendment [criticism of the Hadith narrators] between the Strict and the Indulgent] (Tunis: Al-Dar Al-Arabiya li Al-Kitab, 1997), 253-254.

38 Other expressions are al-ʿāda muḥakamma (custom has the force of legal norm), and al-ta ʿiyīn bʾil-ʿurf kʾal-ta ʿiyīn bʾil-sharṭ (what is dictated by custom has the force of what is dictated by contract). See Ben Ibrahim M., *al-Ijtihād wa al-ʿUrf* [Ijtihad and Custom] (Cairo: Dar Al-Salam, 2009), 156 and passim.

39 See A. Amin, *Ḍoha Al-Islam* (Cairo: Al-Hayʾa Al-Misriyya Al-ʿAmma li Al-Kitab, 1998), vol. II: 221-222.

40 Ellethy, *Geloven*, 17.

41 Ellethy, *Geloven*, 6f.

42 Ellethy, *Geloven*, 5f.

43 T. Modood, 'Muslims and the Politics of Difference,' *The Political Quarterly*, 74 S 1 (August 2003), 100.

44 See E. Gellner, *Nations and Nationalism* (Oxford: Basil Blackwell, 1983), 74 ff.; Idem, *Conditions of Liberty, Civil Society and its Rivals* (Harmondsworth: Penguin Books, 1996), 60f.

45 Gellner, *Nations*, 7f.

46 Cf. Lawrence, op. cit. At the end of his article he concludes that: 'Islamic civilization needs not 'confront' multiculturalism or adapt to it, for it is, of its essence, multicultural.'

47 Al-Ḥujurāt, 49:13.

48 Al-Shaarawi, op. cit., vol. 22: 14475.

49 An earlier version of this paper was published in: Y. Ellethy, *Islam, Context, Pluralism and Democracy: Classical and Modern Interpretations* (London/New York: Routledge, 2014).

13

Chinese Chan Buddhism in the Netherlands as an Example of Multiple Religious Belonging

André van der Braak

This essay covers four topics. First, it addresses the rapidly increasing interest in Buddhism, and Chinese Buddhism, in the Netherlands. Second, it illustrates this with a case study of the Dutch Chinese Buddhist Maha Karuna Chan community. Third, it discusses how the rise of interest in Buddhism in the Netherlands has usually been interpreted in the scholarly literature as a decrease in religious belonging. And fourth, it presents an alternative perspective of multiple religious belonging that also takes into account some Chinese historical notions that may be useful in an analysis of the new developments in Western religiosity.

1   Buddhism in the Netherlands

Recently there has been a surge of popular interest in Buddhism, and especially Buddhist meditation, in the Netherlands. Although there are no reliable demographics on Buddhism available in the Netherlands, a recent study from 2010 suggests that as many as 500,000 people claim to have an affinity with Buddhism or Buddhist meditation.[1]

The German scholar Martin Baumann has attempted to present an analytical perspective on the spread of Buddhism throughout the world.[2] He makes a distinction between the traditional Buddhism of Asian countries, and the more modernist Buddhism that has recently spread outside Asia. In an interesting development, this modernist Buddhism now influences Buddhism in Asian societies as well. A new global Buddhism is arising which has a global agenda: the ending of suffering worldwide, finding solutions for ecological and environmental crises, and seeking methods of bringing about social and political harmony. Whereas in Asia most people are born into Buddhism, in the West most Buddhists are convert Buddhists: they have embraced Buddhism as a new source of religious inspiration.

In the process of such a conversion to Buddhism, Asian Buddhist doctrines often merge with Western philosophical and religious paradigms. For example, the Buddhist notion of *sunyata* (emptiness) is often related to Western discussions on the phenomenon of nihilism. There is a merging of hermeneutic horizons, comparable to what happened when Buddhism went from India to China. As a result, new forms of Buddhist traditions are emerging that incorporate both Buddhist religiosity and Western philosophical sensibilities.

Initially, it was Japanese Zen Buddhism that became popular in the Netherlands. In recent years, however, the Chinese Chan tradition has also established itself. Whereas the Japanese Zen schools tend to be more sectarian, with fixed boundaries between established sects such as the Rinzai and Soto Zen traditions and new movements such as the Sanbokyodan, the Chinese Chan tends to have more fluent boundaries, and to be more interested in dialogue, both between Buddhist traditions, and between Buddhism and other religious traditions. As a case study of this, I will now turn to the Dutch Maha Karuna Chan community.

2   Maha Karuna Chan

Maha Karuna Chan is an informal and fundamentally open community of lay Buddhist practitioners, who dedicate themselves on an individual basis to Chan practice, and its application in their lives. Maha Karuna is Sanskrit for 'great compassion'. Maha Karuna Chan was started in 1987 by the Dutch Chan teacher Ton Lathouwers (Huiyu), who received transmission from the Chinese Chan teacher Ti Zheng Lau He Shang (1923-2002), in Indonesia also known under his Theravada Buddhist name Ashin Jinarakkhita.

Ti Zheng was the first ordained monk in Indonesia, and was responsible for the revival of Buddhism there. Later in his life he was asked to become abbot of the Guanghua Monastery in Fujian Province.[3] The current abbot of Guanghua Monastery, Xuecheng[4], is also abbot of the well-known Longquan Monastery in Beijing. The Chan lineage of the Maha Karuna Chan sangha in the Netherlands, therefore, goes right back to Beijing.

As a professor of Russian literature in Leuven, Belgium, Ton Lathouwers lectured on the work of Dostoyevsky, Sjestov, Nietzsche, and Kierkegaard. He also studied in Japan with Zen masters Shin'ichi Hisamatsu and Masao Abe. Due to these various confluences, a form of 'existentialist Chan' has been emerging in the Netherlands as an important new religious tradition, which is a significant source of religious and cultural renewal.

Maha Karuna Chan organizes five Chan meditation retreats a year: four that last five days, and one that lasts ten days. Throughout the Netherlands there are

weekly meditation evenings in local centers. There is relatively little emphasis on ritual, and a strong emphasis on meditation practice. The Maha Karuna
Chan has a loose institutional structure, and places strong emphasis on the
individual encounter from heart to heart. The visitors to the Maha Karuna
Chan retreats and meditation evenings are not monastic, but lay practitioners.

In Buddhist teaching there is less emphasis placed on traditional Buddhist
doctrines such as karma and rebirth, and a very creative approach to mixing
notions and images from various religious traditions. For example, the Buddhist image of Guanyin bodhisattva is connected with the Christian image of
the Virgin Mary (both in Western Christianity and in Russian Orthodox Christianity). As another example, the Chan notion of The Great Doubt (the necessity of doubting any and all religious certainties in order to break through to
a liberating insight) is mixed with existentialist notions of descending into
despair and nihilism and completely living through such nihilism.

By having such a creative mixing of various traditions, students of the Maha
Karuna Chan not only learn more about Chinese Buddhism, but they also discover new perspectives on their own religious and philosophical traditions.
Many are surprised to learn, for example, that so-called 'anti-religious' existentialist philosophers such as Nietzsche and Dostoyevsky are in fact quite
compatible with the radical Chan Masters from the Linji tradition. Just as Chan
Master Linji (d. 860) said, 'Meeting the Buddha, killing the Buddha', Nietzsche
and Dostoyevsky spoke of the death of God—not as an expression of atheism,
but in an attempt to revitalize the Western religious tradition.

The Buddhist image of Guanyin bodhisattva, who has a thousand arms to
reach out to the suffering and needy people in the world who cry out for her
assistance, and who sheds a tear because she can never help enough, offers
many Western religious practitioners a new way of approaching compassion
and solidarity—not as a moral obligation but as a spontaneous resonance that
arises in the heart when confronted with the suffering of others.

Many visitors to Maha Karuna Chan retreats do not call themselves Buddhist. Although they are quite committed to practicing meditation and applying the Buddhist teachings to their own lives, they do not formalize their
belonging to the community. In this regard, they have quite an existentialist
attitude to Buddhism. Even so, Buddhism is just as important to them, perhaps
even more important, than other religious traditions are to their followers.

3   Dutch Interest in Buddhism in the Scholarly Literature

The massive interest in Buddhism and Eastern spirituality in general has puz-
zled religious scholars. Because of their refusal to be categorized as Buddhists,
such existentialist Buddhists often do not show up on empirical research
results. In an influential report by the WRR, the Dutch Scientific Council for

Government Policy, such Buddhist meditators were labeled as 'unaffiliated spirituals' (ongebonden spirituelen):

> The world view of the unaffiliated spirituals is characterized by a transcendent, spiritual orientation, that doesn't conform itself to doctrines. This emancipated category is empathetic, aimed at harmony with the world, and trusts its own intuition.[5]

A book on religion in Britain since 1945 carries the subtitle 'believing without belonging'. Should we perhaps describe the Maha Karuna Chan visitors as involved in 'meditating without belonging'? It seems that, generally, membership of religious institutions is giving way to free-floating, individualized spiritual seeking without commitment. In the scholarly literature, this phenomenon is often described in a negative way, as a form of consumerism, spiritual shopping, or 'patchwork religiosity'. The Buddhist practitioner of today is seen as part of this larger movement. He is a consumer who creates his own religion by picking and choosing from various traditions, based on his own preferences. In this way, it is said, Buddhism becomes a marketing commodity, a superficial fashion.

The assumption behind such an interpretation, however, is that one cannot adhere to more than one religion simultaneously. According to Western theological assumptions, religion is about committing oneself to the divine, fully and totally. One cannot be half-hearted or divided in one's commitment. A different and innovative trend in modern religion research, however, investigates this interest in Buddhism from the paradigm of *multiple religious belonging*.[6]

Many Western theologians and scholars of religion have assumed that individuals naturally 'belong' to a single religion, exclusive of other religious options. Such an interpretation of religious belonging as the individual committing, or refusing to commit, to an entire, single package of beliefs and practices of an official religion, fails to properly describe how individuals engage in their religions in their everyday lives. In reality, people construct their religious worlds together, often sharing vivid experiences of that inter-subjective reality.[7] What is approached as 'individual religion' is therefore also fundamentally social in nature. Religious belonging is not a consumer choice, but draws upon shared meanings and experiences, learned practices, borrowed imagery and imparted insights. Nancy Ammerman criticizes the overtly simplistic assumptions some prominent sociologists of religion make about religious actors' motivation and orientation. The relationship between human and divine is not only about maximizing rewards, but is also oriented toward belonging and communion.[8]

However, multiple religious belonging does not necessarily mean that people 'belong' to multiple religions in the standard sense of having several affiliations (although a small minority may do so). It means that contemporary individuals construct their sense of religious belonging using beliefs, experiences, expressions and practices of various religious traditions, without even bothering whether they would be recognized as 'belonging' to those traditions by the traditions themselves. Therefore, the 'multiple' in multiple religious belonging means that belonging itself is becoming multiple in character.

Strictly speaking, religious belonging is always inherently multiple in the sense that it is made up of diverse, complex, and ever-changing mixtures of relationships, commitments, and communal practices. Thomas Tweed defines religion as 'confluences of organic-cultural flows.'[9] Therefore one needs to question the definitional boundaries that distinguish the religious practices of one religious group from another's, even to the extent of viewing them as being mutually exclusive.

Such definitional matters seem merely theoretical, but they can have large implications for government policy. The unclear identity of Dutch Buddhists poses a challenge for government policy on Buddhism in the Netherlands. Last

year, for example, when VU University Amsterdam applied to the Ministry of Education for a subsidy for a new study track for Buddhist spiritual care workers (chaplains), it had to specify in the application form how many Buddhists there were in the Netherlands. It was very difficult to explain that in the Netherlands, many Buddhist practitioners don't like to call themselves Buddhist. They combine practices and rituals from many religious traditions, not just Buddhism. Therefore, counting Buddhists in the Netherlands is a very problematic affair.

It may be, however, that counting other religious adherents is also becoming problematic. Dutch religious society is changing rapidly. The old model of 'pillarization' can no longer accommodate the changes in the Dutch religious landscape. Traditionally, the secularization thesis explained the changes in terms of a process of de-religioning. However, it is becoming increasingly apparent that the process of de-churching does not lead to de-religioning.[10] New forms of religiosity and spirituality appear, and almost all of them exhibit some form of multiple religious belonging. It is therefore crucially important to understand this new phenomenon, and discover ways of addressing it socially.

Meredith McGuire challenges the assumptions of scholars of religion and theologians that there is a cognitive consistency between individuals' religion, as institutionally framed, and a person's actual religion, as lived.[11] Actually, people's everyday religious practices rarely resemble the tidy, consistent, and theologically correct packages that official religions promote. The phenomenon of multiple religious belonging shows that standard notions of religion and religious belonging are wholly inadequate for describing how religion is actually expressed and experienced in the lives of individuals today. The new paradigm in the sociology of religion of 'lived religion' distinguishes the actual experience of religious persons from the prescribed religion of institutionally defined beliefs and practices.[12] It focuses on how religion and spirituality are practiced, experienced and expressed by ordinary people, rather than official spokespersons, in the content of their everyday lives. At the individual level, religion turns out to be 'an ever-changing, multifaceted, often messy—even contradictory—amalgam of beliefs and practices that are not necessarily those religious institutions consider important.'[13]

4   Multiple Religious Belonging in Asia

Multiple religious belonging has been the norm rather than the exception in several East-Asian cultures.[14] Van Bragt has suggested, in his discussion of multiple religious belonging in Japan, that the Western conception of religion is losing its monotheistic rigidity and is drawing nearer to the Japanese traditional sense of religion, in which the idea of exclusive affiliation to one religious group does not constitute the norm. In such a situation, multiple religious belonging should no longer be viewed as a deviating state of affairs as opposed to a presupposed normative pattern (exclusive belonging to a single religion, conceived as a particular system of beliefs in a bounded community).[15]

Many Chinese freely engage in rituals and practices from Confucianism, Daoism and Buddhism, without feeling that they have to make a committed choice for one of these traditions. Historically, it has always been recognized that the various Chinese religious traditions each have their own contribution to make to spiritual and moral well-being. Confucianism provides ethical guidelines that contribute to social cohesion, Daoism stimulates and improves physical health, and Buddhism offers many resources in philosophy and spirituality.

This situation of religious plurality has been expressed in the Chinese discourse of *sanjiao*, the three teachings, which, since the 6th century, has frequently been applied by Chinese governments as a religious policy. Characteristic of the *sanjiao* discourse is that, on the one hand, the unity of the three teachings is asserted, and their principles and concepts are affirmed as equally valid whilst, on the other, no attempt is made to combine them in a conceptual synthesis. This differs from the Western pluralistic-theological perspective, where different religious doctrines and practices are interpreted as historically and culturally determined expressions of a single transcendent reality that can always only be partially expressed.[16] It is hard to find a 'theology of religions' in the Chinese intellectual tradition. There is a strong sense that ultimate religious truth can never be adequately expressed in words and concepts, but must be personally experienced. In Buddhism, for example, Nagarjuna's two truths theory distinguishes between conventional truth, which can be expressed in words and concepts, and ultimate truth, which must be experienced through meditation or other means.

The government policy of *sanjiao* (the assertion of the unity of religions without actually theoretically justifying this unity on a conceptual level) has been described by Joachim Gentz as a 'behaviorist religious policy'.[17] Just as the behaviorist psychologist refrains from attempting to look into a person's head to see what he thinks, but looks at his actual behavior, the hermeneutical paradigm of *sanjiao* avoids trying to solve doctrinal differences, but looks in a pragmatic way at their efficiency.

I want to investigate now whether this Chinese model of dealing with religious diversity could be helpful for the Western European context. Another and perhaps more interesting interpretation of Dutch Buddhists would be that they are not so much spiritual seekers without belonging, but religious practitioners with multiple religious belonging. In this view, Buddhist practitioners in the Netherlands do feel the need to belong; they just don't want to belong to one religion only. They also practice a form of religious behaviorism: they are not so much interested in knowing whether the Buddhist doctrines are true, but practice meditation for its practical effects. However, this does not mean that they lack a sense of belonging to Buddhism as a tradition: they merely do not see the need to formalize this sense of belonging.

Contemporary Western scholars of religion often state that religious traditions are losing their importance in the West, and that people are turning away from religious institutions in order to experiment with forms of individual and subjective spirituality. However, what is taking place in the West is not that people are turning their back to tradition, but that they are dissatisfied with their own religious tradition, and are seeking new inspiration in foreign traditions. As a result, what often happens is that they discover a new connection with their native Western Christian tradition through making this 'detour' into Asian Buddhist traditions.

Contrary to public opinion in the West, it might be that religious belonging is not so much disappearing as it is in the process of transformation (from singular belonging to multiple belonging). And it could very well be that this multiple belonging will be an important part of Western religiosity in the future— as it historically might have been in China (although there are also important differences between Chinese and Western notions of religious belonging). Perhaps in this regard, Western Europe has something to learn from the Chinese perspective on religion.

5 Conclusion

When we speak about religion as a source of social cohesion our perspective on religion is very important. The one-sided interpretation of Dutch Buddhist practitioners as 'unaffiliated spirituals' suggests that they experience religion as a private affair, and that they do not need to make any contribution to social cohesion. However, many Dutch Buddhist practitioners are actually very involved in contributing to the improving society and establishing more harmony. For them, this is part of their Buddhist bodhisattva practice. It is my view that a perspective of multiple religious belonging is more able to recognize and explain such commitments, and is therefore a more constructive way of speaking about Buddhism in the Netherlands than the perspective of 'without belonging'.

The currently influential one-sided interpretation of interest in Buddhism and spirituality in the West as representing a decrease in religious belonging affirms religion as a private affair, with no need for social engagement and social responsibility.[18] However, many religious seekers are actually very committed to social engagement. The paradigm of multiple religious belonging is better able to recognize and explain such commitments, and is therefore a more constructive way of speaking about hybrid religiosity than the perspective of 'without belonging'. The paradigm of multiple religious belonging could possibly set the standard for the future of religion in the West, and could therefore be of great significance for the social meaning and shaping of religion, and for new forms of social connectivity.

The Western image of religion as a unitary, organizationally defined and relatively stable set of collective beliefs and practices, is challenged by the phenomenon of multiple religious belonging. Extensive religious blending and within-group religious heterogeneity may be the norm, rather than the exception, as they have been and still are in Asian cultures. Scholarly theories of religion have long depicted religious belonging at the level of the individual in terms of commitment to the relatively coherent beliefs and practices of a single, received faith tradition. The contemporary phenomenon of multiple religious belonging might not be new, but might suggest that scholars' earlier depiction of individual religious belonging was no more than an artifact of their definitional and methodological assumptions. Therefore, multiple religious belonging forces us to reconsider established conceptions of religious identity and belonging and reveals that the borders of religious identity and belonging are as contested, shifting and malleable as the definitional boundaries of religions themselves.

Interestingly enough, many Dutch Buddhist practitioners are also recognizing the importance of being embedded in an Asian Buddhist tradition. The Maha Karuna Chan sangha has recently been seeking to strengthen the connection to its Chinese Linji Chan lineage, and to make its Chinese Buddhist identity more visible. The value of tradition is increasingly recognized. Just as the secularization thesis, that religion would cease to be of importance in the society of the future, has proved premature, perhaps the individualization thesis, and the paradigm that assumes a turning away from traditional religiosity towards subjective spirituality, will also prove to be premature. The human tendency to belong, and to contribute to the greater good of society, also through religious practice, is perhaps greater than the scholars have assumed so far. And, as the case study of the Maha Karuna Chan in the Netherlands shows, the meeting between Asian and Western religious traditions can play an important role in bringing about new perspectives on religious diversity and multiple religious belonging.

1   P. Hek, *Resultaten enquête boeddhisme in Nederland* (Hilversum: NPO Media Onderzoek en Advies, 2010), http://www.boeddhistischeomroep.nl/uploadedDocs/Resultaten_Enquete_Boeddhisme_in_NL_definitief.pdf, accessed September 12, 2013.

2   See M. Baumann, 'Global Buddhism: Developmental Periods, Regional Histories and a New Analytical Perspective,' *Journal of Global Buddhism* 2 (2001): 1-43.

3   Guanghua Monastery is widely connected with the Buddhist society in Southeast Asia. Before 1949, more than twenty monks of Guanghua Monastery started to build monasteries in the Southeast Asian countries to spread Chinese Buddhism. Now, Guanghua Monastery has seven branches in the Malay Peninsula and Indonesia.

4   Master Xuecheng is a well-known Buddhist master in China, who holds various public posts.

5   W. B. H. J. van de Donk, A. P. Jonkers, G. J. Kronjee and R. J. J. Plum, *Geloven in het publieke domein. Verkenningen van een dubbele transformatie* (Amsterdam: Amsterdam University Press, 2006), 185.

6   See C. Cornille, ed., *Many Mansions? Multiple Religious Belonging and Christian Identity* (Eugene, OR: Wipf & Stock Publishers, 2002); C. Cornille, Double Religious Belonging, Aspects and Questions, *Buddhist-Christian Studies* 23 (2003): 43-49; H. Egnell, *Other Voices. A study of Christian Feminist Approaches to Religious Plurality East and West* (Uppsala: Swedish Institute of Mission Research, 2006); J. May, ed., *Converging Ways? Conversion and Belonging in Buddhism and Christianity* (St. Ottilien: Eos, 2007); R. Bernhardt and P. Schmidt-Leukel, eds.,

Multiple religiöse Identität: Aus verschiedenen religiösen Traditionen schöpfen (Zürich: Theologischer Verlag Zürich, 2008); M. Kalsky, 'Het flexibele geloof van Pi. Meervoudige religieuze identiteiten als toekomstvisioen,' in *Buigzame gelovigen. Essays over religieuze flexibiliteit*, ed. by C. Doude van Troostwijk et al. (Amsterdam: Boom, 2008), 64-73; R. Drew, *Buddhist and Christian? An exploration of Dual Belonging* (London: Routledge, 2011).

7   R. A. Orsi, 'Is the Study of Lived Religion Irrelevant to the World we Live In?,' *Journal for the Scientific Study of Religion* 42/2 (2003): 169-173.

8   N. T. Ammerman, ed., *Everyday Religion: Observing Modern Religious Lives* (New York: Oxford University Press, 2006), 227.

9   T. A. Tweed, *Crossing and Dwellings: A Theory of Religion* (Cambridge, MA: Harvard University Press, 2006), 54.

10 J. de Hart, *Zwevende gelovigen: oude religie en nieuwe spiritualiteit* (Amsterdam: Prometheus, 2011).

11 M. B. McGuire, *Lived Religion: Faith and Practice in Everyday Life* (Oxford: Oxford University Press, 2008), 185-213.

12 See D. D. Hall, ed., *Lived Religion in America: Toward a History of Practice* (Princeton, NJ: Princeton University Press, 1997).

13 McGuire, *Lived Religion*, 4.

14 See M. Garrett, 'The 'Three Doctrines Discussion' of Tang China. Religious debate as rhetorical Strategy,' *Argumentation & Advocacy* 30/3 (1994): 150-161; P. C. Phan, *Being Religious Interreligiously. Asian Perspectives on Interfaith Dialogue* (Maryknoll: Orbis Books, 2004); J. Gentz, Multiple religiöse Identität in Ostasien, in *Multiple religiöse Identität* 115-135.

15 J. van Bragt, 'Multiple Religious Belonging of the Japanese People,' in *Many Mansions?* 7-19.

16 E.g. P. Schmidt-Leukel, 'Multireligiöse Identität: Anmerkungen aus Pluralistischer Sicht,' in *Multiple religiöse Identität* 243-265; M. von Brück, 'Identität und Widerspruch. Bemerkungen zu einer Theologie multipler religiöser Identität' in *Multiple religiöse Identität* 291-328; K. Baier, 'Spiritualität und religiöse Identität,' in *Multiple religiöse Identität* 187-218.

17 See J. Gentz, *Multiple religiöse Identität in Ostasien*, 130.

18 See K. Gabriel, ed., *Religiöse Individualisierung oder Säkularisierung. Biografie und Gruppe als Bezugspunkte moderner Religiosität* (Gütersloh: Kaiser, 1996).

14

In Search of a 'New We' in the Netherlands: Interreligious Multimedia Projects and their Contribution to Social Coherence

Manuela Kalsky

In 1968, the famous sociologist Peter Berger ventured the following forecast on the future of religion in a New York Times article: 'By the twenty-first century, religious believers are likely to be found only in small sects, huddled together to resist a worldwide secular culture.'[1] In the beginning of the twenty-first century, however, we have come to the conclusion that his prediction was wrong. The secularization theory, which was not only embraced by Berger but by most of his colleagues in the field of social sciences, has revealed itself to be a Western myth, based on a Eurocentric worldview. The secularized countries in Europe appear to be small islands surrounded by a vast ocean of religions; at the top of the list, Christianity with 2.2 billion believers, followed by Islam with circa 1.4 billion, Hinduism with 890 million and Buddhism with 390 million.[2] And the number of believers is only going to grow even more in the future. According to *World Christian Trends*, in 2050 there will be more than 3 billion Christians, some 2.2 billion Muslims, 1.1 billion Hindus, 424 million Buddhists and 16.6 million Jews.[3] Peter Berger changed his opinion along the way too: 'The assumption that we live in a secularized world is false: The world today, with some exceptions […] is as furiously religious as it ever was, and in some places more so than ever.'[4]

1 Transformation

The secularization theory predicted that religion would disappear as a result of increasing wealth and the ongoing developments in science and technology. Even though this prediction proved to be false in a global sense, the fact cannot be denied that secularization and individualization have made a decisive impact on European societies. The Netherlands, for example, has undergone a radical transformation of religious identity.[5] The so-called 'pillarization' of Dutch society[6] has almost come to an end. It is not only the churches as institutions which are under pressure, but political parties, trade unions and other associations are losing members too. The Dutch have become assertive citizens and will no longer be told what, or how to believe. As a matter of fact a lot of people turned their backs on the Christian churches during the last century. While two hundred years ago nearly everyone in the Netherlands was a church member, nowadays only forty percent of Dutch citizens feel connected to a church,[7] and the number of church members is still in decline. Today many young people in the Netherlands have no clue as to what Christianity is about.

Surprisingly enough, nearly sixty percent of Dutch people still claim to be a believer. Only four out of the ten people who state this, however, are referring to the traditional Christian faith. The remainder falls into the category: 'unaffiliated spirituals'. These new believers are patching together their own religion from the wisdom of various traditions. According to surveys, seventy-five percent of the Dutch people are convinced that this hybridization is the way forward for religion in the future.[8] A large number of the Dutch citizens no longer want to take part in a religious community in the classical sense. They are not the only ones; this trend can be seen all over Europe today. Citizens of Europe are developing multiple religious identities in everyday life through their encounters with people of other faiths and through the information flow on the worldwide web. These identities no longer conform to the law of purity and unity. Boundaries are blurring and identities are becoming fluid. In general, Europeans do not want to be identified with a religious group anymore. They prefer to represent just themselves, or at most two or three others around them.[9]

With trepidation, Dutch people observe Muslim solidarity and their sense of a religious 'we'. They are afraid of the radicalization of Muslim believers, a fear fueled by events which occurred at the beginning of this century. Three years after the terrorist attacks by Islamic extremists on 9 September 2001 in the United States, the Dutch filmmaker Theo van Gogh was murdered in the streets of Amsterdam by a young radicalized Muslim, born and bred in the Netherlands. This brutal murder was a big shock for the Dutch people; they were very proud of their open and tolerant society and their way of dealing with 'the other'. After this traumatic event, fear of the political Islam and fundamentalist Muslims increased and Dutch society became more closed and inward-oriented. Suddenly the Muslim neighbor became a potential 'enemy' and the already existing gap between 'us' and 'them' widened. During the last decade it became very obvious that people didn't know much about the religious other. Stereotypes of 'the Islam' as a monolithic and very static religious system set the tone, even in the serious media.[10]

As a result of these developments, the staff of the Dominican Study Center for Theology and Society decided to put the focus of their research on the diversity within the various religious traditions. They also wanted to highlight the growing tendency in the Netherlands today for individuals to develop their own multiple religious belongings.[11] In Asian countries it is not uncommon to be a Christian and a Buddhist at the same time, and even perhaps a Hindu.[12] In an originally Christian country, however, this 'syncretistic behavior'[13]—the mixing of elements from different religious traditions—practiced by a growing number of Dutch citizens is something new and for most of the official churches unacceptable.[14]

Europe today is facing the challenge of a paradigm shift, from a mindset of unity to a mindset of multiplicity. The present attempts to recreate a long-gone European culture of nation states, based on the unity of language, territory and religion, seems to be a nostalgic enterprise doomed to fail. A concept of culture which integrates multiple identities, and includes religion too, seems to be a more realistic endeavor.[15]

The hermeneutical and epistemological key for what is important in life and faith today lies in the experiences of people who live and 'survive' in a multi-ethnic and multi-religious society. This means we have to intensify mutual relations and forge connectedness instead of fearfully avoiding one another. We have to find answers to questions which are important for the creation of common future for Europe, such as: how can we create a peaceful and just society which enables people to live together in a multi-ethnic Europe? How can prejudice against and fear of other faiths be dismantled without denying the problems that arise when people from different cultures and religions live together? How can we help ourselves and our society to benefit from the fruits of cultural and religious differences, in order to guarantee *the good life for all*?

2   The Multimedia Projects of the DSTS

Revolutionary developments in the field of communication technology have changed the world dramatically. The Internet has created a global 24/7 network in which boundaries disappear and everybody can be in contact with everybody. The cyber-based network society[16] opened up new ways of communication and relatedness. In less than three years more than 350 million people have joined Facebook, searching for connections with one another, searching for a new sense of belonging—crossing cultural and religious borders.[17] Network societies produce network religions. In this sense the internet facilitates ongoing processes of negotiation and changes in religion and religious identities.[18]

The rapidly advancing digitalization of Dutch society led the research team to connect the DSTS research programs to multimedia websites. The first website the DSTS established focused on the interreligious dialogue in the Netherlands and the rise of multiple religious belonging.

On the multimedia website Reliflex.nl, six portraits of Dutch people from different religious traditions were published: Kaouthar Darmoni (Islam/Sufism), Ton Lathouwers (Buddhism), Jan Lagas (Baha'ai), Narsingh Balwantsingh (Hinduism), Petra Katzenstein (Judaism) and Annemiek Schrijver (Christianity). The format of Reliflex was founded on the insight that interreligious dialogue is not an encounter of 'religions' but one of flesh-and-blood people. Thus the portraits of these six persons were situated amid their daily reality. Their personal history was central, their relationships, their social context and the choices they had made with respect to their religion. With the help of their stories and the added background information on the website in the shape of articles, weblogs and interviews with experts, the visitor received more information about present-day (inter)religious questions on sacred texts, emancipation, fundamentalism, the religious education of children, circumcision, mixed marriage—and in what way the religion in question played a part in the life of the interviewees. From the day-to-day living with religion it became clear that religious traditions are not static and monolithic entities, but are in themselves flexible in nature. The internal diversity in opinions and traditions was greater than outsiders usually think. And—the internal diversity of voices and views did not stop at the religious traditions in question.

Three of the six persons who were portrayed on Reliflex no longer drew the ingredients for their religious identity from one religious tradition only, but from two or three. The Dutch Chan master Ton Lathouwers (Emeritus Professor of Slavonic Literature at Leuven University and founder of Maha Karuna Chan) appeared to be rooted in the Catholic Christian tradition *and* the Chinese Zen tradition.[19] Also Annemiek Schrijver, a Dutch TV presenter, feels at

See trailer: http://www.youtube.com/watch?v=AMWoWvdOjlk.

home in two religious traditions: the Protestant Christian tradition and, under the guidance of her spiritual teacher Sogyal Rinpoche, Tibetan Buddhism. Elements from both traditions nurture her daily life and teach her how to enrich her spirituality. Kaouthar Darmoni, born and bred in Tunisia, fled to Europe to escape her father who was increasingly influenced by Wahhabism, making the atmosphere in the family more and more fundamentalist. She ended up in the Netherlands where she married Gerard, a non-practicing Catholic who calls himself secular. They have a son whom they are raising bi-culturally. As a sign of this hybridity they gave him a name which is both Western and Eastern: Sacha-Shams. On the doorpost at their home's entrance, following the Jewish custom, they have affixed a *mezuzah* and a statue of Mary to welcome visitors on entering. 'A double protection,' Darmoni explains in the interview, laughing. The sacred texts of the various religious traditions flank each other in the bookcase and she deliberately takes her son to a synagogue, mosque, church and temple to familiarize him with all the different religious practices in a Dutch society which grows ever more multicultural and multireligious.

There are articles next to the portraits enabling the visitor to learn more about the people presented and weblogs, columns and audio recordings with well-known Dutch men and women, on the theme of the week. A permanent feature on the website was a self-assessment of one's religious flexibility. As well as the portraits, there was a new video each week of two young Muslims asking young people about their experiences, impressions and views on intercultural and interreligious topics, such as: What do you think about fundamentalism? What do you believe? What gives direction to your life? Are you religious? What do you think of the fact that people are inspired by different religious traditions, is this multiple religious belonging an issue in your life as well? The visitors to Reliflex.nl were invited to respond to the content.

Hetty Zock, Professor of Religion/Philosophy and Mental Health at Groningen University, rightly remarks that the persons who are featured on Reliflex are highly educated and that a conscious cultivation of religious multivocality such as this requires a high level of self-awareness and self-reflection. Zock was one of the twelve scholars who were connected with the Reliflex project and who conducted research into the usability of the concept of 'religious flexibility'. Her critical remarks notwithstanding, in her contribution to the book *Buigzame gelovigen* ('Flexible believers'), which pulled together the results of the Reliflex research, she comes to the conclusion that the only way to live together in a constructive way within a culturally and religiously diverse society lies in the promotion of people's ability to reflect, which means taking on the 'me' position, in which one reflects on internal and external dialogues and is attentive to any possible asymmetry and conflicts of interests.[20]

Our aim with Reliflex.nl was to acquaint the general public with ideas and views concerning multiple religious identity and religious hybridism and to show that religious traditions are not static monolithic blocks, but are instead diverse, dynamic and flexible. By picturing a personal story, and hence the practical day-to-day living of concrete religious people, the website enabled the visitors to put their own story next to what they saw and heard there. In this way, similarities and differences with the story of their own life and faith came to light. The added background information on the site served to enlarge the knowledge about the various religious traditions. One person functioned as an example of the religious transformation that is going on in society. By using the new media we created a platform where everyday life and scientific insights met and stimulated visitors to form an opinion of their own and exchange their views with others. Reliflex collected living material for the study of shifting identities—from a mindset of *either/or* to a *both/and* approach.

Apart from the infotainment content, which was also used in schools, the site also had a research section. Twelve scholars from different disciplines—sociology, philosophy, theology, culture, literature, religion and religious psychology were invited to reflect upon the usefulness of the concept of religious flexibility. What are the opportunities and the limitations of religious flexibility in a dynamic society? Can religious flexibility make a contribution to better interreligious communication? For a month, each scholar wrote a weblog on Reliflex in which they described the development of their insights. The idea was to create a kind of a laboratory of scholars which the visitors of Reliflex could employ to gain new insights. At the end of the project each of the scholars wrote an article in a book they published together: *Flexible Believers. Essays on religious flexibility.*[21]

After this first internet project, which put the individual and the new phenomenon of multiple religious identity building in the Netherlands on centre stage, we decided to ask the question about how to find social cohesion in a highly individualised and, at the same time, multicultural and multireligious society. How can we create a peaceful and just society that enables people to live together in a multi-ethnic Europe? How can the prejudice and fear projected towards people of other faiths and cultural backgrounds be dismantled without denying the problems that arise when people from different cultures and religions live together? How can we help our society to benefit from the fruits of cultural and religious differences in order to guarantee *the good life for all*? In short: What is needed for a 'new we' that binds people together and makes differences fruitful?

2.2   *Nieuwwij.nl: a New We in the Netherlands*

These questions indicate the direction of the present research programme of the Dominican Study Centre entitled 'In search for a new *We* in the Netherlands'.[22] Once again a multimedia website seemed a perfect tool and platform

See trailer: http://www.nieuwwij.nl/index.php?pageID=26

for this ambition. It was built with support of the Dutch Ministry of Housing, Spatial Planning and the Environment (VROM). This website project on inter-religious and intercultural communication was launched on 1 December 2008. To date the site has become one of the most visited sites in the field of religion, culture and spirituality in the Netherlands, with nearly 30,000 unique visitors a month.

What kind of *We* do we have now and what kind of *We* do we need in the future? How can the gap between 'us' and 'them' be bridged? How can we find a new *We* which takes diversity in all its guises (gender, age, race, religion, etc.) seriously and doesn't strive for exclusive unity by drawing a line between 'us' and 'them'? What ingredients are needed to create a new *We* that can value differences positively and connect them in a serious, yet flexible, way?

The *We* project uses the slogan *Let's connect the differences* and allows (young) people with different cultural and religious backgrounds to work together. The philosophy behind this slogan is that differences must be faced before something new can be built together.

Accepting diversity means learning to think 'in plural'. This is particularly difficult for the western mindset which is based on binary and unifying concepts. After all, it is not only the concept of culture of the modern age that is modelled on the idea of (national) unity. In Christianity, as well, unity is a central notion. 'We are all one in Jesus Christ', Paul said in an attempt to strengthen the cohesive powers of the first Christian communities. But, in the name of that same unity, those who had a different interpretation of faith than those who believed in the power of the Church were declared heretics. Unity is not only a uniting concept, but is often also a violent one. But can a community be based on diversity? Is it possible to not put 'truths' in the forefront as a uniting element, but instead embark on a common search? Can we not imagine a truth which can be discovered by and through encounters with the 'other'; a truth that includes people with multiple or other religious identities?

Project *We* is not first and foremost about giving answers but about asking questions. It strives to create a picture of the creativity and energy of people in the neighbourhoods of towns and villages and to stimulate their ability to find their own solutions, making new common initiatives possible on a small scale. The project's goal is to prompt people to take their responsibility and to show their strength instead of taking the role of the victim. The 'Generation Y' video team, for instance, records projects and people who are still working on this 'new we', making them accessible to a wider Dutch-speaking audience. Besides virtual connections the website also features real life interfaith encounters. One of the most successful activities involves Muslims and Christians staying in a monastery together over a weekend. The aim is getting to know each other better, building friendships and understanding the religious values which are important in each other's lives. Much of the material is also used in schools and other multicultural meetings, as well as in lectures about 'a new we in your neighbourhood'.

Without denying that living amidst all those differences is problematic, Project *We* focuses on the positive developments that are being made in an increasingly plural country. By doing this, *We* wants to motivate people to work on shaping their own lives and society in a constructive and creative way—for words and images are not innocent. They are not only a reflection of reality, they create reality themselves.

Instead of fostering fear and cynicism, Project *We* wants to promote the development of a common culture, in which mutual differences are made fruitful through participation. The right to 'be different' is an achievement within liberal democracy. The struggle about the question as to which values should define society is part of this democratic process. The debate on this question, in my view, should not be seen as a problem but as a privilege. In an open society which strives for individual emancipation as a human right, there will always be conflicts of interests. The common ground is that people comply with the law, with the rules that are laid down in the Constitution.

3   Connecting Differences

As long as diversity is associated with loss of identity and relativism of values, and the convictions of 'the other' are seen as a threat to one's own identity, there will be no room for a new *We*. Mutual acceptance and equality, while retaining and respecting differences, are indispensable ingredients for the development of new sustainable connections. This is why we chose the motto '*We*—connects the differences', as it underlines the necessity of not downplaying the differences in favour of commonalities in the search for mutual connections. *We* advocates facing these differences and making them fruitful—moving away from the *either/or* thinking and searching beyond the prejudices and with an open mind for an *and/and* approach.

How can we conquer fear of the other? How can we connect without having to become the same? What is at stake is not the search for a new big *We*, but rather the existence—side by side and mingled—of small 'we's', dependent on mutual communication and making connections. There is no ready-made recipe for a new *We* on the site. There are, however, inspiring ideas, conversations, information and opinions about what is required. The *We* team asks people in the street, in neighbourhoods, young and elderly people, people with lower education and those who are highly educated, the well-known and the lesser-known Dutch people. People and their initiatives are all part of the picture. Sceptics get a voice too. Project *We* aims at mutual communication. It wants to promote an exchange of views about what is valuable and what could give direction to a new 'We-land',[23] which all Dutch people can contribute to, and where everyone can feel at home.

Breaking down prejudice by having encounters, promoting knowledge about and providing inspiration from the various religious traditions, and stimulating communication about them with a view to creating a peaceful and just society: this is Project *We*'s goal. It is an expression of the longing for new ways of connectedness.

A theology which takes the signs of the times seriously and seeks God's salvation amidst 'the messiness' of our daily life must allow space for multiplicity;[24] multiplicity not only in one's own Christian circle—no matter how important and relevant this may be—but a multiplicity which provides space for the voice of the religious and spiritual stranger in our midst to be heard.

The burning question is: Will I allow this? Will I allow this 'other' to interrupt my own narrative and disrupt my peace? Will I let this 'other' expose the assumptions in my thinking and acting, and question my complacency? Do I have the courage to allow my own limited view of the world to be expanded, which could mean I have to face things I would rather not see? In short: do I make the other into an alter ego, into a projection of my own desires or do I sustain the opaque unicity of every human being? Together with Emmanuel Levinas I would plead for the latter: no 'egology', no determining the other from my own ego and reducing them to myself, but letting myself be surprised by the opacity of the other. For the Heidelberg theologian and missiologist Theo Sundermeier, who lived and worked in Africa for many years and who is an expert in the field of intercultural communication, wonder is the beginning of all hermeneutics. He writes:

> In wonder, I am open for the little, the humble, and in this I discover otherness, beauty, multiplicity. He who is surprised, is capable of enduring dissonance with resignation and will not look for harmony too easily. For the dissonant, as well, belongs to the fullness of life.[25]

Today, doing theology means going to the virtual marketplace, where people meet each other in very different ways, playing with identities, narratives, imagination and desires and seeking God in many spiritual guises. The game of theology has changed. The (non)religious other becomes a *locus theologicus*, which means that the slogan 'unity in diversity' should be replaced by 'diversity in search of connections', the search for a new *We*. Or, better still, the search for lots of small *We's* which are able to connect in a network which does not cherish the desire for fusion but can make a difference by building a society in which everyone can feel at home.

Whoever thinks that this is a utopian and naive idealism is mistaken. It is the reality of the twenty-first century. A century in which the neo-liberal market thinking within a nation state—and the related excesses of egocentric wealth accumulation at the expense of both the majority of humankind and the earth's natural resources—is running on empty. Creating social cohesion needs new and just connections at a local and global scale. A spirituality of the good life for all is an urgent necessity. Maybe it's time now to look beyond the borders of the Netherlands, using the motto: Looking for a global new *We* by connecting the differences.

1   A Bleak Outlook is seen for Religion, *New York Times*, 25 February 1968, 3.
2   Source: CIA *World Fact Book* 2008.
3   D.B. Barrett, G.T. Kurian and T.M. Johnson, *World Christian Encyclopedia: A Comparative Survey of Churches and Religions in the Modern World* (Oxford: OxfordUniversity Press, 2001), 4.
4   P.L. Berger, 'The Desecularization of the World. A Global Overview,' in *The Desecularization of the World. Resurgent Religion and World Politics*, ed. P. Berger, (Grand Rapids 1999), 1-18.
5   P. Nissen, 'The Holistic Revolution. Contemporary Transformations of Religiosity in the Netherlands,' in *A Glance in the Mirror. Dutch and Polish religious cultures*, eds. M. Kalsky and P. Nissen (Münster: Lit Verlag, 2012), 23-37.
6   For more information on the 'verzuiling'-structure of Dutch society: http://www.encyclopedia.com/doc/1O88-pillarization.html. See also: M.A. Thung, G.J. Peelen, M.C. Kingmans, 'Dutch Pillarisation

on the Move? Political Destabilisation and Religious Change,' in: *West European Politics*, 5 (1982) 2, 17-148.

7   For an overview of religion in the Netherlands at the beginning of the twenty-first century see: *Religie aan het begin van de 21ste eeuw,*Centraal Bureau voor de Statistiek, Den Haag 2008.

8   T. Bernts, G. Dekker, J. de Hart, *God in Nederland: 1996-2006* (Kampen: Ten Have, 2007).

9   Religionsmonitor 2008, Gütersloh 2007; L. Halman, R. Luijkx, M. van Zundert, eds., *Atlas of European Values* (Leiden 2005); see also M. Kalsky, 'Die Dialogfähigkeit des Christentums in der pluralen Gesellschaft,' in: S. J. Lederhilger, ed., *Den Himmel offen lassen. Der christliche Glaube in der Herausforderung des wissenschaftlichen Weltbildes* (Frankfurt a. M.: Peter Lang Verlag, 2010), 92-111.

10 About seven percent of the Dutch population is of Muslim origin.

11 C. Cornille (ed.), *ManyMansions? Multiple Religious Belonging and Christian Identity*, Maryknoll/New York 2002; R. Bernhardt, P. Schmidt-Leukel (Hrsg.), *Multiple religiöse Identität. Aus verschiedenen religiösen Traditionen schöpfen*, Zürich 2008.

12 A. Sharma, K. M. Dugan (eds.), *A Dome of Many Colors. Studies in Religious Pluralism, Identity, and Unity*, Harrisburg 1999; P. C. Phan, *Being Religious Interreligiously. Asian Perspectives on Interfaith Dialogue*, Maryknoll/New York 2004, 60-81.

13 On the concept of syncretism see: R. Bernhardt, 'Synkretismus als Deutungskategorie multireligiöser Identitätsbildung,' in: R. Bernhardt and P. Schmidt-Leukel, eds., *Multiple religiöse Identität*, 267-290.

14 M. Kalsky, 'Embracing diversity. Reflections on the Transformation of Christian Identity,' in: *Studies in Interreligious Dialogue* 17, 2 (2007), 221-231.

15 See M. Kalsky, 'Wahrheit in Begegnung. Die Transformation christlicher Identität angesichts kultureller und religiöser Pluralität,' in: *Christian Identity/Christliche Identität I* (Forum Mission, Jahrbuch Band 2/2006; Brunner Verlag, Luzern 2006, 29-52.

16 See Manuel Castells' systematic theory of the information society and the new social and economic developments brought by the Internet and the 'new economy': M. Castells, *The Rise of the Network Society*, (Oxford: Blackwell Publishers, 1996).

17 P. Levitt, 'Redefining the Boundaries of Belonging. The Transnationalization of Religious Life,' in: N. T. Ammerman, ed., *Everyday Religion. Observing Modern Religious Lives* (Oxford: Oxford University Press, 2007), 103-120.

18 H. A. Campbell, 'Understanding the Relationship between Religion Online and Offline in a Networked Society,' in: *Journal of the American Academy of Religion*, 80 (2012) 1, 64-93.

19 See also the contribution of André van der Braak to this volume.

20 H. Zock, 'Het dialogische zelf. Identiteit als dialoog tussen collectieve stemmen,' in: C. Doude van Troostwijk, E.van den Berg and L. Oosterveen, eds., *Buigzame gelovigen. Essays over religieuze flexibiliteit* (Amsterdam: Boom, 2008), 74-83.

21 Doude van Troostwijk et al., *Buigzame Gelovigen.*

22 The research programme on a new *We* in the Netherlands started in 2009 and will run until the summer of 2013.

23 B. Brandsma, M. Kalsky (red.), *W!J-land. Voorbij de bindingsangst*, Ten Have 2008.

24 See H. Egnell, 'The Messiness of Actual Existence. Feminist Contributions to Theology of Religions,' in: A. Esser, e.a. (eds.), *Feminist Approaches to Interreligious Dialogue, Journal of the European Society of Women in Theological Research* 17 (2009), 13-27, here 25-26; L.C. Schneider, *Beyond Monotheism. A Theology of Multiplicity* (London/New York, 2008); C. Keller and L.C Schneider, eds., *Polydoxy. Theology of Multiplicity and Relation* (London/New York, Routledge, 2011); M. von Brück, 'Identität und Widerspruch. Bemerkungen zu einer Theologie multipler religiöser Identität,' in: *Multiple religiöse Identität*, 291-328.

25 T. Sundermeier, *Den Fremden verstehen. Eine praktische Hermeneutik* (Göttingen: Vandenhoeck and Ruprecht), 184 f (transl. MK).

179

15

Comparative Scripture and Interreligious Dialogue: Taking the Chinese Experience as a Starting Point

Bin You

Scriptures have been usually considered the heart, or the original resource, of a culture. Whenever a culture is encountering crises, there will be a voice saying 'Back to the Scriptures'. It has been widely acknowledged that the supremacy and purity of scriptures should be safeguarded as seriously as possible, and that scriptures can only be studied and interpreted in their own tradition. With the development of globalization, however, religions encounter each other at an unprecedented level of depth and width. This raises a new question: how do we read or interpret these different religious scriptures in interreligious dialogue? China has provided some inspiring answers for this question in its age-old diversified cultural context. It would be proper, therefore, to start with the Chinese experience of dealing with religious diversity and interreligious dialogue during the sixteenth and seventeenth centuries, the later Ming Dynasty.

1   The Chinese Experience of Comparative Scripture

In autumn 1595, Matteo Ricci, an Italian Jesuit staying in Nanjing at the time, was planning to write a book to introduce Catholicism to Chinese people. The first idea that came into his mind, was that he would imitate the way of intellectual writing used in the Chinese tradition, which highly respected the Confucian works *The Four Books and the Five Classics*, which he could also take as his cultural resource. He was going to prove that 'the Lord' had already been there in the Confucian works, but that most contemporary people were oblivious to this. In his work *The True Meaning of the Lord of Heaven*, *The Book of Changes* is quoted 6 times, *Shang Shu* 18 times, *The Book of Songs* 11 times, *The Book of Rites* twice, *Zuo Zhuan* twice, *The Great Learning* 3 times, *The Middle Mean* 7 times, *The Analects of Confucius* 13 times, and *Mencius* 23 times. Moreover, the *Lao Zi* and the *Zhuang Zi* were both quoted once.[1]

Matteo Ricci did not realize that he was not alone in his time. There were a great many of his contemporaries who were also doing comparative scripture, such as Lin Zhao'en (the founder of the Three-in-One (Confucianism, Daoism and Buddhism) Religion), Xu Guangqi, Li Zhizao and Yang Tingyun, the so-called 'Three Pillars of the Chinese Church', who were the first generation of Chinese Christians who tried to integrate Confucianism and Christianity and Wang Daiyu, an Islamic Confucian who had combined Confucianism and Islam.

Unlike the 'conversion' policy that was pursued in Europe, the Chinese authorities followed a cultural policy of 'cultivating a people with its own religion as well as keeping its customs; unifying in politics but keeping their own traditions' in dealing with ethnic and religious others. It is the very fact that various religions coexist in China that produces a 'post-modern' phenomenon: mixed ethical groups with religious diversity are woven together in an ancient country, where religions communicated and engaged with each other often. Furthermore, a solution to the current problems of cultural dialogue and inter-religious coexistence might be found in the particular Chinese experience.

A very important principle of this Chinese experience is 'to enrich one's own tradition through reading others' scripture'. If we put this in modern scholarly idiom, it is a way of practicing comparative scripture. In all three major Chinese religions (Confucianism, Daoism and Buddhism), each of them has immersed itself into the other two. Representatives of each tradition are all well-versed in the other two traditions as well. For instance, Zhi Xu (1599-1655), a famous monk in the later Ming Dynasty, wrote his commentaries on the 'Truthful Impartment of Sixteen Characters', which was regarded as the primary doctrine of Neo-Confucianism in the Song and Ming Dynasty. This impartment comes from a verse in *Dayu Mo*, a chapter of the *Shang Shu*: 'The heart of the human is in crisis; the heart of the Dao is in the depths; concentrating on the perfection and the Oneness; observing faithfully the Middle way'. Zhi Xu commented on it as follows:

Are there two hearts? Due to the confusion about Oneness, the human heart is in crisis, as water becomes ice. By claiming that 'two' is wrong, the heart of the Dao is in the depths, as ice becomes water. Moving from confusion to comprehension is therefore called 'concentrating on perfection', as boiling water is poured on ice. Confusion and comprehension are both empty in nature, and therefore it is called 'concentrating on Oneness', as water and ice share the same quality of moisture. He who is deeply trapped between confusion and comprehension does not belong to either one. This is called 'the Middle way', which is the true nature of understanding. Once having comprehended the truth never falling back to confusion, this is called 'observing faithfully'. It is the result of the work of concentrating on perfection.[2]

Through such a practice of interreligious commentary, the core of the Confucian classical texts is thus 'Buddhicised', and interpreted as a Buddhist theory of 'truth and karma'. This kind of boundary-crossing interpretation between different scriptures is a common feature shared by Confucians, Daoists and Buddhists in the later Ming Dynasty, when comparative scripture was widely practiced and bore great fruits. To take a popular example, the *Dao De Jing* is not only a scripture within Daoism, but it also serves as a rich resource within both Buddhism and Confucianism. It was a popular scripture to write a commentary on for both literati and Buddhist monks.

In another so-called foreign religion in China, Chinese Islamic scholars followed a similar path, building their Islamic theological system with inspiration from Confucian scriptural resources and terms. On the one hand, they were committed to the Islamic tradition; on the other, they sincerely entered into the Confucian scriptural system as well. Take Wang Daiyu as an example. He approved the ethical injunction in *The Great Learning*, which holds that a noble person should be righteous and honest, and should behave well in four domains: personal, household, civic and national. He applied this ethical injunction to the Islamic human-God relationship,

> Therefore, once the right relationship between the Master and us, as His servant, has been established, the true injunction is implemented. Thereafter, the origin of Bright Virtue will be known. Once you know the origin of Bright Virtue, you can understand Bright Virtue itself; once you know Bright Virtue, the true knowledge is accessible; once you grasp the true knowledge, you can understand yourself; once you know yourself, you can be righteous; once you are righteous, you can be honest; once you are honest, you can speak properly; once you speak properly, you can behave well; once you behave well, you can make your family peaceful; once you make your family peaceful, you can rule the country.[3]

According to these Islamic scholars, a Muslim's absolute obedience to Allah would make him understand what Bright Virtue is, and would help him to fulfill the ethical injunction in *The Great Learning*.

It is the same with the Christian missionaries in China, such as Matteo Ricci. They went back to the Confucian scriptures, using their resources to build their theological system. Under their influence, both visiting missionaries and converted Chinese literati were proud of going back to the Confucian classics, quoting from *The Four Books and the Five Classics*. Paradoxically and amazingly, the first Christian theologies were built up with resources from the Confucian scriptures.

Practicing comparative scripture through boundary-crossing reading and interpretation, this model of the Chinese experience of interreligious dialogue can be inspiring for modern generations when we encounter religious others. First of all, reading, or even performing exegesis upon the scriptures of another religion requires a profound understanding of them, all the way back to their origins. It also requires having profound respect for them. We can take Matteo Ricci as an example again. He finished the Latin translation of *The Four Books* and set about translating *The Five Classics* twelve years (1593 C.E.) after arriving in China. Called 'natural theology', this ethical philosophy, derived from Confucian intellectualism and humanism, was then well known to Europeans. Leibniz even asked the Chinese government to send some saints and sages to Europe in order to teach 'the art of governing the country' and 'the highly perfected natural theology'.

Secondly, boundary-crossing reading and interpretation between two cultures is always accompanied by a 'double renaissance', which means that during the mutual reading and interpretation, A is revived by drawing new resources from B; meanwhile B can rediscover itself because of the new encounter with A. This is also exemplified by the dialogue between Christianity and Confu- cianism in the later Ming Dynasty. Matteo Ricci's great effort to build a Sino-Christian theological system, rooted in his textual authentication, re-interpretation and re-reading of Confucian scriptures, was not only foundational in the history of Chinese Christian theology, but also had a great theoretical impact on the Confucian camp in the late Ming and early Qing Dynasty. Due partly to his contribution, the 'Song Xue', which mainly focuses on philosophical construction, was transformed into the 'Han Xue', which mainly aims at textual authentication and exegetics. Liang Qichao (1873-1929) once said that, 'the overall thoughts of Dai Zhen (1724-1777) come from the Western world, but he himself claims that his thoughts derive from Confucius.'[4] Hu Shi (1891-1962) also claimed that, 'the philological works of the early Qing scholars, such as *The Five Books of Philology*, written by Gu Tinglin (1613-1682, the greatest philologist in the Qing Dynasty), and the textual criticism of the *Shang Shu* undertaken by Yan Ruoqu (1636-1704), are both influenced by Matteo Ricci.'[5]

Although it might be a little exaggerated to assert that all their methodologies were affected by Matteo Ricci, the comparative scriptural practices employed by Jesuits missionaries and Chinese intellectual Christians in the Ming and Qing Dynasty, undoubtedly stimulated early Qing scholars to go back to the Confucian scriptures and to foster these philological works.

It was the re-interpretation of Confucian scriptures that produced a dynamic, through which many Confucians were pushed back to their ancient classics in the Confucian traditions. As a result, quite a number of famous scholars of the Pu Xue (Plain Reading School) appeared, such as Mei Wending (1633-1721), Jiang Yong (1681-1762), Dai Zhen, Ruan Yuan (1764-1849), Jiao Xun (1763-1820), and so on, The Qian Jia School also started in the Qing Dynasty. In other words, the re-reading and re-interpretation of the Confucian scriptures from a Christian perspective not only benefited the rise of Christian theology in a Chinese cultural context, but also offered an opportunity for revival to Confucianism, a chance to reexamine itself in order to explore new roads and new dynamics.

Finally, boundary-crossing reading or interpretation of scriptures from other religions or cultures is the best way of dissolving the self-assurance that is the largest impediment to interreligious dialogue. As is well known, scriptures are usually the authoritative representative of a religion. Some declare themselves to be orthodox, and claim that the right of interpretation should only be in their hands. Nevertheless, the experience of Chinese interreligious dialogue had shown us that the meaning of scripture is multi-dimensional, abundant, and generative. The Confucian scriptures can be re-interpreted by Muslims, and integrated into an Islamic theological system; they can also be interpreted by Christians and become an integral part of a Sino-Christian theology. Both Christians and Muslims have the right to interpret *The Four Books and the Five Classics*. The legitimacy of interpreting *The Four Books and the Five Classics* won't be reduced or devalued, even if the interpretation takes place in a Christian or an Islamic context. In fact, the case of Matteo Ricci and his impact on the development of Confucianism proves that, probably, the so-called 'outsiders' can sometimes get closer to the truth of the scriptures.

2   Comparative Scripture as a Method of Interreligious Dialogue

If we use the metaphor of a hydrographic net on earth in order to describe the various religious cultures, the scriptures would be the origins of the rivers. The history of religious development is a history of the interpretation of these scriptures. The religious encounter is, in fact, the encounter of different scriptures; interreligious dialogue is the dialogue between different scriptures as well. The religious diversity of today's world offers a new possibility for scriptural reading: all religious scriptures can be read together by different religious persons, be they professional or amateur. These readings can be engaged in an interactive pattern by inviting the scriptures of the other to enter into a deep dialogue. It will open up the most authoritative scriptures of those religious others that they have ever encountered before. In this way, new and creative effects can be achieved.

It is not difficult to organize practices of interactive boundary-crossing reading. It can be done in the form of 'scriptural reading groups', inviting the representatives and researchers of various religions to join.[6] In every reading group, there could be a theme, such as creation, righteousness, forgiveness, or even a concrete one such as 'women', selecting verses from scriptures from Judaism, Christianity and Islam, and from Eastern religions such as Buddhism, Daoism and Confucianism. People can expound their own understanding of these verses to each other, in accordance with their own tradition or interpretations.

This practice could be divided into three stages. The first one is *exegesis*: a brief introduction to these texts. For instance, if we want to discuss a theme like 'the origin', we could invite a Jewish scholar to introduce *Genesis*, a Christian one to introduce *The Gospel of John*, and a Confucian one to introduce *The Explanation of Tai Ji Schema*. At this stage, the main purpose is to understand their textual meanings, as well as the sophisticated interpretative history of a particular tradition. The next stage is *dialectic*: participants are allowed to ask questions about the specific meaning of some words, or the theological framework of a particular religion, or propose some new interpretation from other religious perspectives. The last stage is *dialogue*: people can more freely offer comparisons or re-interpretations of the verses of the different religions that are being discussed.

Throughout the whole process, people can agree or disagree on some certain ideas in one tradition. It reveals to us the possible abundance that a piece of a verse could have, and how a piece of a verse is able to generate so many different meanings in various different traditions. Through this kind of reading practice, an open attitude towards scriptures can be cultivated naturally, refusing any arbitrary scriptural explanation, and encouraging self-reflection. At the end of the reading, it is unnecessary to reach a consensus, and new possibilities are always there.

This interactive reading practice involves some basic ideas. Firstly, it pursues 'the encounter with the unknown'. When the various religious passages are read together, people not only respect the other religious texts as strangers, but also their own familiar ones are set in a new frame of reference, which transforms them into strangers as well. Basically, the production of meaning in interactive reading is an ever-progressing endless encounter with the ultimate 'unknown'. Secondly, it pursues the concept: 'to promote the quality of difference between each other'. It reveals not only cultural differences, but also the root of such differences, where they come from, and where they are going to. Thirdly, it respects the diversity of religions and cultures. In our globalized world, diversity is not merely a challenge, but rather an opportunity for every religion and culture. It encourages all religions to know and learn from each other.

Comparative scripture could be a new discipline with its inherent tension between humanity and theology. At first, it is reasonable to take comparative scripture as a branch of the humanities as is commonly understood, just like comparative literature or the comparative study of religion. In this sense, the purpose of comparative literature or the comparative study of religion is applicable to comparative scripture as well: to improve the understanding of other cultures, to seek the response of others' religious traditions, to extend the spiritual worlds of various religious traditions, to help those who participate in this practice to reach mutual understanding and self-reflection, and so on.

However, comparative scripture could be a special form of 'theology' for a certain religious purpose. That is to say, comparative scripture not only serves the purpose of inter-faith dialogue, or merely mutual understanding. It also searches out new resources from other religious traditions which could benefit it, whether this religion is Christianity, Buddhism, or Confucianism, with the purpose of improving or developing the ability of this religion to face the challenges of modernity. In this sense, comparative scripture is rooted in and devoted to a particular religion.

In conclusion, comparative scripture is a discipline between the humanities and theology. In terms of the former, it is comparative study or interfaith dialogue, aiming at comparing scriptures in an objective and detached way. In terms of the latter, it serves to deepen the understanding of the particular religion, a new form of 'faith seeks understanding' in a multi-religious context.

3 Comparative Scripture as Reciprocal Interreligious Hermeneutics

The emergence of comparative scripture has raised new questions to a hermeneutics that is confined to one religious tradition. A basic question here is how to develop a kind of 'interreligious hermeneutics'.

To do this, some crucial problems must be taken into account: is it possible for an 'outside' religion, which has a different worldview and knowledge system, to faithfully and honestly understand another religion, both in theory and in practice? For the religions that have made exclusive truth claims, will they allow others to cross over religious borders? The aim of interreligious hermeneutics is not simply to comprehend other religions, but also to attempt to integrate elements of other religions into one's own system. If so, then what kind of ethical principle should be followed in the appropriations or re-interpretations of other religious texts? And what is the dynamic? Can different religious hermeneutical frameworks be commensurate, and allow for mutual exchange?[7] And the last crucial question would be: who has the legitimacy to judge the result of interreligious hermeneutics? Should it be the religion that is doing the interpreting, or the one which is being interpreted?

A good interreligious hermeneutics, that follows the way of faithfulness and reciprocity, should be interactive and mutually beneficial. The way of faithfulness means to be as respectful and honest as possible in entering into the interpretation of another religion; the way of reciprocity is to benefit both religions involved in interreligious hermeneutics.

Such a hermeneutic would be reciprocal, because it can produce two distinctive effects: one is 'to cast off cliché'; another is 'to start a new journey'. 'To cast off cliché' firstly means an attempt to cast off the misunderstanding of religions towards each other, to understand a religion from the inside. Secondly, this also means that when one is interpreting another religion, in the mirror of that other tradition, the clichés about one's own tradition could be cast off, and some elements of one's own tradition which had sank into oblivion could be rediscovered. 'To start a new journey' means that, for one thing, many new elements and frameworks of other religious traditions, and even the principles of hermeneutics itself, could be absorbed or woven into one's own religious system as new materials or new illuminations. Also, in the process of interreligious hermeneutics, with the reference of other religions, a new system could be set up in realizing its own creative transformation.

Compared with other interreligious dialogue models, this model of comparative scripture has basically three characters. The first one is that of particularity. Comparative scripture always takes a certain religious scripture as its study object. Therefore, it has to probe deeply into the details of a classical or scriptural text, tracing back the hermeneutical traditions that interpret and enrich the text. In the process of absorbing this text and its interpretative traditions into another religious system, a 'grafted' creation could be brought about. Secondly, it is provisional. Unlike systematic theology, comparative scripture as an interreligious hermeneutics is to understand or interpret a religious text in light of another religion. It is not meant to be a strict, well-organized system. Its outcomes would be open to criticism, supplementation and perfection. Lastly, would be the element of surprise. To a great extent, comparative scripture breaks down old-fashioned thoughts and frames. It attempts to illuminate the blind spots of the past, to graft new materials onto an age-old tradition. Therefore, its results can be literally unimaginable, and could astonish many people.

Owing to the great tension between Chinese and Abrahamic religions, whether this is with regard to their linguistic nature, their thinking model or their worldview, the novelty of the results of doing comparative scripture and religious dialogue, and of consequently developing an interreligious hermeneutics, must be astonishingly inspiring.

187

1 M. Ricci, *True Meaning of the Lord of Heaven* (Tien-chu shih-i), trans. Edward Malatesta et al., (Taipei: Institut Ricci; St. Louis: Institute of Jesuit Sources, 1985), see Index of Chinese Classical Texts.

2 Zhi Xu, *Complete Works of Zhi Xu*, Vol II, Book V.

3 D. Wan, *The Islamic Great Learning, the Outline*, commented by Yu Zhengui (Yinchuan: Ning Xia People's Publishing House, 1988), 230.

4 Q. Liang, *An Introduction to Scholarly Works in the Qing Dynasty* (Shanghai: Shanghai Guji Publishing House, 1998), 89.

5 This assertion was paraphrased by Xu Zongze, referred to in his *A Summary of Jesuits' Translation in Ming and Qing Dynasty* (Beijing: Zhonghua Books, 1989), 8.

6 This kind of reading practice, the movement of Scriptural Reasoning, has been used by an Anglo-American scholar circle for nearly 20 years. For a discussion of the history, theory and practice of Scripture Reasoning, see B. You and D. Ford: Cross Cultural Dialogue and Religious Study in Scriptural Reasoning: An Interview with David Ford, *Journal of Comparative Scripture*, 1 (2013): 231-246.

In the past, scriptural reasoning always happened within the Abraham traditions. Recently, in the last three years, with the cooperation of David Ford and Peter Ochs, Bin You has started this interactive reading between Eastern and Abrahamic religions.

7   For reflections and formulations on these questions, see also C. Cornille, 'Introduction: On Hermeneutics in Dialogue,' in C. Cornille and C. Conway, eds., *Interreligious Hermeneutics* (Eugene, Ore.: Cascade, 2010), ix-xxi.

16

Migrant Churches: Chances and Challenges for Society and Politics

Kathleen Ferrier

1   Introduction

This article focuses on my experiences of, and the developments in, migrant churches based here in the Netherlands. From this experience, I argue that these churches could play an increasing role in maintaining the social cohesion of Dutch society both now and in the future. Migrant churches in the Netherlands started an association in the early nineties of the last century called SKIN, Samen Kerk in Dutch, which means Together Church in the Netherlands. I have had the privilege of being the Coordinator of this association for eight years, from the time it was founded. After these eight years, I became a member of Dutch parliament where I experienced the uneasiness, and later the xenophobia, in political debate and in society about migrants, multi-culturality and multi-religiosity.

China plays a role in worldwide migration. Many Chinese people work and live abroad, in Africa, Latin America, Europe, and the United States. I met a lot of Chinese people, and shared with them, in Suriname where I grew up, in the Dutch speaking church in São Paulo, Brasil, and later, of course, in the Netherlands. There are also migrants in China, in this case, from the Philippines, Vietnam, and Thailand. And, from a Chinese friend of mine, I understand that Chinese people who move from the countryside to the cities are called migrants too. We have to deal with issues related to migration and human dignity all over the world.

This text is a personal one because it is based on my own experiences, and is structured in three parts: my experiences in Suriname, my experiences as a Coordinator at SKIN, and my experiences as a Member of Parliament on behalf of the Christian Democratic Party in the Netherlands, an office I held for ten years. Finally I would like to draw some conclusions related to the theme of this conference: religion and social cohesion.

2   Suriname

As I said before, Suriname, the country where I was born, is a multi-ethnic, multi-cultural and multi-religious society. People from all over the world have come to live and stay in Suriname. It is the only place in the world where one can find a mosque and a synagogue next to each other on one site. Many times I was asked: how is it possible, in a world where there are so many wars and conflicts because of different religions and cultures, that you manage to live together so peacefully in Suriname? My answer is: because in Suriname we have always, since the abolition of slavery appreciated and still do appreciate how much we need each other. If we do not work together, we will not be prosperous; we may even not survive.

The knowledge that no one can live by his or her own efforts alone, of course, has religious roots. In all religions people are not only called upon to look after each other, but in religious texts, reference is often also made to the need to work together for the world to be prosperous. But of course, it is not only religion that calls for people to work together for the benefit of the country. Politicians and economists call upon people to work together too. In these times of economic crisis, national governments of many countries seek to understand and collaborate with governments of other countries. Nowadays, Europe is struggling to survive a severe financial crisis. The 27 small countries that form Europe all need each other but still, it is not always easy to speak with one European voice, or to act as one strong continent. China is a country with promise and has economic figures that North American and European leaders could only dream of. They seek contact with China, and the other BRICS-countries,[1] to explore whether there are any possibilities for co-operation. This is often not as easy as it seems, as there are deep differences and suspicions, on both sides. Some 160 years ago, the first Chinese people migrated to Suriname and today we are witnessing a new migration movement from China to Suriname. These new Chinese migrants will experience in Surinam what we learned centuries ago, that it is important to respect each other, be honest, and try to have an open dialogue, even if this is from very different points of view.

3   SKIN

In the Netherlands we have a total population that is about the size of the population of Beijing, around 17million inhabitants. Traditionally, the Netherlands is a Christian country, consisting of Catholics and Protestants. Today, of the 17 million inhabitants, 800,000 to one million are Muslim. Most of these came as migrants to the Netherlands during the 1960swhen they were brought in to supplement the labor force. It was thought, at that time, that the men from—mostly—Northern African countries would only stay for a limited time, and then return to their home countries, but most of them decided to stay, so policies were developed to allow their families to join them. The general idea, of politicians and policymakers at that time was that these people would 'automatically' adapt to the Dutch system, learn the language, participate in society and forget about the archaic curiosities of their home countries, like being a religious person. Modern Dutch society would help them to be part of modernity and thus forget about religion.

This turned out to be a mistake, as we now know. Nothing happens 'automatically' and becoming part of a new society even less so, with its different culture, language, and its way of looking at basic things like education, healthcare, dress, behavior, eating habits and the way parents educate their children Migrants started to live together, in specific neighborhoods, speaking their own language and not feeling part of Dutch society. Autochthonous Dutch people started to move out of these neighborhoods and, by the end of the last century, there was an increasing fragmentation and segmentation of Dutch society which created many problems. Finally, policy makers and politicians understood that integrating into a new society never happens automatically. It demands efforts, both from the autochtonous population that has to give space to newcomers and of migrants. It is vital that people learn the language of the country they are going to live in, and that participation in Dutch society is demanded of them.

Of course there is freedom of religion and freedom of speech, so everybody has the right to worship in a proper religious building, a church, mosque, synagogue or temple, but the bottom line is always the Dutch Constitution. Honor vengeance, for instance, is not permitted in the Netherlands.

Apart from Muslim migrants, there is also a large community of at least 800,000 migrant Christians living here: people who have come from all over the world, for many different reasons, but who now live in the Netherlands where they want to build up a respectable life for themselves and their children. Oddly enough, this group is still rather unseen and unheard in Dutch society. People assume that they will fit easily into Dutch society, because they are Christians, like most Dutch people, and so will easily find their way. This, however, is not true.

In the early Nineties, leaders from several different Christian migrant churches decided to join forces and start working together so that they could be heard and seen in Dutch society. They also pledged to come together around a number of common issues; with many voices one is able to speak much louder. For this reason an association of migrant churches was founded, called SKIN: 'Together Church in the Netherlands'.[2] Since the foundation of SKIN (1997), the important role that migrant churches play in Dutch society is becoming more and more visible. Unfortunately this role is not often seen clearly enough. Some migrant churches take over many important tasks that other groups or services have stopped doing. I refer here to both the mainline churches and the Dutch government. Social welfare tasks that were traditionally done by churches can no longer be executed on the same scale. This is primarily because mainline churches are suffering increasing losses of congregation and means but also because some of their social welfare tasks have been taken over by the government.

Over the last decades, Dutch governments, which are traditionally coalition governments, and often formed with the participation of the social democrats, developed a strong state-influenced welfare system; the state owned elderly homes, it organized social welfare, and funded social welfare money systems. The problem today is that this entire system is no longer sustainable as governments have less financial capacity. In short, mainline churches lack people and the government lacks money. In this situation migrant churches play a vital role. They organize voluntary work, as the most natural thing there is, and take care of the elderly, and the physically challenged, for example. Most migrant churches have hardly any resources. That is why they seek collaboration and support or subsidies from the government.

4   Separation of State and Religion

One of the strongest pillars of Dutch democracy is that state and religion are separate. There is no involvement of the state or politics in religious affairs, and no involvement of religious leaders or organizations in state affairs. But does this mean that there cannot or must not be any relationship at all between the state and religion? Does this mean that there can be no financial support or subsidies for churches which do important work promoting social welfare and social cohesion?

It is my conviction that that would be a great and severe mistake. Of course there has to be a separation between state and religion in relation to religious or political content. But, when it comes to welfare, political parties and governments that are wise collaborate with religious organizations, because they take over the welfare work formerly done by the state like taking care of elderly, orphans and physically challenged people, for example. What could be wrong with a government facilitating or financing religious organizations that do precisely what needs to be done, and what the government can no longer do itself? A government that gives space to religion and that gives power to church-related social activities, creates a strong win-win situation; a relationship of 'give and take', religious organizations doing what they are good at and what the state is (no longer) able to do, for whatever reason: promoting social cohesion.

Valuable examples can flourish when churches are challenged to participate, form part of the society they have arrived in and when they are given
space.. As mentioned earlier, migrants, with either a Muslim or Christian background, have problems finding dignified ways of integrating in Dutch society,
and of creating a balance between the country of departure and the country
of arrival. Can you ask people to assimilate and just forget about the country
and culture they left? I don't think so. On the other hand, can we accept people from abroad, with a different language and a different culture, who do not
participate in the country they have come to live in? I don't think so. I want
to share with you the example that one of the Chinese churches in the Netherlands, has given. Since I began working as the Coordinator of SKIN, I have
noticed that little to nothing is known about the important contribution that
these churches make to Dutch society, so I decided to write a book on migrant
churches and to describe five of them in more depth.[3] One of these five is the
Chinese Church in the Netherlands. I chose the Chinese Church because the
members of this church have a very interesting concept of integration. The
want their young people to learn Dutch and integrate as soon as possible into
Dutch society; study hard and take important positions in society, as doctors,
lawyers, engineers. But they should never forget where they came from, where
their roots are. So they have to attend classes every Saturday and learn to speak
and read Mandarin.

I find this a very important example of how to make a dignified integration in society. Of course it is not always easy; there are as many differences
between migrant churches and mainline churches as there are between
migrants in Dutch society and native Dutch people. Migrant churches also differ a lot between themselves.[4] What I learned is that it is vital to have contact, to
speak and to work together. Migrants and migrant churches are often seen as a
threat: 'they break down our achievements'. This is a very narrow view because
it does not see that migrants, and religious people generally, play an important
role in the social cohesion of a society. I am sorry to say that, right up to this
present day, many people in the Netherlands, including politicians and policy
makers, see migrants as second class people, and a threat.[5]

There is even a political party in the Netherlands, ironically called the
Party for Freedom, which views migrants as a threat, and states that Islam is
not a religion but a political ideology that we should fear and banish from the
Netherlands and Europe. I have been a Member of Parliament for ten years, a
spokesperson on foreign affairs and development co-operation, and on issues
that relate to the multicultural society. I was a Member of the Parliamentary
Assembly of the OSCE (Organization for Security and Cooperation in Europe)
where I was nominated as a Special Representative on migration. In this role
I have traveled a lot over the last years: to Kazakhstan, Kyrgyzstan, Armenia,
Turkey and the Ukraine. There I have seen how important it is for governments

to recognize the role of migrants and the importance of the role of religion. Religion should be taken seriously because it acts as a strong driver for people and, therefore, a strong driver for change.

Politicians and policy makers sometimes consider religion a threat. In China too, religion and the state are, by definition, two entities that have nothing to do with each other. What is more, I have met people in China who cannot imagine religion being a driver for political action, or for the development of political views and convictions or for political action, that it was for me, when I was a member of parliament. Keeping religion out of public life is a mistake, because religion is a strong driver of change and a strong force in achieving social cohesion. That is why governments in general, and the Chinese government, in particular, can profit from, or one might even say, 'need', religious organizations for maintaining social well-being, providing care for an aging population, orphans, the physically challenged etc. It is, therefore, wise for a government to seek to co-operate with religious organizations for the benefit of the people. Giving space to religion and to religious organizations and facilitating the efforts they make to provide social welfare services can lead to a win-win situation for both the state and the religious organizations, even in a country such as China.

5   Conclusions

I would like to draw two conclusions, one about Europe and the other about China. We are all aware that we live in a world that is rapidly changing. Power relations are changing radically. China plays a crucial role in these shifting power relations. We are moving from a bi-polar world to a multi-polar one where Europe will play a less and less important role. It is very difficult for Europeans to accept that the time when Europe ruled the waves, and when the West made all the important decisions about what goes on in the world, are over now. It is very difficult for Europe and Europeans to let go of their deeply-held feelings of superiority. Govert Buijs mentioned the five Ps earlier, and one of them was pride. I dare to say that there is more than pride. Pride is positive but often pride turns into superiority, which is not a positive driver. In Europe there are strong feelings of superiority. But these European feelings of superiority will have to change—and they will change because Europe is in crisis. Not only a financial-economic crisis, this one goes deeper, it is also a political and a moral crisis. There is no political leadership, and it is not inconceivable to imagine Europe, as a continent, falling apart into a number of small—and globally insignificant—countries. Add to this the serious demographic crisis that Europe is also facing as an aging society, and it becomes very clear that Europe needs migrants if it is to maintain its current standards of living. Without young people who are able and willing to work to keep up the level of prosperity that it has achieved, there is no possibility of maintaining the levels of peace and prosperity, and the concomitant moral standards, that it has achieved over the past fifty years by working hard. Europe needs migrants to maintain this social cohesion.

China does not need migrants, but it definitely needs social cohesion. China, like Europe, faces many challenges; one of these is dealing with an aging population. In our globalizing world, China is also changing rapidly and people are making their own choices— of religion too. I would strongly suggest that religion should not be seen as a threat but as the strong driver of social cohesion and welfare that it is. This is certainly true of Christianity, which is growing rapidly in China. I am convinced that looking for better ways to develop more and closer ways of co-operation will be to the benefit of both the state and the religious organizations because it will be to the real and enduring benefit to the Chinese people.

1 Brazil, Russia, India, China and South Africa.
2 See also http://www.skinkerken.nl, accessed September 23, 2013. Members are 74 migrant churches, with an estimated total of 65,000 believers.
3 K. Ferrier, *Migrantenkerken* (Kampen: Kok, 2002).
4 See also J. A. B. Jongeneel, R. Budimanand J. J. Visser, *Gemeenschapsvorming van Aziatische, Afrikaanse en Midden- en Zuidamerikaanse christenen in Nederland: geschiedenis in wording* (Zoetermeer: Boekencentrum, 1996).
5 See also K. Ferrier, 'Migranten in ontwikkelingssamenwerking: Weinig pretentie en veel ambitie,' (The Hague: Seva Lecture, 2010).